# Contents

## Part Four: Treatments for Depression

# Acknowledgments

I would like to thank several people who made this book possible and made it better than it would have been otherwise. First I want to thank Ms. Jane Nevins, editor in chief of the Dana Press for providing the editorial guidance for this project; and William Safire, Chairman of the Dana Foundation and the Dana Press for giving me this wonderful opportunity for a second book on depression. Working with patients who are ill with depression or manic depression is one of the most rewarding jobs in medicine. With the possible exception of delivering a baby, there is no professional experience more satisfying than seeing a patient emerging from an episode of severe depression. I happily work every day for this. And since it is in one sense all I do, it is also the only topic today that I could write a book about. I also thank Mr. Tom Miller and Ms. Lia Pelosi at John Wiley & Sons for their editorial work.

I also want to thank Mr. Les Horvitz, who has helped me immeasurably to make a message into a book. We met for nearly three hundred hours and worked on our own much longer than that to produce this manuscript. Les was an active, engaged collaborator, reading the hundreds of source papers I selected; going over them with me to prepare for a chapter and accepting my interpretation of them (for better or for worse). Les came from New York to Baltimore regularly to discuss with me the book and all its extensions. I held stacks of papers in my hand, lead him through one-on-one seminars of two to three hours duration, and then loaded the papers and chapters into his satchel and asked him to return with the draft. His patience and sage advice were a great help and I am grateful to him.

I also wish to thank at the top of this acknowledgment Ms. Anne E. Phillips, who will be entering medical school this fall. Anne came to work with me as a research assistant shortly after getting her master's degree in biomedical technology. She came at a time when I had been doing much more editing than writing. Her talent and my weaknesses as an essayist created her major work, namely, helping to get me back to writing again. It involved her reading new papers and picking ones I should read. She edited out the duplications and basic flaws in my writing, developed a bibliography, and helped access expert advice as needed. She became a one-woman Kiretsu. Without Anne there would be no *Understanding Depression*. Thank you.

I owe particular thanks to my chairman Paul McHugh M.D., for being a wonderful mentor and strong supporter for twenty-six years and to Kay Jamison Ph.D., for her encouragement and enough ideas for three books as well as a foreword for this one. I take courage from both their work as teachers of students and advocates for patients and families. I thank Barbara Schweizer R.N., B.S., for her support and unflagging friendship; and I thank Dr. Virginia Willour Ph.D. and Ms. Jennifer Coughlin for reviewing the manuscript and giving helpful advice. I also want to acknowledge my colleagues who have helped me develop ideas included in this book: Michael Kaminsky M.D., John Lipsey M.D., Karen Swartz M.D., Melvin McInnis M.D., Sylvia Simpson MPH, M.D., Dean MacKinnon, M.D., Todd Cox M.D., James A. Potash M.D., and Frank Mondimore M.D.. I want to thank the many dedicated staff members on Meyer 4 including Trish Caruana LCSW-C, Sharon Walsh Esterbrook C.O.T., Rachel Tajenstein, M.S.W. and the nursing staff especially Chris Boyle RN and Deborah Brown RN. I also want to thank the members and staff at DRADA (Depression and Related Affective Disorders Association) especially, Sallie Mink, RN, Wendy Resnick, RN, Cathy Pollock, Anne Hilgartner, Vicki, Paulette Finck, and the members of the Roland Park and Timonium DRADA Family Support Groups for their advice and helpful insights. I also want to acknowledge and thank all of the research assistants who have kept our genetics research going and who have provided countless valuable questions and critiques: Krista Vishio, Jennifer Chellis, Erin Miller, Brandie Craighead, Katie Aman, Gwen Walker, Colleen Clarkin, and Lizza Gonzales. To Jen Coleman, who did so many tasks so that I could get started in this effort, thank you.

I acknowledge and thank Mr. Ken Heyman for the medical illustrations contained in the figures. I wish to acknowledge that about four chapters were derived from the "Grand Rounds" discussions I have presented over the last ten years at Johns Hopkins.

To my patients and their families, thank you for encouragement, advice, and for agreeing to see a better future when faced with today's conspicuously fallible enterprise.

Lastly to my wife, Joanne Althoff, who has been patient and encouraging, and critical only when I asked her to be one of my "readers." I offer heartfelt thanks.

# Foreword

Depression, for those who have it, is a painful and inextricable illness; for those who do not, depression is simply inextricable. Depression and manic-depression (bipolar disorder) are common illnesses in adolescents and adults and not uncommon ones in children. Suicide is one of the leading causes of death for those dealing with depression in virtually all age groups. Yet, where there should be open and informed discussion, there is a terrible silence. Depressive illnesses are highly treatable but most who suffer from them never receive any kind of treatment at all. Of those who do, most receive far less than ideal care. We know a tremendous amount about the symptoms, causes, and treatments of depression, but there remains an indefensible gap between what clinicians and scientists know and what the people who are depressed know. This is unfortunate and potentially dangerous.

*Understanding Depression,* written by Dr. J. Raymond DePaulo, Jr., a Professor of Psychiatry at the Johns Hopkins School of Medicine, is an excellent bridge between medical science and the sufferer. It presents in a direct and compelling way the most important things that patients and their families need to know about the symptoms of depression and mania; what depression and mania feel like to those who experience them; and what the best and most effective pharmacologic and psychotherapeutic treatments are. Dr. DePaulo covers the advantages and disadvantages of different treatment options, as well as medication side effects and how best to manage them. He also deals with the co-occurrence of anxiety, alcohol, and drug use, and other common problems that affect the treatment outcome of depression. Dr. DePaulo's approach to the clinical management of mood disorders is based on taking a long-term perspective on the illnesses, rather than focusing on just the presenting episode of depression. This is critical to providing excellent clinical care, and it is a perspective strongly supported by what we know scientifically and clinically about depressive illnesses.

I have been privileged to work and teach with Dr. DePaulo at

Johns Hopkins for the past fifteen years. He is, without doubt, one of the best clinicians and clinical teachers I have ever known. His understanding of depression is deeply grounded in science, and his treatment approach is characterized by compassion, pragmatism, subtlety, and an obvious affection and respect for the many thousands of patients he has so effectively treated.

None of us has a choice about becoming depressed. We do, however, have a choice about becoming informed about our illnesses. *Understanding Depression* is the best place to begin the process of becoming informed.

Kay Redfield Jamison, Ph.D.
Professor of Psychiatry
The Johns Hopkins School of Medicine

# A Clinician's View of Depression and Manic Depression: Progress, Ignorance, and a Promise

This book presents my experience—as a psychiatrist who has seen in consultation, teaching, research, and treatment settings some 8,000 people—with clinical depression and manic-depressive illness. I've also had a chance to meet thousands of other patients and their families in a variety of forums around the country including support groups and educational meetings.

Since many books have been written about depression you may be wondering for whom this book is written. First, it is for people who think that they may be suffering from depression or manic depression (bipolar disorder) and who want to know more about it. Second, it is for people who have already been diagnosed with depression (or bipolar disorder) and are in treatment, but who want to understand more about it in order to deal with it more successfully.

Third, I am writing for people who are concerned about a family member or loved one who may be in treatment or who is not receiving any medical care but probably needs it. Those of you in this category are very likely looking for advice on how to go about persuading the individual who might be depressed to go for help. On the other hand, you may be in a situation in which you feel shut out of the communication loop (as happens too often) between a family member and the doctor. It is very difficult to know what you can do to help (or what you shouldn't do) when you don't know how the treatment is actually progressing or what outcome can reasonably be expected. I hope this book will help you to participate more effectively as a patient or as a family member. Some readers may be oriented toward self-help, which is truly important as a part of all treatment plans. Nothing in treatment in my experience is more powerful than the efforts of patients and families who understand what they can do.

Finally, this book is for anyone who is interested in the problem of depressive disorders and other common disorders of mental life. You will learn what we know today about the causes (genetic and environmental) of depression and about treatments of all types as well as where I see the next advances coming in genetics, brain science, and treatment research. It is my hope and belief that, armed with the information about what we know and what we need to know, you will be more effective in helping yourself and others. The advocacy for research to make diagnosis and treatment more effective and available will ultimately come from patients and families affected with these conditions.

Not all the material in this book will be equally pertinent to all readers. People who are feeling down but unsure whether they're depressed will find what we as clinicians look for when diagnosing depression. What can you expect when you go to a doctor for an initial consult? What kind of outcome can you hope to achieve if the doctor does diagnose depression? For those of you already in treatment I've included information on what you can do to improve your chances of recovery. At the same time you will find out what you can expect from your doctor or other professional caregiver. Getting well isn't a one-way street—it isn't simply a matter of talking or taking medication. It is a process that works best as an active collaboration among the doctor (or other professional), the patient, and the family.

I'm covering both depression and manic depression in this book because they are closely related brain diseases that manifest themselves in clinical depression. There are many more patients with recurrent depression who never have manic attacks (unipolar disorder) than there are patients who have both depressions and manias (bipolar disorder), but perhaps one-fourth of the depression cases have a close genetic kinship to manic depression. So to understand the paths leading across depression we will have to travel to both of these terrains.

All the more reason to address the bipolar as well as the more common unipolar form of this illness.

My message to all readers is that you should know what the experts know and you should know what we *don't* know about causes, precipitants, and treatments for depression and manic depression. The critical value of knowing what we don't know is that the still unanswered questions allow us to frame what we *do* know, and to recognize what we need to prioritize for research. As clinicians, we know a great deal about the clinical presentations of signs and symptoms— as well as the long-term outcomes—of depression and manic depression. We know a great deal about today's treatment options, including medications, psychotherapies, and ECT. We know the odds of success are fairly good and we know the major complications of treatment. In sum, we know how to help patients and their families, which is the heart of our work in the clinic.

But our ignorance about these conditions is profound. I'm not talking about health professionals who just haven't kept abreast of the latest developments in research and treatment. I mean that we are *all* in the dark about the fundamental brain and genetic mechanisms underlying these conditions. And to be honest, we have very little knowledge about how our treatments for depression work even though we've found that they are usually quite effective.

My objective in this book is to try to give you a picture of what we know about depressive illness and its treatment and to point out where we're still in ignorance. Since 1988, when I coauthored with Keith Ablow, M.D., an earlier book, *How to Cope with Depression,* I've seen many more patients and used newer treatments that were still unknown when that book was published. That has given me a different, more nuanced perspective on depression than I had then. But even more influential in shaping my view of these conditions is my experience working with patients and their families over the last thirteen years in three settings: the clinical Affective Disorders Program at Johns Hopkins University (with an inpatient unit, an outpatient treatment clinic, and an outpatient consultation clinic), the Depression and Related Affective Disorders Association, or DRADA (an organization of 1,200 families, with 75 mutual support groups and school outreach programs); and our genetics research program (in which 1,500 families have volunteered for the study of the genetic causes of depression and manic depression).

In spite of the great advances made by science, some things have stayed the same or nearly so. As a group, for instance, patients have the same symptoms and signs of their illness as they did ten or twenty or fifty years ago. They experience the same fears, the same behavioral complications, and the same kinds of stress in their relationships as people with these illnesses always have. What has changed—aside from a few new treatments—are my views about how the disease may be caused by the interplay of genetic and environmental factors. I've also developed a greater appreciation of the role of self-destructive behaviors (abuse of alcohol and drugs to name two) in interfering in treatment. Finally, I've also come to understand the greater need for structured plans to foster the rehabilitation of patients who have been functionally set back by successive episodes of illness. You could say that I have more wisdom about what the critical steps in treatment should be.

In my first book, we focused on depression much more than on manic depression, an approach that was taken by many books like mine at the time. We emphasized that depression can be diagnosed using easily understood criteria, and that treatment was straightforward—and very effective. Those principles still hold true for half the patients with depression and half with bipolar disorders. We can treat them successfully and in a straightforward way, so long as their illness is typical and they understand their condition and comply with the treatment program.

In some ways, I'm more optimistic than I was when I wrote *How to Cope with Depression,* primarily because we have a larger array of medical treatments to tap. In 1988, I estimated that about 20 percent of patients with depressive illness were resistant to all medications and therapies. While doctors still use this figure, I now see that this is misleading and overly bleak. At the same time I realize more than I did before the enormous courage that most patients have in the face of the many treatments that have not helped them.

Nonetheless, I have to admit that finding an effective treatment for about 20 percent of all patients is a very time-intensive and painstaking task. Because I tend to see patients who have already failed many treatments before they come to Johns Hopkins, my overall view of the illness might be somewhat skewed toward this 20 percent. When it becomes clear to me that a patient has already gone through several adequate treatment trials without deriving any benefit from them, I try to approach the treatment realistically. I tell the patient that, as a first goal, we will seek an 80 percent improvement, and that, if this can be maintained for about 80 percent of the time, then we should seriously consider holding onto this treatment at least for a while. I read many papers recently that argue that it is wrong to settle for less than full remission and I am sympathetic to this view. However, for patients who have been depressed for years in spite of many efforts at treatment, then, when they reach 80 percent, I counsel against pressing our luck too quickly. Treatment changes, after all, can make patients worse as well as better. I usually counsel patients to stick with the mostly effective treatment for a time and see what other ways we can find to reduce symptoms and improve functioning. I have found that several life changes, such as a more rewarding relationship or a better job—or even the experience of helping others—often keeps the progress going, even when medication mediated improvement slows or stops.

So that's my view from the trenches, working with patients and their families. But the battle is also being fought in the labs, too. What events or problems in the brains of my patients were responsible for the disorders we are treating? We didn't know in 1988 and it's almost as much of a mystery today. Back then, I was reluctant to get into a speculative discussion of what might be happening in the brains of depressed or manic patients. (These speculations or "models" are what I term neuromythologies of the brain.) We now have more information, derived from newer brain imaging and other research methods, which bode well for eventual resolution of the mysteries of these disorders.

Many patients persuaded me that when it came time to write this book I should engage in some informed speculation. They argued that these models serve useful purposes (so long as I don't present them as revealed truth), even if none of the current ones turn out to be correct. These models point to the direction that scientists are taking as they search for the causes of depressive disorders. For some patients, just knowing that serious research in the causes of these conditions is being pursued offers reason for hope. And make no mistake: for most people struggling with a depressive disorder, research is *hope*.

What I want to do is provide you with a road map of depressive illness. How far have we come in our search for its cause and successful treatment? I will be describing where we are today in our ability to explain and treat depression and manic-depressive disorders. At the same time I will try to bring you up to date about what we've learned from the most recent research and draw on my own clinical observations as well. I will discuss the theories that hold the most promise in genetics and brain science. But, as I mentioned at the outset, there are still real gaps in our knowledge, and I will try to be clear about what they are. Still, you'd expect any road map to offer direction, and so you'll also find my advice about recognizing the symptoms, getting treatment, dealing with medical coverage, and obtaining helpful information from a variety of books, web sites, support groups, and relevant organizations. As I proceed, I also intend to emphasize just how devastating these disorders can be, in both personal and economic terms. Shamefully, depressive illness is still neglected at every level of our medical enterprise—not enough clinical resources are available, education about these conditions lags behind, and funding for research remains inadequate. That this neglect persists is unjustifiable, in view of the enormous potential of today's scientific tools to illuminate the basis of depression and bipolar illness. If this book can help change the situation in a positive direction then I will consider it much more than a success.

So now that you have the map, we can begin.

# PART ONE

∞

# Understanding Depression

In this first part I will try to convey as much as words will allow what it's like to experience depression and bipolar disorder. What is the difference between being clinically depressed and the normal feeling of discouragement you might expect, for example, if you lost your job or a friend? Which of us are more susceptible to depression? For instance, are women more prone to all forms of clinical depression than men are? We'll discuss the reality that the types of depression requiring medical attention are far more common than most people think. They come in a variety of shades and colors, sometimes posing as other conditions (psychiatric or physical), so that even psychiatrists and other health professionals often don't recognize they're related to depression.

Even if depressive disorders are prevalent all over the world, do they really matter other than to those who have had depressions? In other words, if you're not depressed and no one in your family is, why should you be concerned about it?

I believe (and I tell audiences wherever I speak) that the problem of depression and bipolar disorders matter to everyone. Identifying people who are in need of care and getting them the treatment they need is truly important to all societies. And here's why.

As an illness, depression exacts an enormously high cost in both human and economic terms. At least one in every 10 Americans experiences a clinical depression or manic-depressive episode in his or her lifetime. About 15 million people (10 million women and 5 million men) in the United States at any given time have major depression or some form of manic depression. By comparison, about 6 million people suffer from coronary disease.

By 2020, depression is expected to be the second most debilitating disease worldwide, after ischemic heart disease, and one of the

## Leading Sources of Disease Burden
## in Established Market Economies, 1990

| | | Total DALYs* (millions) | Percent of Total |
|---|---|---|---|
| | All Causes | 98.7 | |
| 1 | Ischemic heart disease | 8.9 | 9.0 |
| **2** | **Unipolar major depression** | **6.7** | **6.8** |
| 3 | Cardiovascular disease | 5.0 | 5.0 |
| 4 | Alcohol use | 4.7 | 4.7 |
| 5 | Road traffic accidents | 4.3 | 4.4 |

*Disability-adjusted life year (DALY) is a measure that expresses years of life lost to premature death and years lived with a disability of specified severity and duration. By this measure, major depression alone ranked second only to ischemic heart disease in magnitude of disease burden. Bipolar disorder, schizophrenia, obsessive-compulsive disorder, panic disorder, and especially alcoholism also contributed significantly. (Source: U.S. Surgeon General's Report on Mental Health, 2001.)

leading causes of death, as suicide takes more lives than traffic accidents, lung disease, or AIDS. Most of the people who commit suicide suffer from major depression or manic-depressive illness. Of the thirty thousand suicides annually in the United States, two-thirds or more have some form of depressive illness. Well, you might ask, isn't everyone who commits suicide depressed? The answer is no—at least not clinically depressed. Many people who take their lives are suffering from schizophrenia or other conditions that cause delusional beliefs that lead them to suicide. For instance, one of my patients with schizophrenia believed he would be ritually murdered and attempted suicide in order to avoid this, which seemed to him worse than death. Others attempt suicide when intoxicated with drugs and alcohol and become despondent and impulsive.

Depressive disorders can be lethal in other ways, too. Several recent studies have shown a link between heart disease and depression; a significant proportion of people with depression (but without any history of heart disease) will develop a heart attack within several years after an episode of depression. And people who have heart attacks or strokes when they are depressed are two to four times more likely to die from them than are people who have them but are not depressed.

The economy, too, takes a real hit from depression. Depression alone costs more than $44 billion in the United States economy each year. The impact on society includes decreased economic productivity because of days of work lost due to illness as well as increased health costs. And because few people with depression receive the diagnosis and treatment, the costs for them, their families, and their employers is even greater. Of the 11 million who suffer from depression each year, about 7.8 million (72 percent) are in the workforce. Major depression carries the greatest risk of disability days and days lost from work. (A disability day is defined as a day during which a person spent all or part of the day in bed due to an illness or was kept from usual activities due to feeling ill.)

Even so-called mild depression has a significant cost. A RAND Corporation study noted that the impact of depression on day-to-day functioning was "comparable to that of a chronic heart condition" and is responsible for more days in bed and more physical pain than hypertension, diabetes, or gastrointestinal problems. In terms of a person's ability to function physically—even to perform such simple tasks as walking or dressing, not to mention strenuous sports activities. Depression is more debilitating than many common medical conditions such as diabetes and arthritis.

What's being done about the problem? Clearly not enough. For one thing, the money being devoted to research to find the causes and devise new treatments isn't keeping pace with the need. Cardiovascular disease receives the largest amount of government funding, 25 percent; diabetes gets about 8 percent and cancer a little over 6 percent, while all mental illnesses (which includes Alzheimer's disease, schizophrenia, and several other conditions besides depressive illness) receive just 4 percent. Only one in three people with depressive illness ever gets diagnosed and treated for depression, according to government studies. In one survey, 78 percent of the respondents said they would simply continue to live with depression until it passed. Only half of those with the illness who ask for help get the correct treatments, usually because their physician fails to recognize their condition.

Now I've told you why I think the problems of depression and bipolar disorder are problems for all of us, not just for people with the illness and their families. But before you can do anything about the problem you have to understand what you're dealing with—what depression is and why it can be so difficult to recognize—and that's what we'll be doing in the next five chapters.

# CHAPTER 1

∞

# The Experience of Depression

What is it like to be depressed? The experience varies widely but to put it simply: when you're depressed you might feel as ill as when you have the flu, but it's a mysterious process because there is a sense that although you should be able to shake it off, you learn that there is little you can do to overcome it. If you're depressed, you may feel so isolated that the world seems a strange and hardened place. No matter what you do, it doesn't seem to help you or anyone else. Your natural habits of thinking and behaving calmly are not there when you need them. You wonder, "What is wrong with me?" What's worse, you don't see any way out; you could become convinced that you are going to remain in this state of discontent the sinkhole forever. The idea that it will pass on its own or that there might be light at the end of the proverbial tunnel seems to go on and off until you stop believing it.

What if you're not depressed yourself, but someone close to you is? As you may already know, depression isn't a disease that affects only the person who has it. Depression can drain the confidence that family members, loved ones, and coworkers have in the person. That loss of trust would be bad enough, but most people suffer from depression, often for years, without any idea that they are ill.

In the pages that follow, I'll be talking about the progress we're making in treating patients with depressive illness restoring them from the seemingly hopeless situations. Slowly—too slowly—the world of medicine is recognizing clinical forms of depression and manic depression as devastating diseases which benefit from treatment. The good news is that we are actually able to help increasing numbers of patients. But it's not enough. Greater understanding of these illnesses through research will allow us to help a greater number of people who are suffering. In the meantime, though, we need to redouble our efforts to reach many more people with depression and manic depression. The fact is that most people in need of help are never diagnosed, and, thus, never treated. We can talk all we want to about statistics and rigorous scientific studies, and we'll be referring to them as we go along. But I also hope to describe the people with depression: what it's like to experience the gnawing pain and terror in the faces of those with the illness. I want readers to understand how difficult it can be for patients to accept the slow progress of treatment and rehabilitation.

## How Do You Know If You're Depressed?

What we know about the experience of depression often comes after a depressed person has gotten better. The fact is, it's difficult for many depressed patients to give an account of their illness when they are depressed. They are working hard trying to manage their feelings and their responsibilities, and at the same time trying to figure out what is wrong with them. At their most despondent they feel overwhelmed. There are also unpredictable times when they may feel better, and they assure themselves that the episode has passed and they are okay. But then suddenly it is back, worse than before. Inevitably, these changes and moodiness can confuse and disrupt any continuity in work or in relationships. The confusion of the illness affects their ability to see things as they are.

Depression is an episodic illness. Episodes can last for weeks or months or years, and are interspersed with more or less symptom-free periods. They often wax and wane with external (seasons) or internal (hormonal) changes.

One of the most disabling aspects of depression is that often you don't know that you have it all. That doesn't happen with most other painful diseases that are usually quick to announce their presence and location. But depression can sneak up so insidiously that you literally don't know what it is, sometimes until years later. This was what happened to late night talk show host and writer Dick Cavett. Newly arrived in New York City, an aspiring actor, he was eager to launch his career on the Great White Way. The only trouble was that he couldn't get out of bed. "I'd stay between the sheets until three the next afternoon. And if I were really brave and heroic I would haul ass out of the apartment and take the laundry down, and that made for a big week. And that lasted six weeks. It seemed like spring cured it. I was sure I had a degenerative disease from looking at my face in the mirror, and most of my organs were rotting inside."

Once the depression was over, though, he says, "It was inexplicable. I couldn't remember that I'd had it or why I'd had it. It didn't even seem real that I'd had it." He described the experience as being under a "horrible black heavy dreary authority." The depression, he said, seemed impossible to lick. "This will last the rest of your life, you're the exception to the rule and the drugs won't work for you. You will die unloved and despairing in a garret even if you're a Rockefeller." He admitted to envying cancer patients he saw when he was at Columbia Presbyterian Hospital. Even though they had little time left, they were still interested in life. They cared about their families and their friends and still rooted for the Yankees (or prayed fervently for their comeuppance). But Mr. Cavett couldn't summon the energy or the will to care about anything or anyone.

Although being economically and socially deprived may play a role in the development of some depression, celebrity status, worldly success, good looks, and intelligence offer no protection from it. Most people who have lost a spouse to divorce or death or a friend or a cherished coworker will go through a period of bereavement, the length and intensity of which is related to how close they were to the deceased. However, this painful experience is not a clinical depression. Bereavement is normal and it serves as a catharsis; death brings people together in mourning but also in love. In some ways the rituals surrounding death are intended as celebrations of the life of the deceased. There are happy memories to be shared, and laughter as well as tears. Going through these rituals makes it easier for people to say good-bye to their loved one and then get back into their lives, even if their lives are never the same again.

On the other hand, for people who are genetically predisposed to depressive illness, even a small loss—a stolen camera, a raise, or a promotion delayed by two weeks—can trigger a ferocious depression. Those who are predisposed to depression, no matter how successful they are, can wake up one day unable to get out of bed and wonder how on earth they got to that point.

For someone who has never been hit with the illness before, it's difficult to distinguish between simply feeling down and being clinically depressed. Art Buchwald, the noted humorist and syndicated columnist, had a period of depression, but because he'd never had anything like it before, he assumed it was just a case of the blues. "Then," he said, "the blues went away." He soon learned, though, that depression wasn't just a matter of feeling low on a rainy afternoon.

The next episode of depression hit him so hard that it left him thinking that something was "seriously amiss." Having come through one episode without much trouble and then being struck down by a second left him confused and worried, Buchwald noted, "So you really don't know where you are in this business."

So exactly where are we in this "business"? How can anyone know when they have depression before they wind up collapsing or being hospitalized? You may imagine the worst but, it's important to remember that depressive disorders vary enormously in severity, duration, and frequency of episodes.

Doctors and patients who have lots of experience with the disease would say they judge the clinical meaning of the symptom by the company it keeps. With any depressive illness certain themes recur. We know, for instance, that in clinical depression, mood is usually down but—and this is important to note—not necessarily sad. Self-esteem and self-confidence go down, often dramatically.

We have to acknowledge that diagnosing depression is not as simple as it is with many physical ailments. A doctor might examine you and conclude with reasonable accuracy that you have heart disease or diabetes. To be sure, he or she must order blood tests or X rays or CAT scans, whatever is warranted. When it comes to depression, there's a significant difference. Clinicians can distinguish the symptoms of depression and if they're trained and observant, they can make a diagnosis that will serve as the basis for successful treatment. I cannot stress often enough that treatment is usually quite effective. What we do not have, though, are lab tests that can confirm the diagnosis; no blood test, X ray, or CAT scan will greatly increase the certainty of a clinical diagnosis of depression. This is not to say that we never use these tests. We often do so to find a cause for the depression when we suspect that a stroke or low thyroid functioning might be the cause. Whether the head MRI is normal or abnormal it doesn't change the diagnosis of depression. They simply say that a stroke did or did not produce it.

On what basis then can we assess whether someone is depressed? We have three basic criteria. Depression is characterized by 1) symptoms that involve changes in mood, vitality (physical and mental liveliness), and self-regard (self-esteem and self-confidence; 2) that it runs an episodic course, and 3) that it tends to run in families.

## Feeling Low

The hallmark of severe depression is an inclination to despair. If you're depressed, you tend to feel worthless and that it's only a matter of time before everyone else finds out. The prospect of receiving help may fail to lift your spirits. As Mr. Cavett put it, "you know you're depressed when you see a pill on your dresser that would cure you, and yet you don't have the motivation to get out of bed and take it." When a depression is severe, the patient truly feels worthless, useless, and possibly hopeless about the future. "Everything was black," recalls Buchwald, "the trees were black, the road was black. You can't believe how the colors change unless you have it. There's just no color. It's scary."

How do most doctors (and patients who have had depression already) know that clinical depression isn't the same as being in a bad mood? How do they know that depression doesn't represent a normal response to some terrible event? Maybe your dog did die, maybe you did lose your job—those are the kind of events that would probably make you feel bad. But depressed? If you haven't been there, then you might not suspect that there's much of a difference. Sooner or later, you'd suspect, you'd pull out of it, pick up the pieces, and get on with your life. Even physicians can be guilty of not being able to distinguish the difference. "I once went to a psychiatrist," Cavett recounted, "and I said, 'I'll do anything, get me out of this.' And he said, 'I know what you're going through. When one of my parents died I went through awful grief.' 'Do you think grief is anything like depression?' I told him. Go with the grief, it's better. In grief, you're at least feeling a rich, deep feeling. In depression you don't even have that, it's just that awful drone of nullity."

*An awful drone of nullity.* That's not sadness. It's worse than that. For many people, when they have depression, it's hard to feel *anything*. "I was totally without feeling," Cavett says. "I went to the dentist. And I thought, 'This is great: I won't take any Novocain and it will hurt and I'll feel something.' And it did. But not as much as if I were not depressed. So in some sense I was already anesthetized." And that sense of being anesthetized or deadened is what I mean by the soul of depression. You feel despondent with no hope for the future.

## Feeling Drained

Depression saps your ability to concentrate or think clearly. People with depression often find it difficult to comprehend what they're reading. They have to read the same lines over and over because nothing sticks in their minds. One of my patients complained that he could only read "words"—one at a time—but was unable to take in a whole paragraph. For some people with depression, it's even a struggle to keep track of what's being said in a conversation. In a very severe depression, thinking becomes muddled and confused.

When you're depressed, physical vitality also declines and you tend to feel fatigued much of the time. You lack the energy or stamina you are used to having. Getting started in the morning is extraordinarily difficult, and you don't have the energy to do things that normally would be second nature to you. You have decreased ability to perform tasks that demand concentration or a mental effort. This inability can transform even minor challenges into major crises, especially at work. Depending on the severity of depression, you'll probably get through most days, but with difficulty. It might take six hours to accomplish what you would normally have done in two or three. You might make more errors, and your performance may become inconsistent. Your physical and mental vitality also varies depending on the time of day. The most typical pattern in depression is to feel worse in the early morning hours and better during the evening.

The change in vitality can take the form of physical symptoms, too. People who have arthritis or are prone to headaches may find that their symptoms worsen. In some cases they may develop new symptoms. People with depression will often become overly preoccupied by a medical condition that they previously might have thought to be merely an inconvenience. Inconsequential aches and pains are viewed as harbingers of a serious threat to their health. In the most severe forms, depressed individuals might become convinced that they have a fatal illness like terminal cancer or AIDS.

Usually depression causes sex drive to diminish or disappear altogether. Pulitzer-prize–winning novelist William Styron, who suffered a severe bout of depression, reported that he lost confidence in his psychiatrist when the psychiatrist hesitated to use a particular antidepressant because it might diminish Styron's sexual functioning: Styron admitted to being bewildered by the psychiatrist's attitude. "He couldn't possibly have any idea of what I had, if he thought that I was interested in a little carnal fun."

Appetite can also change in depressive illness. In the most severe depressions, patients were classically thought to lose their appetite, restrict their eating, and experience considerable weight loss as a result. But, at least an equal number of depressed people, including many people with bipolar disorder who are in their depressed phase, will actually overeat and gain significant amounts of weight. Overeating is also seen in people who have seasonal depression cycles or who have long-standing but moderate depressions. (This can be particularly problematic for whose self-esteem is closely tied to their weight, who might require medications that increase their appetite.) About one-third of the people with depression, however, have no particular change in eating habits or weight.

Sleeping habits during depression vary considerably; sleeping can increase as well as decrease. Sleep often increases for people who suffer from seasonal and chronic depressions compared to episodic and extreme forms of clinical depression, in which loss of sleep is more common. Typically depressed individuals have fewer problems falling asleep but find that *staying* asleep is a real problem. They'll often wake up by three or four A.M. and find it very difficult to get back to sleep.

## Feeling Worthless

Our feeling of self-regard or self-esteem is a part of our everyday inner life. It normally varies, even if only by a little bit, depending on the challenges and frustrations we encounter. *Was I a good mother today? Did my wife really understand that I didn't mean to forget her mother's birthday? If I work overtime will I feel like a fool if the boss doesn't notice?* These are the types of situations into which self-criticisms from depression can creep without raising any alarms. Only when significant and obvious changes occur are we finally warned that a real problem exists.

The sense of worthlessness for depressives can be so pronounced that the most heartfelt reassurances of their closest friends and families will fall on deaf ears. Some of my patients have told me that their depression warps reasoning, so that they will think friends are secretly angry at them but won't come right out and say so because they're too polite. That's why close relationships are difficult to sustain. Take, for example, a patient of mine who brushed off his wife's reassurances that she loved him in spite of his illness. "I know it's irrational," he said, "but I thought she must be insincere or stupid. If she really knew how hollow I was she wouldn't want to stay with me."

## Other Signs of Depression

In addition to the symptoms of depression I've mentioned, there are also the signs of depression that doctors discover by examining and observing patients. In some depressed patients, I can see a change in facial expression and a loss of muscle tone that causes them to look exhausted all the time. When some patients become depressed, they will walk or talk more slowly so that it's like watching a film meant to be shown at thirty-two frames per second running at sixteen per second. The most severely depressed might take one to two minutes to answer a simple question, even one requiring a yes or a no. It's difficult for me to watch a patient going through such a painful experience. It's much more painful for the patient who feels so paralyzed. I can actually see the anguish in the patients' faces as they start to give an answer, then hesitate, then resume again, repeating this cycle many times. It is the psychiatrist's equivalent to what a surgeon has to do when palpating an extremely sensitive part of a patient's body. The surgeon knows that he or she will produce pain, but it's necessary to find out what's wrong.

Sometimes the physical signs are quite dramatic. I had one patient who developed a Parkinsonian-like syndrome. He had typical stiffness, slowness, and tremors that would appear only when he was depressed. The same syndrome had reappeared six times over the course of thirty years, showing up whenever he became depressed and vanishing as soon as he was better.

Some patients may even fall into a stupor when they're depressed, becoming unable to move. One of my patients remained in a stupor for twenty or twenty-two hours a day, becoming alert only for a couple of hours in the evening when he'd improve and have a bite to eat. There are patients so immobilized that you can lift up their limbs and unless you put them back down again, they will remain suspended in the air. Other patients exhibit what we call waxy flexibility because their limbs are like warm wax candles that you can "mold" into a new position and that will then maintain their new shape. Physicians call these catatonic signs. Although we used to think that all these patients had catatonic schizophrenia. We now know that most of them did not and that they can make full recoveries.

Once they recover, though, many of these patients will remember a lot more than you would have thought by looking at them during their illness, since they appear so unaware of their surroundings. They may tell you that they were so uncertain as to what to say or do that they simply couldn't act.

## Jumping Out of Your Skin: Depression and Anxiety

Depression is associated with a high frequency of anxiety symptoms or anxiety disorders. In fact, anxiety is the most common of the syndromes that cluster with depression as well as with manic depression.

With both illnesses, a person often has a high degree of anxiety. In that sense, severe anxiety can be seen as a manifestation of depression. But I don't mean to suggest that all people with anxiety have depression. Anxiety disorders can also affect patients who have never had a clinical depression. However, we know that there is a link between depression and anxiety. Neuroscientists tell us that many of the same nerve pathways and brain regions are involved in both.

In his account of his depression, novelist William Styron described how, for months at a time, he was in a continual state of panic. He was so intensely agitated that he felt as if he were jumping out of his skin. The experience, he said, was like a brainstorm. He wasn't referring to a burst of inspiration; what Styron meant was being in the grip of a raging storm—a cyclone or a hurricane—that rips through the mind, leaving destruction and havoc in its wake.

When we talk about anxiety, what do we mean exactly? There are several specific types: panic attacks, phobias, and obsessive-compulsive symptoms. The phobias include agoraphobia (fear of the marketplace, literally), social phobias, fear of water, fear of heights, fear of driving, fear of speaking or eating, or being scrutinized by others in public, and so on. But there are hundreds of phobias, most of them not so severe, including a fear of the number thirteen. People can often live perfectly normal lives with these phobias, even if it means missing out on some opportunities—they might simply avoid going to the top of the Empire State Building. But in some instances phobias become so debilitating that they prevent someone from leading a normal life. This is especially true when a person is in a state of depression. Depressed people can become so fearful of scrutiny that they feel that other people are staring at them. Even walking into a room to exchange a few words with someone may overwhelm them.

Patients with depression may develop agoraphobia. Agoraphobia is usually taken to refer to an intense fear of going out in public. But most are also actually afraid to be alone so that their spouse or partner cannot leave them at home and must accompany them outside of the home.

Panic attacks which come out of the blue often occur in depression. These attacks are typified by a rapid onset of extremely unpleasant symptoms—rapid heartbeat, sweating, tightness in the chest, lightheadedness, and shortness of breath. When the panic attack is over, many people fear another attack. They will avoid putting themselves in the situation that seemed to have brought on the first attack. Some of my patients report that there are few more terrible experiences in their life than having an anxiety or panic attack. If you have a panic attack in a store, you might hesitate to enter that store again for fear of having another panic attack. In this way panic attacks and phobias can be linked together. If the attacks continue in other settings the patient might further restrict their movements. This ironically makes them more vulnerable to an attack the next time they are exposed to any circumstances that cause them anxiety. Their activities can become so restricted that they become virtually housebound for fear of another attack.

For many patients, when the depression lifts, so does the anxiety. But, for some individuals, even when the depression clears, the anxiety disorder, improves without going away entirely. Fortunately, though, we've found that most antidepressants are also inherently good treatments for anxiety disorders. even in patients who have never been depressed.

## Hallucinations: Seeing Is Believing . . . or Isn't It?

When I began my practice I found it relatively easy to observe and comprehend some of the symptoms of depression such as a loss of self-confidence and self-esteem. But other symptoms of the disease are not constant; that's to say they occur in some patients but not in all. Even the same patient will have some symptoms during one episode of depression that may not arise during the next episode. The most alarming of depressive symptoms, however, are delusions and hallucinations. They occur frequently enough so that we recognize typical forms of them as symptoms of a depressive or manic illness. But while they are not uncommon, they are very upsetting and confusing symptoms for patients and their families all the same.

Anyone who watches TV or goes to the movies is familiar with the term *hallucination*. A hallucination is a perception without a stimulus. By stimulus we mean the object (e.g., a chair) you see. By perception we mean the normal function of the five sensory systems (vision, hearing, touch, smell, taste). We distinguish hallucinations from a distorted or misinterpreted perception and firm images. Images are often powerful but they are seen in the mind's eye and thus don't have the concrete quality of true perception. In the case of a distorted perception, something is truely present (a stimulus); the problem is you thought it was one thing when in reality it turned out to be something else. That accounts for why someone could observe a cloud formation or the twinkling lights of a satellite and think it's a flying saucer. We call these illusions or misinterpretations. By contrast, a hallucination has all the properties of a normal perception except that there's nothing out there. When we evaluate patients it can take a while, but we want to be very clear to differentiate these three events: images, illusions, and hallucinations.

In such cases the experienced psychiatrist's examination becomes an art form: The patient must be persuaded that the psychiatrist is intent on understanding their experience. They don't want to be thought of as crazy. After all, any of us can misinterpret what we perceive through our senses. We need to get a description of the *qualities* of the patient's experience. When we are examining the qualities of a perception we can do it after the fact. Usually we cannot determine after the fact whether a stimulus was present in the patient's bedroom when they heard the "voice." Proceeding this way will help us determine whether the patient's experience was more like a perception or like a vivid image. Where did the event take place? Was it outside or was it inside my head—in the mind's eye? Was mental work necessary to see it or was it effortless or automatic. In general, when patients tell me they saw something as clearly as they are seeing me but the room was in total darkness, my conclusion is that this was probably a hallucination and not an image or normally perceived event.

Hallucinations are much more common and more elaborate in schizophrenia than in depression. One summer day, a patient I'll call Sarah was riding on a city bus, and even though the windows were closed and the air-conditioning was running at full blast, she told me that she could hear people at the bus stop, a hundred feet behind the bus, muttering, "There goes Sandtown Sally." She was certain that the comments were directed at her because she'd come from Sandtown, where they used to call her by the name Sally. And she was convinced that these comments were derogatory, even somewhat threatening. These people at the bus stop, Sarah said, were warning her about the things they would do if she should ever come that way again. Her hallucination was so persuasive to her that she stopped riding the bus for the next two months in order to avoid that particular bus stop.

## Delusions: Unshakeable Ideas Against All Evidence

Unlike hallucinations that occur in depressive episodes, which are usually not very elaborate, delusions in depression can take on extraordinarily intricate form. We define a delusion as a fixed false, idiosyncratic idea, or judgment that is almost always so self-absorbing that it doesn't leave much room in the mind for anything else. When I say that a delusion is fixed I mean that you can marshal the most convincing evidence in the world to prove that the idea is false but it won't do any good. The person with the delusion is absolutely convinced despite all evidence that he or she is in possession of the truth. A delusion is idiosyncratic in that it is deeply personal and not shared by the patient's family, church (if the delusions are religious), or coworkers. The final requirement is that the judgment is false. How do I assess falseness? Sometimes it's very easy to do, but occasionally it is extremely hard.

Psychiatric history offers an intriguing example of the way in which delusions can occur along with depression. Clifford Beers, who later founded the National Mental Health Association, became ill in 1900. During his long bout with depression he suffered from a number of delusions, the most prominent and persistent of which was his unshakable belief that he had epilepsy and was doomed to a fate worse than death. He reasoned that because his brother had epilepsy, he, too, must be developing the illness. No one else believed this to be true, including the doctor who was treating him. Beers, however, could not be swayed from his conviction. In fact, he was quite certain that his illness was so catastrophic that it would be easier for his family and himself if he died rather than to endure his excruciating deterioration. His delusion was so compelling that he decided to take his own life and spare his family further agony. He attempted suicide, disrupting an afternoon party at his parents' home by jumping from a third-floor window. Fortunately, he survived.

One of my patients was president of a bank and very secure financially. When he was depressed, though, he was sure that he was impoverished; he was convinced that he'd be on the street in a week or two looking for a handout. He discounted any reassurances that his wife or I tried to give him; everything we said made him even more upset. He'd constructed several *almost* plausible scenarios in which he'd fall into destitution. His accountant acknowledged that in theory he could see the logic of one or two of the scenarios, but that they were not realistic worries. We call this symptom a delusion because it was a fixed false idiosyncratic judgement. He was unable to be persuaded that he was not going broke, and he was totally consumed by the idea. Trying to get him to talk about anything else was pointless.

Negative or nihilistic delusions, on the other hand, are fixed false ideas that plague and torture the most severely ill depressed patients. Typically, people with these delusions believe that their insides have rotted away, that there is literally nothing inside their bodies. They may even have the idea that their brains have degenerated and that their skulls are empty. If you ask them to explain how they still manage to walk and talk without any brain, they'll tell you that that they are the object of a cruel joke. While it may appear as if they are walking or talking, they know for certain that they are, in fact, dead. To have a glimmer of their inner life, try watching some of George Romero's horror movies populated by zombies, the living dead. There are patients who, like those who condemned women to death in the Salem witch trials, believe they are possessed by the devil.

Delusions can take on another form in people with depression, as William Shakespeare understood when he wrote *Othello*. There we find these lines: "But jealous souls will not be answered so/They are not even jealous for the cause/But jealous for they are jealous/'tis a monster begot upon itself, born on itself." The green-eyed monster of this passage is familiar to us all. In extreme cases jealousy can become pathological, a delusory condition known as morbid jealousy, what some psychiatrists call the Othello Syndrome.

Morbid jealousy doesn't require the presence of a depression or any other form of mental illness to occur, but it is more common than you would think among people with depression. Some healthy people develop jealousy based on suspicions that have no basis in reality. When is jealousy abnormal? The answer is that at its extreme it can become not only abnormal, but truly delusional.

Morbid jealousy takes on a particular complexion in people who are depressed or manic. In depression the jealousy often seems to grow out of feelings of inferiority or worthlessness that come with depression. An eighty-five-year-old patient told me (after many denials) that he was convinced that his seventy-two-year-old wife was having an affair after fifty-five years of faithfulness! "Of course, she is, Doctor," he insisted. "I've lost her interest now and compared to me she is a young woman who doesn't want her life to end like mine is."

Sometimes people's suspicions about their partners grow out of their conviction that anybody who professes to love them must be faking since, as bad as they are, no one could really love them. Then they begin to mull over the possibilities. *Why is my wife so satisfied? Could it be that she's off with someone else and doesn't want me to suspect it?*

Morbid jealousy can suddenly strike in people who have never been jealous before, or it can be an aggravation of a long-standing but milder jealous inclination. The jealous spouse might ask questions that are thinly veiled accusations, but as time goes on will begin to make accusations: *Why were you out so late? Who were you just talking to over the phone?*

Although patients with depression (and mania) are usually not dangerous to others there are exceptions. People overcome by delusional jealousy can be intensely suspicious of everything their spouses do and everyone they see. Those suffering from this condition may be so overwhelmed by the power of the delusion that they become preoccupied with a loss that hasn't occurred and contemplate harming themselves or their spouse or the spouse's imagined consort. When this pattern develops, immediate psychiatric help is critical.

Sadly, too many people do not realize the need for help or understand the potential for danger if their preoccupation continues to intensify. Spouses, families, even police and judges often fail to appreciate the significance of the disorder, with terrible consequences ensuing as a result.

There's yet another delusion that is in some sense the mirror image of morbid jealousy, called erotomania. Writing in the waning years of the nineteenth century, a French physician named de Clerambault discussed a phenomenon he'd observed in one of his patients who'd formed a fixation on a man she'd only seen from afar in church. "From this distant view alone, she asserted that she had absolute proof that this gentleman was in love with her and thought of no one but her. She laid siege to him till in exasperation he lodged a complaint and she was committed to a mental hospital." The woman was suffering from what we now call a delusion of passion or erotomania. Strange as it may seem, this type of delusion can occur in a depressive disorder, a manic episode or in mixed states.

People who are consumed by this delusion come to believe, against all evidence, that the person they are fixed on is really the pursuer or at least was the one who fell in love first. This is a psychiatric condition that is sometimes associated with what's called stalking. The stalker may shadow the object of desire unrelentingly, sending letters and gifts or show up at the person's house at all hours of the day or night. Sometimes the pursued person will mistakenly think that he or she can solve the problem by reasoning with the pursuer. When the pursuer is delusional this approach usually has the effect of encouraging the pursuer even further.

In these cases, my recommendation is first to treat the depression or mania or other underlying condition. However, sometimes it seems that the depression or mania resolves but the erotomania will still persist or recur with the recurrences of the illness.

In 1895, before the age of modern medicine, an eminent psychiatrist named Emil Kraeplin concluded that the best treatment for erotomania was "geographic." The deluded person had to move away (or be moved if necessary) from the person he or she was pursuing. Even today this is sometimes the best solution.

Now that you've read this chapter I hope you can see that depression can often be a confusing illness to identify, diagnose, and treat. Yet I've also tried to show you that together mental health professionals and patients—are making a good deal of progress against this terrible illness. While we do not have physical criteria to diagnose depression, like CAT or MRI scans or blood tests, we nonetheless have some fairly reliable markers for the disease. If several major symptoms are present we can, with a fair amount of reliability, determine that someone is depressed. These symptoms include a dramatic change in mood (often characterized by a sense of numbness rather than sadness), a depletion of vitality, an inability to concentrate, muddled thinking, and a loss of self-regard or self-esteem. Depression is also marked by troubling changes in appetite, sleep, and sexual drive. In many cases, anxiety and panic disorder can occur as a manifestation of the depression and disappear when the depression does. Many people with depression also experience hallucinations and delusions. In addition to these symptoms, there are signs of depression that express themselves physically, in a slowing down of speech or movement, or in certain instances in stupor or immobility.

In this country depression affects about 6 to 12 percent of the population at any given time while a separate but related illness, manic depression, affects about 1 percent of the population. However, in order to get a clearer picture about depressive illnesses, we will need to consider manic depression, or bipolar illness, as well. And that's the subject of our next chapter.

# CHAPTER 2

The Experience of Mania:
Bipolar Disorder

The central feature or essence of mania is a state of excitement with an inflated sense of self. You may feel highly valued, omnipotent, or omniscient. Manias produce many other symptoms, but that sense of autointoxication is the essence. This type of intoxication needs no alcohol or drug to cause it. In effect, you get high off yourself. But as you'll shortly find out, not all mania is capable of making you giddy with happiness any more than all depression makes you sad.

Syndicated columnist Art Buchwald was first hospitalized for severe clinical depression. Several years later he was hospitalized again, but this time he was in a manic state. Manic episodes are the most dramatic expressions of classic manic depression or to use the more preferred name, bipolar disorder. When he was in a manic phase, Buchwald didn't think anything was the matter with him. On the contrary, he'd never felt better; he was on top of the world. "There's a power that comes with it and you love and cherish it." The downside is . . . well, the downside. Many manias are followed by severe depressions. If you don't "crash" into depression you might still experience the reentry to a more normal mood as painful. You might find out that, because of the episode, you have lost your friends, your credit, your marriage, and possibly your reputation. Art Buchwald had a sense that something might be wrong and got help promptly. Sadly, most people with manic depression are not willing to get help, and so they and their families end up paying a terrible price.

Manic depression is now generally known as bipolar disorder because it has two phases. (It was given the colorful label "manic-depressive insanity" by the nineteenth-century psychiatrist Emil

Kraepelin.) Bipolar disorder has so much in common with severe unipolar depression that they used to be thought of as variants of the same condition. These two illnesses—depression and manic depression—are alike and very different. They both catch you by surprise. They will strike at times you might expect them to—when you are under a lot of stress, or if you're already being treated, when you stop taking your medicines—but they can also hit when everything seems to be going well, when "morning is at seven and God's in heaven." Episodes of depression and mania last for weeks, months, or even years. They usually occur between longer symptom-free periods, but for 20 percent of the patients they rarely go away completely. For many people with manic depression, the depressive phases wax and wane with seasons or hormonal rhythms. Both depression and mania have a disruptive effect on sexual drive, appetite, and sleep. We used to think that anxiety disorders were more common with unipolar depression, but we now know that they frequently appear in both depression and manic depression. In about 20 percent of the families with manic depression, several family members had attacks of panic disorder as well as unipolar depression.

Nonetheless, manic depression has some distinct characteristics all its own, and we now consider depression and manic depression as separate but similar conditions. Manias, like depressions, can assume many different colorings, but they are generally characterized by elation, irritability, hyperactivity, hyperexcitability, and accelerated thinking and speaking, almost always accompanied by a loss of good judgment. In addition to these classic manias, there are relatively mild manias, which we called hypomanias.

What can we say about mood, vitality, and self-regard in people with manias or hypomanias? For the most part, the mood in mania is almost a complete reversal of what we've just said about depression. Just as a descending sense of self-worth and self-confidence is the central experience of the depressed state, an ascending or inflated sense of self is the crux of the manic state. One of my manic patients put it like this: "I have a sense that I have just discovered something important. I'm not sure what it is, but I am certain that it is very important." He had just gone through a serious operation and had been asleep the whole time. However, when he awoke, he experienced a sense of euphoria that puzzled him. He felt as if he were navigating a maze searching for an elusive goal. "I feel too good to have had the surgery you told me I had," he said. "So you must have lied, and brought me in for some cosmetic surgery, and [admiring his scar] it does look good. You are pretty clever."

As a recognized condition, mania has a history extending back to ancient times. But it was only in the late nineteenth century that Emil Kraepelin put the disorder on the map as a modern disease. Kraepelin based his theories on his experience treating about 3,000 patients. He was one of the first psychiatrists to conceptualize mania and depression in terms of diseases, meaning that they both exhibited a set of symptoms that could be explained by a broken or malfunctioning body part. He maintained that clinical forms of depressions and manias and mixed states (a combination of the two) should be understood as "a single morbid process," but that he couldn't say what the morbid process was or in which part of the brain it was occurring. He also admitted that he was unsure about a practical treatment for these illnesses. Although he'd tried sedation to alleviate his patients' symptoms, he recognized that it wasn't particularly effective. He expressed the hope that in the future these conditions would be understood and treated as illnesses. Seeing depression and manic depression as an illness would have two benefits, he said. For one thing, it would prompt physicians to treat patients with psychiatric illness more humanely. For another, it would influence the direction of medical research in finding the ultimate causes of the illness.

## How Manias Speed You Up

Manic patients have a lot of *energy*—too much energy. It's the kind of energy that can carry you on a thrilling coaster ride but ends by throwing you off. Unfortunately, this can literally be true. A number of patients, believing that they could fly, have leapt to their deaths from windows or roofs of tall buildings.

Manias get people revved up for a period of time. They sometimes perform with such efficiency and act so enthusiastically that others around say with admiration, "Look at that guy go! He's never looked so good!" But that impression is mistaken. When someone has a severe manic episode, judgment can be warped. So the person will tend to do things that he or she would never do under normal circumstances: going on spending sprees, indulging in drugs, or deciding on the spur of the moment to get on the next plane to Las Vegas to drop a life savings in one night, and give the rest away on the street.

Many people with mania, though by no means all, will experience a physical sensation best described as a feeling of racing (as in a car race). They may feel in complete control, just about to go out of control, or feel out of control. Those who feel in control say their minds are locked in and as focused as, say, a basketball player in a game where he can't seem to miss a shot or an actor who loses himself in the role. Athletes call this experience being in the zone while an actor might call it getting into character. A golfer who seemingly can't miss a putt calls it "seeing the line." (I don't mean to suggest that great athletes are manic; truly manic athletes cannot perform well at all.) In severe mania the speed of thinking increases dramatically. Patients not only refer to racing thoughts but often speak in a way that reflects this. Many of my patients will tell me that they make more intuitive and more frequent "connections" between events. They even find it frustrating that the rest of us can't seem to keep up with them. For these patients the racing sensation is usually pleasant but for those who feel they can't keep up with the speed, the sensation can be very unpleasant. For them the sensation is more like riding a tiger: they're barely able to hold on, but the experience is so thrilling that they don't want to get off.

Manic patients also feel that what they're doing is volitional, that they really are in charge. And, of course, they are "making decisions," it's just that their ability to form accurate and prudent judgments about themselves and their situation is impaired, a little in hypomania and a lot in mania. Nor do they have a realistic sense of the consequence of their actions. Some people who have a mania will seek out new stimuli wherever they can find them. That may mean taking on a risky new investment, making an extravagant purchase, or using illicit drugs. Ironically, one of the main psychological principles in managing manic patients is to decrease stimuli.

It's not hard to spot people when they're in a manic state. Once they start talking they often won't stop; you won't be able to get a word in edgewise. Their words tumble over one another at lightning speed. Some patients talk so fast that you can't follow them. They jump from one topic to another. The abrupt changes in topic can seem senseless, but it is often possible to discern their logic if you can slow the patient down. One patient startled me by saying, "Aha, there goes Beethoven," when he saw another patient walk past us carrying a cup of coffee. What could this mean? I asked the patient why he'd called the man Beethoven. He said that the coffee was brown, and brown was symbolic of the Nazis since there was a Nazi paramilitary group known as the Brown Shirts. The Nazis were German and so was Beethoven. So that's how he figured out that the patient carrying the coffee was Beethoven! The last step was patently illogical, but at least he had made the first three connections flawlessly. Speech that jumps so fast from topic to topic, often filled with rhymes or puns is called "flight of ideas" and is a classic sign of mania.

## Hypomanias

What about those milder forms of mania known as hypomania? (Literally, hypomania refers to a state "just under" mania, along the lines of the term hypochondria, which originally referred to patients with discomfort in the area just below their sternum called the hypochondrium.) In fact, these manic states are so mild that most people who have them think of them as normal. But though they may not last long, these states are *not* normal. After a while, even some of the mild cases have unhappy social consequences that can jeopardize friendships and close relationships. One patient told me that his wife felt that he acted as if he didn't like her during these spells, which he called "periods of false happiness."

The feeling that they are "in the zone" like basketball players who can't miss can be more than a feeling for some people with hypomanias, at least temporarily. Some athletes can perform herculean tasks. One patient persuaded a bank to give him an unsecured loan of $500,000. After his family found out, but before they could stop him, he put it into speculative developments. By the time they caught him he had lost some but not all of the money. His investments were not great but his persuasive abilities were fabulous. On the other hand patients who make these investments while they're manic usually end up losing all their money and go deeply into debt.

When a person goes into a mild manic state, he or she will often feel immensely relieved simply not to be depressed after several months of feeling awful. Some hypomanic patient will truly feel normal. The families of these people often see it that way, too, at least at first. The problems may develop later on, when these individuals expect to feel and function at a high level of energy all the time. This has a serious implication for treatment, because, in their craving for the high, they may discard medications that don't get them to that pleasant high state.

Let me give you an example of what it means to be in a hypomanic state. One of my patients is a young woman who, when she gets into one of these mild states, is suddenly seized by the urge to clean. And clean. And clean. When she's in the midst of a depression she'll let a lot of things slide and then one day, when her mood improves, she'll decide "to make up for lost time." These sudden bursts of energy come on her about three times a year. She'll stay up until two in the morning cleaning like mad. At one in the morning she'll just be getting going when anyone else in her situation would be exhausted. In fact, she'll be operating at peak efficiency at one or two A.M. That's another characteristic of these mild manias: It feeds on itself. The more active hypomanic people get, the more energy they seem to have. What distinguishes hypomania from full mania is the degree of intensity of the experience, the severity of the problems that come from their actions. Hypo means "just under." So a hypodermic needle goes just under the skin and a hypomania is just below mania. Such states are also marked by what looks like compulsive behavior. My patient told me that when she got focused on the closet, she would begin to organize her hangers, dividing the hangers by their color and whether they were metal, plastic, or wood. And once she gets going there's really no stopping her. If she started the night thinking she was going to get the closet done, by the time she's nearly finished cleaning and rearranging the closet her thoughts are traveling to the cellar or to the attic, where more cleaning and unpacking await her. No matter how much she's already accomplished, she'll keep readjusting the goal, setting more tasks for herself.

When she's hypomanic, she will go over the top of what she knows to be her normal standards of conduct. She'll switch on the TV and turn the volume way up. She'll turn on the stereo and play that fullblast as well. Then if someone phones, she'll take the call but make no effort to turn down the volume on the TV. She thinks she can hear just fine. However, she isn't really inclined to listen to what the person on the other end is saying anyway; she's too distracted. She'll shout into the phone unaware that she isn't herself. If anyone points this out, she will tell them where to get off and not give it another thought until she realizes a day or two later that she'd behaved improperly.

Now, she doesn't ever become convinced that she is God or about to move into the Oval Office. Nor does she make rash purchases. On the other hand, she has been known to tell her boss to go to hell and becomes irritable with her husband and sister over perceived slights.

How these hypomanic states express themselves depends on the individual involved. Another patient of mine, for instance, a physician, will get this kind of mild hypomania whenever he's called upon to write a paper for a leading medical journal. He'll work feverishly on it for two weeks straight until he's gotten the article done, and invariably it's beautifully written. But no sooner has the last page rolled out of his printer than he realizes that he's not said hello or good night to his wife or children for two weeks. He regrets these even though they are mild and calls them his periods of "false happiness."

## Are Manic Depressives More Creative?

The feeling of being in total command, is usually an illusion, because performance most often deteriorates in mania and to some extent in hypomania (depending on the task). Many years ago I had a manic patient who was a young up-and-coming artist. When he was hospitalized he continued to paint but faster than ever. He was able to complete as many as three to six canvases a day and do so with astonishing facility, at least to my untrained eye. But when he declared each new painting to be his best ever, I began to realize that his judgment was off. As his manic energy ebbed during his treatment with lithium, he calmed down considerably, spending his nights sleeping rather than whipping out paintings at his easel. One morning as I was at work in my office I heard someone scream out in the corridor. When I looked out to see what was going on I found my patient standing in front of a large stack of his paintings with look of shock on his face. "Who painted these?" he demanded. (I think he suspected the truth.) "You did," I replied. He was clearly distressed to hear this. Shaking his head, he muttered, "These are awful." All twenty-five to thirty paintings, produced at such a furious clip, were abandoned to the junk heap.

This is an appropriate point to bring up a subject of interest to many: lithium, the medication most often prescribed to treat mania. Patients and sometimes people who care for them worry that the medication will impair their creativity. While creativity is very hard to define, some researchers have studied several established artists who suffered from mania and were put on lithium for a year or more. Of the twenty-four artists surveyed in one study, two-thirds of them reported that their work had improved since they started lithium. Only a few felt that their work had gotten worse or that there had been no change from before they entered treatment.

## A Burst of Energy: Losing Judgment and Inhibitions

While people with either mania and hypomania become more energized, this is more the case in cases of mania. Manic individuals might go several nights or weeks with little or no sleep. They also can exhibit more outlandishly unpredictable behavior. One of my first manic patients simply left our inpatient ward and took a walk . . . and what a walk it was! The police picked him up on the interstate after he'd covered nearly half the distance from Baltimore to Washington. And he'd done it all barefoot without realizing that his feet were bleeding. The episode was frightening for me and presumably very painful for him, but it could have been even worse. The manic and to a lesser extent hypomanic states change the person's perceptions, including the perception of pain. Like my runaway patient, people with mania often feel so invulnerable that they can go for hours or even a day or two before they notice that they have injured themselves. Just as their perception of pain is diminished, people in the manic state often experience heightened perceptions of color, motion, and music. (These perceptual changes tend to occur in the reverse direction in depressive states.)

The impaired judgment in mania is usually severe and is most appreciated as a reduction or complete loss of normal inhibitions. People in such a state fail to grasp the consequences of their behavior. They can make calamitous choices—squandering large sums of money, for instance, or indulging in sexual excesses, or making spectacles of themselves in public—and in the process create wildly embarrassing scenes for friends and family. Sometimes the consequences of their actions can be devastating. In her 1998 memoir, *Personal History,* the late Katherine Graham, former publisher of the *Washington Post,* described what it was like to be married to someone suffering from manic depression. Once, addressing a large public gathering of publishers, writers, and politicians in California, her husband, Phil Graham, went into an incoherent tirade that was so embarrassing his friends had to drag him off the stage. They put him on a plane back to Washington, where he was admitted to a hospital.

Interestingly, men and women with manic depression perceive some benefits from their highs although almost all would not want to behave as they did when they were manic. Dr. Kay Jamison surveyed patients who described their "silver linings." Males on the average say that they missed the social ease that came about as a result of their manic states. They can relate to other people better when they're high. Women, on the other hand, don't rate social ease as a particularly unusual consequence of their highs. Rather they say that their highs heighten sexual intensity.

How sexuality is expressed depends on a person's temperament, personal values, circumstances, and—most of all—the severity of the manic (or depressive) state. Manias cause some people to lose their sexual inhibitions and feel that they are sexually irresistible. On the other hand a number of individuals in the manic state cease sexual activity altogether. Either they have too much else to do of great, even cosmic, importance or else they can't find anyone of sufficient stature worthy of them.

Weight gain poses another difficult problem for people with mania, who may develop a voracious appetite and eat prodigious amounts of food in periods of extreme hyperactivity. More often, though, I see patients who tell me they don't have time to grab a bite or literally forget to eat. Even so, they seem to make up for their caloric deficits when they finally do eat, so they usually don't lose much weight.

Nearly all people with mania feel that they have less need for sleep than usual and can get by on little more than a couple of hours a night. The lack of sleep, which is commonly seen in manias, can actually aggravate the condition. A hypomanic who stays up a couple of nights reading or trying frantically to get a project finished may induce a full-blown mania without knowing it. In more serious cases, manias may cause people to go for a few nights without sleep and feel euphoric; but after several sleepless nights they may become very irritable and agitated or even fly into a rage. For some less euphoric, more inhibited people with mania, these periods cause them to feel that everything is spinning out of control.

Another manic patient of mine continued to insist for three days straight, and always at eight A.M., that he had just won the lottery (a new lottery each day!). I asked what number or ticket he had and he'd admit that he didn't know because the winning tickets were at home. Well, I asked, was there anyone home who could tell him what his ticket said? No, but he just knew it—he felt that good.

## Becoming God for a Day: Hallucinations and Delusions in Mania

In cases of mania, hallucinations are not as common as delusional ideas. When present, hallucinations are more often auditory than visual. People with mania may report hearing the voice of God, telling them that great things are in store. But, when I question them closely, they don't actually *hear* God speaking the way they hear me. Most of them will say that they receive messages from God through telepathy or signs such as seeing the sun. This would be a delusional experience (a fixed, false idiosyncratic judgment) rather than a hallucination.

Of all the classic manic delusional ideas that occur in a Western country, the belief that they are God is one of the most common. But not all manias look the same if they share a belief about being God. One day my chairman, Dr. Paul McHugh, and I examined a patient who was sitting on the floor weeping uncontrollably. When Dr. McHugh asked why he was crying, he said it was because he was overcome with "the realization" that he was God. It was exhilarating at first, he assured us, but then he would become very frightened because of the awesome responsibilities he had to discharge. The content of delusional ideas is often related to the culture of the person as well as his or her own life history. In our culture, grandiose delusions in which people feel that they are omnipotent, or acting for some greater cosmic purpose, often get expressed in terms of God or Jesus Christ. Several years ago, I had three male patients at the same time who were all convinced that they were Jesus Christ!

I had one most unusual patient who was in a stupor for several days. We took her for an electroencephalogram (an EEG or brain wave test) to look for evidence of seizure activity or a metabolic brain disturbance that might cause her stupor. To relax her we gave her some amobarbital. All of a sudden she came to. To our surprise, she had a big smile on her face. "Oh," she said, "It's so wonderful, it's incredible! You can't believe how fantastic it is!" Heaven knows where she'd been in her reveries for the last two weeks, but she was clearly ecstatic without the aid of any artificial substances. She went on to describe her experience, which was typical of mania, even though we had seen none of the outward signs that would have indicated it. No matter how many patients I've seen, there's one thing about which I can always be sure: Mania and depression are diseases that hold many more surprises.

## The Worst of Both Worlds: Mixed States

Finally we turn to another type of illness, which is called a mixed manic state because it simultaneously combines elements of both depression and mania and so it is by definition a manifestation of manic depression or bipolar disorder. On the face of it, it seems impossible since we call it a bipolar illness? How can you reach both poles at once? After all, in typical manic depression, the phases are distinct and take place at different times. The paradox suggests that our names for these disorders are not in sync with the underlying realities of the illness. But whatever we call it, mixed manic states often create the worst of both worlds—bad depressions and bad manias. Mixed states also come in various shades as do simple depressive and manic states. Trying to determine exactly where the lines should be drawn between mania and mixed mania is probably impossible even for expert diagnosticians. Patients who have mixed states usually feel irritable and on the verge of rage (at themselves or others) almost all of the time. Although irritability is often a part of depression or even classic mania, the mixed state might be the "mother of all irritabilities." In this volatile state, mayhem can occur. Because it is neither a classic depression nor a mania, a mixed state can fool even experienced clinicians. People in a mixed state who have delusions might be diagnosed as having schizophrenia. On the other hand, if they are not beset with hallucinations or delusions, psychiatrists or even police may see them as being very angry, uncaring people or as an antisocial personality. Just as with depressive and manic patients, people who are in mixed states usually don't know that they are ill either.

I've seen some delusions in mixed states mirror the dual themes of depression and elation. One of my patients told me that while he was driving at eighty miles per hour on an eight-lane interstate he became convinced that precisely half the cars on the road were being driven by people trying to protect him while the other half were driven by people who meant to harm him. I've also had several other patients in mixed manic states who believed that they were a combination of Christ and the Antichrist all rolled into one.

Because mixed states tend to last somewhat longer than "purer" manias, Kraepelin said that mixed states should be regarded as "lingering forms" of the illness. Although "lingering," it is rare to see this state persist for more than several months at a time.

## Manic and Unipolar Depressions:
## So Similar, So Different

Manic depression can be even more destructive than unipolar depression, although it affects fewer people. One to 2 percent compared to 6 to 8 percent for unipolar illness. When it is the depressive syndrome that is active the two conditions have a great deal in common—they affect mood, vitality, self-regard as well as appetite, weight, and sexual drive—but the way in which they express themselves can be quite different. The lows of manic depression are more likely to manifest themselves in oversleeping, overeating, and sometimes by intense fatigue even more than by sadness. On average depressions in patients with severe manias (BPI) tend to be even more severe than in patients with BPII or unipolar illness. They are more likely to be complicated by delusional ideas, to require hospitalization, and to require ECT. In a manic state, people make rapid connections that are seldom apparent to outsiders. Gripped in a manic state, people may go on binges, gamble away their life savings, or pursue sexual adventures that they would never think of doing when they're healthy. Similarly, delusional thinking in people with manias tends to take on a grandiose aspect; it's not uncommon to find manic patients who think they are God or who are convinced they can fly. Not all manias, however, have such dramatic manifestations. There are also mild or hypomanias, which may not even be recognized as mania at all, that are characterized by surges of energy, sleeplessness, and unrealistic ambitions followed by a sudden mood swing in the opposite direction. Nonetheless, people with hypomanias can cause a great deal of tumult in their families and at work, without realizing (until they recover) what they were doing. People with manias usually feel as if they are in control, that what they are doing is volitional, even though the illness impairs their judgment and thinking.

# CHAPTER 3

Who Is at Risk for Depression?

You've probably wondered why some diseases seem almost to "target" certain groups of people, leaving others alone. It happens every winter with the flu. We all know some people who never get it and others, who are otherwise healthy, nonetheless end up home in bed for one or two weeks every year. Many diseases are like the flu, striking certain individuals in a certain season or time of year with varying degrees of severity. Some diseases may peak in a particular period, as heart attacks and strokes did in the United States during the 1960s or AIDS did in the '90s. These are illnesses that are especially virulent for several months or even years, cutting a great swath through a vulnerable population, and then running their course. The study of disease, rates, and mortality, among various populations is called *epidemiology.*

Specifically, epidemiology asks which individuals in a certain community are most likely to get an illness and then tries to find out what they have in common that might explain how they became sick. If several people in a community come down with hepatitis the task of an epidemiologist is to investigate the characteristics of who gets it and who doesn't. Did they all use IV drugs? Did they receive blood transfusions, or eat seafood at the same restaurant in the last month? Because depression is also an illness that varies in frequency and severity within our population, the same epidemiological techniques can be applied to find out how common depression is and who is at the highest risk of getting it.

If, as I believe, depression is an illness in the same way that heart disease or cancer is, then it should be possible to learn important things by studying how depression is distributed among populations.

And, in fact, it turns out that we can study it this way, though we still have a great deal to learn about the epidemiology of depression. We can say with certainty, however, that some people are more prone to get it than others are, and those who are susceptible may get it at one time in their life and not at another. For instance, we know that the illness tends to cluster in families and that the peak times of the year for depression are November and May.

Just take a look at the statistics:

- $44 billion annual cost of depression in 1990 in the United States, of which $24 billion was due to lower productivity at work and absenteeism.
- 70 percent of people with major depression in the United States are never diagnosed or treated for depression.
- 30,000 suicides occur per year in the United States; depression and/or alcohol are involved in 70 to 85 percent of suicides.
- Suicide is the second leading cause of death in the United States among 15–24-year-olds.
- 5 to 15 percent of the U.S. population will have at least one episode of major depression in their lifetime (most of them will have multiple episodes).
- Unipolar depression is the second leading cause of disease burden in the industrialized world (1990).
- Bipolar disorder is the sixth leading cause of disability worldwide.
- Severe (Bipolar I) manic-depression affects about 1 percent of the U.S. population (about three million people).

## Are More People Depressed Now Than Ever?

Some research suggests lifetime rates of major depression have been increasing progressively in the United States since the end of World War II. If true, these newly reported findings have serious implications for public health. However, from my perspective it's not clear that depression is increasing.

The data supporting a rise in depressive rates are derived in part from well-conducted population studies that are free from the reporting bias that usually occurs whenever new treatments become available. In other words, when people learn that a drug has come on the market—Prozac is a good example—they may turn up in much greater numbers in their doctors' offices in hope of getting a prescription. Under circumstances like these, the numbers of people reporting depression might go way up.

What we call "true" population studies don't depend on treatment or on a diagnosis made in clinics, since epidemiological research is optimally done in the field by an investigator going door to door and asking questions. However, by relying on people's own recollections—when they might have had a depressive episode or how impaired their function was during an episode—we know that we are contending with a built-in bias. For one thing, people don't like to recall painful episodes in their life; for another, people sometimes are forgetful.

Several true population studies in the last twenty years appear to show there is a higher rate of major depression and bipolar disorder in populations born after 1960 than in earlier born populations. However, they do not tell us why this is happening. A couple of factors could produce this result: 1) Since the study was done over 1–2 years, the people born before 1960 were older and therefore might be more forgetful about their depressive episodes. And even if they were equally as forgetful as the younger people, if they had a depression at age thirty (in 1950) and a thirty-one-year-old (in 2001) had a similar depression at age thirty, the fifty-year interval between the two depressions could explain the reporting difference. 2) Since both genes and environmental factors play a part in causing depression which is the more likely culprit (if the increased rate of depression in the more recently born persons is real, and not explained by differences in time allowed for forgetting due to the age of the person trying to remember)? Most of us would guess that a change in environmental factors in the last forty years is the reason for the change. If I was told this was true and had to guess what environmental factor had changed and made younger groups more prone to depression, I would guess it would be that the greater access of young people to drugs and alcohol might be responsible for an increase in depression and bipolar disease.

## Why Do Women Get Depressed More Often?

More women than men will develop major depression. We know from true population studies that almost one in five women in the United States will have one or more episodes of clinical depression. That rate is two or three times the rate of depressive illness that men have. However, practically no difference can be seen in terms of gender when it comes to individuals with the most severe cases of the depression. We would like to know why women are more at risk for unipolar major depression. Certainly there's no shortage of theories. And not surprisingly, a lot of media attention also has been given to the disparity between the numbers of women who develop depression compared to men. Take, for example, an excerpt on the subject from a web site called PlaneRX.com:

> According to most surveys, women suffer depression twice as frequently as men. . . . In addition, women must cope with the mood-altering hormonal effects of the menstrual cycle, pregnancy, childbirth, infertility, and/or oral contraceptives. "Women are also more likely than men to define themselves in terms of their relationships with others," says Boston-area psychologist Eda Spielman, Psy.D., who teaches at the Massachusetts School of Professional Psychology. "As a result, women tend to experience losses more deeply, which makes them more vulnerable to depression." On the other hand, compared to women who have no children, mothers are much less likely to suffer severe depression or attempt suicide, presumably because the intensity of their relationships with their children shields them against emotional damage from other losses. The differences in hormonal shifts of pregnancy may also play a role. Research suggests that severe childhood emotional trauma plays a role in many women's depressions. The American Psychological Association's Task Force on Women and Depression discovered that 37 percent of depressed women had suffered significant physical or sexual abuse by age 21.

How true are these statements about women generally? Do women experience losses more deeply than men? If so, is this why they are more prone to depression? I don't know and I know that no consensus exists among experts about the cause of the higher rates of depression in women. Even if such assertions about women's emotional lives are true, we cannot say that explanations like these actually account for why more women get depressed. Nonetheless, some of these theories are testable ideas or hypotheses; that is, we have a chance to prove them right or wrong. This makes them useful ideas, even if they turn out to be wrong.

Marital status also differs in depression. It turns out that married men have lower rates of depression than single men, but this is not so for married women. In terms of protection from depression, women who are married are no better off than women who are widowed, divorced, or have never been married. So does that mean that marriage protects men but not women from clinical depression? There is evidence that the risk of depression goes up for mothers with several children at home and no one to confide in. Many studies show that changes in reproductive hormones are important. At the age of onset of menstrual cycles, the rates of depression go up in females. Childbirth is also a high-risk time. We also know that a family history of manic depression, for instance, is strongly associated with severe postpartum depression.

So the truth is that we really don't know why women have higher rates of depression than men or why rates peak in young adulthood. While we have some important studies that guide us in care of our patients and aid in finding the causes of depression, we don't have enough good studies that would allow us to answer such vital questions.

Let's turn the situation around. How would young men act if they were obliged to raise two to four young children at home? It's hardly surprising to learn that we don't have enough young men performing the role of principal caretaker to carry out a study. Certainly I have no problem imagining the high stress of raising children in isolation but that kind of stress might be irrelevant in terms of its impact on major depression. There are many ways to put the puzzle together to assume we know how it "must have" happened. To be sure, some evidence suggests that young women with confiding relationships with their husbands, with living mothers, and with no more than two young children at home are *less* likely to be depressed. Certainly these are issues that are worth researching, but we don't have a working theory that would be able to withstand vigorous challenge. We can only say that higher rates of depression in women is a reality and that it may involve genes, the hormone system, the brain structure, the home environment and other factors.

## Getting Depressed at a Younger Age

What do we know about how depression affects children and adolescents? Before age thirteen, depression is fairly uncommon in both boys and girls. For many years scientists even considered childhood depression too rare to pay much attention to it. In the last twenty years, though, we have come to realize that childhood depression may not be so rare, after all. Now many studies are underway to investigate the problem. The biggest factor for severe depressive illness in children appears to be genetic. But it is also the case that both parents of severely depressed children often have depression. For a parent almost nothing is more stressful than having an ill child; it's not like the mumps or chicken pox that has an obvious cause and a quick and obvious remedy. A child who is already susceptible to depression also may be more at risk because the parent is depressed at that time.

The situation is somewhat clearer among adolescents, who have been more extensively studied. (It's also easier—though not easy—to recognize depression in teenagers than in small children.) During puberty the incidence of depression shoots up quite markedly. At thirteen, at least as many boys as girls are clinically depressed, but after menarche girls suffer from depression twice as much as boys do. Although we suspect the explanation involves the hormonal changes that take place in puberty, too many things are happening at the same time in adolescence for anyone to know with certainty what the explanation is.

From our studies we've found that early onset of a depression is often predictive of a more severe recurrent course of the illness later in life. That pattern is similar to that found in juvenile forms of rheumatoid arthritis and diabetes. We don't know yet exactly why, but it appears that this recurring pattern is probably related more to genetic influence than to environmental factors. Fortunately, all this has a positive side. Studies are now being conducted in hope of demonstrating that early treatment can offset the probable genetic disadvantage. This raises another problem for professionals and most parents. How do you know when an adolescent is depressed? It can be very difficult to distinguish between normal adolescent behavior and symptoms of depression. Even abnormal "rebellious" behaviors, such as delinquency and drug abuse, can be manifestations of depression.

## When Depression Strikes the Elderly

As of today we don't know as much as we need to about the prevalence and nature of depression in children, but the same holds true for depression and mania in the elderly, maybe more so.

More than a million Americans age sixty-five and older—nearly one in twelve—suffer from serious forms of major clinical depression. Approximately 15 percent of people aged sixty years or older in long-term facilities have major depression, although much of it goes undiagnosed and untreated. Too often, depression is overlooked in older persons because it is seen as "understandable" in light of advancing age or medical problems that an older person is likely to have. Depression is mistakenly perceived as a natural, even inevitable response to aging, serious physical illness, or the death of a spouse.

Because depression in the elderly is so poorly recognized, even fewer depressed elderly Americans receive needed treatments compared to younger patients—3 percent as compared to nearly 10 percent in the general population. However, keep in mind that depression is not more common among all older persons than in young adults. Aging doesn't cause depression. But several brain diseases, which are more common in the elderly, do cause depression.

Some of these brain diseases have a direct physiological role in causing mood disorders. Parkinson's disease and strokes that occur in particular brain regions are the most common ones. As many as 40 percent of stroke victims experience major depression, which may be due to changes in brain chemicals following the stroke. Medications of several types cause depression in older and younger adults, but older adults take about twice as many medications as younger people do, so they are more at risk.

How can we judge whether an older person is depressed? One way, of course, is to determine if that person has had an episode of depression or mania in the past. But with older people that becomes a problem. People may not recall a depression they had twenty years earlier especially if they got through it without treatment. It becomes a bad memory, and then maybe no memory at all. There are some objective criteria, of course, such as hospital records. I've conducted research studies on older patients who have allowed access to their records. Even though I could see that they'd been treated for depression, they often had relatively little recollection of ever being treated for a mood disorder. Several of these patients will hasten to assure me that it hardly matters now. *"Don't worry about me, sonny, I made it."*

Because we know that the rates of depression derived from epidemiology studies usually rely on memory, we recognize that they are not perfect, especially since most depressions are never diagnosed or treated. However, we should take at least some encouragement from this finding. If it proves nothing else, the ability of older persons to forget their severe depressions must mean that even painful emotional scars tend to heal with time.

Untreated depression in the elderly, however, is a major problem in human and in economic terms. Depressed people of any age make more medical visits and require more medical tests and get more prescriptions and side effects than younger persons do. If they are hospitalized for their heart or arthritic condition and they are depressed, they tend to stay longer in hospitals than patients without psychiatric disorders and they are twice as likely to die.

Perhaps the biggest obstacle that hampers effective treatment is the belief on the part of doctors and even the patients' own families that depression is the least of an older person's problems. If depression is an inevitable result of growing older, as so many people feel, then it follows that there's not much you can do about it. Of course, that kind of thinking is misguided. Being well at any age, whether at twenty-five or at eighty-five, is a blessing. So it is extremely important to make the diagnosis of depression and to give patients (young and old) constant encouragement to stay with the treatment long enough to give it a chance to work. After all, the natural tendency for depressed patients (young and old) is to believe that nothing can be done to help them and that they were mistaken even to seek help in the first place.

Treating the depression also has the added benefit of alleviating many of an elderly patient's other medical problems, not the least because it gives them back their confidence and optimism. Once the diagnosis of depression is correctly made, there are many antidepressants that have proven remarkably safe and quite successful among the elderly. So the result is restoring hope to people who had resigned themselves to spending years in despair. Even patients with Alzheimer's disease can benefit by being treated with antidepressants. Not only does their depression improve, but so can the ability to reason and remember. Among patients with heart disease and those living in nursing homes, treating depression improves their outlook and physical functioning and actually decreases mortality rates. At the same time, treatment for depression helps the pain that is related directly to diseases like osteoporosis, arthritis, and the like. That's not a bad investment of about two dollars a day, the daily cost of the more expensive antidepressants.

## Does Deprivation Equal Depression?

Are the poor more likely to be depressed than the well off? Epidemiology studies have observed links between severe depressive disorders and low socioeconomic status for more than a hundred years. As far back as 1855, Edward Jarvis, a Massachusetts epidemiologist, reported, "The pauper class furnishes, in ratio of its numbers, sixty-four times as many cases of insanity as the independent class." Although we now measure and express socioeconomic status in different ways (sociologists no longer refer to people as paupers) and our views about psychiatric illness have changed, Jarvis's basic findings still hold up. The association between socioeconomic deprivation and overall rates of depression, at least in women, has proven remarkably consistent. However, two differing explanations have been proposed to account for it. One is the social causation theory and the other is the social drift theory. Social causation says that poverty and the adversities that come with it cause depression. Social drift holds that, if you have severe depression, you will become poor and you will tend to "drift" into a lower socioeconomic level. Neither explanation alone is satisfactory, and there is probably some truth to both of them.

Several lines of research tend to confirm that socioeconomic factors do play an important role in depression occurring in women. The standard measures of socioeconomic status include financial, educational, and occupational status. A study in Israel, for instance, found that current and lifetime rates of major depression were significantly higher among persons of North African origin than among Israelis of European background. Because of a variety of factors—prejudice, or lack of education or job opportunities—even second- and third-generation Israelis of North African descent continue to occupy a lower social status than Israelis descended from families who migrated from Europe.

The hardships imposed on people because of prejudice could lead to the conclusion that society is to blame for depressive illnesses. But there are many reasons to question this. African American and Puerto Rican populations do not have higher rates of depression in the U.S. This is not to say these groups cope with fewer burdens from prejudice in the United States or that it plays no role in predisposing individuals to depression. That we don't see more cases of depression among these groups—though they may be prone to other types of physical and psychological impairments—only underscores the fact that depression is no more exclusively a product of environmental causes than it is of genes. We can conclude that we have as much to learn about how socioeconomic status and minority status influence the development of depressive disorders as we do about how genes might interact with these and other environmental factors.

The distribution of severe unipolar depression as well as manic depression is still not well understood. Nonetheless, studies show that three populations are more at risk for these disorders: females, postpubertal adolescents and younger adults, and patients with selected neurological disorders such as stroke and Parkinson's Disease. Women who suffer from low social status and economic deprivation they may also have higher rates of depression, but interestingly, those

populations who confront racial prejudice do not suffer dispropor-
tionately from depressive illness.

Even after identifying those populations and individuals who are
more at risk for depression, we still need to ask some other important
questions. *When* do the people who are most vulnerable to mood disorders tend to develop the illness and *why* do they get it at one time
in their lives and not at another? The answers, when we eventually
find them, will help immeasurably in getting the people into treatment who have so far fallen under our radar screen.

# CHAPTER 4

Recognizing Depression
in All Its Forms and Guises

One of the most bewildering and fascinating aspects of depressive illness is its capacity to take on different forms and masquerade as other seemingly unrelated conditions. People who have this illness aren't the only ones who are confused; clinicians are often baffled by it, too. For a start, we need to be able to distinguish between one kind of depression and another. Then we need to be able to recognize depression when it appears to be another illness altogether. Let me begin with a story.

The patient was a psychotherapist. All her life she'd done well; she was a prize student and had an outstanding career. She was about as nice and caring a person as you could ever hope to meet. Yet she realized that something was wrong and didn't know what "it" was. Over the last five years, she told me, she'd become more downcast for two or three months each year. Twice she'd had very severe periods lasting up to an entire year, during which she was continuously depressed, unable to concentrate, and would be so tired that she'd stay in bed and skip work three to six days a month. She admitted that during these bad periods she suffered from very low self-esteem but attributed this to the fact that she had not been successful in her marriage. She and her husband separated, she said, because they just didn't make each other happy. Aside from a couple of coworkers and a younger brother, she really didn't have any close and confiding friends. She had been in therapy for almost twenty years working on "relationship issues." In spite of all the time that she'd put into her therapy without any real improvement, her psychotherapist regarded her as a "very good patient."

She had all the classic symptoms of recurrent depressions (and so, she recalled, did her grandmother). Fortunately, when I told her my diagnosis, she was ready to accept it. While she'd been in treatment with her previous therapist, she'd operated under the assumption that her bad mood "made sense." But she'd gotten her reasoning backward, mistaking the effects of depression for its causes. None of us, even if we are trained clinicians, are so objective that we should depend on our own judgment about whether depression makes sense as a response to an event or circumstance. In such cases we all need professional guidance.

Three weeks later, while taking the first antidepressant she had ever tried, she phoned to tell me that she felt normal for the first time in two years. While she was grateful, she also she felt an odd sadness. She'd lost twenty years and a good husband by her "own choice" because she didn't understand that her depression was the underlying cause of her problems.

Over the years doctors and scientists have made many efforts to classify the forms of mood disorders, such as depression and manic depression (the two best known), according to a variety of criteria so as to make them easier to diagnose and treat. I don't like the term *mood disorders* since the symptoms of depressed and manic patients involve much more than their moods. In fact, sad and elated moods are not the most prominent symptoms for as many as half of the depressed and manic patients. Instead of "mood" I find the term *affective*—a general term used to cover moods, emotions, and appetites—best captures the most critical problems that these patients have. The characteristic central features of an affective disorder are changes not just in mood, but also in vitality and self-regard.

Let me return to my main point: why should a classification system matter? I hope to convince you that such a system matters a great deal in how we diagnose and treat patients. Before I can do that, however, I will try to give you an idea of how good our classification system actually is and explain what its limitations are. The system, as you'll see, has many advantages, but we also have to be wary of relying on it too much.

Why is developing a system of classification so important? Though disorders of mental life are kindred, they are also quite varied, involving different considerations and requiring different treatments. A good classification system offers a framework in which to evaluate and treat these differences. A system not only offers a simple and powerful way to approach the treatment of patients, but serves as a guide for research as well. It becomes an immediate tool to study the impact of a condition on a society. A classification system allows us to count how many people have it, how many are treated, and what is the cost per person of the disease. In spite of these obvious benefits, we know that psychiatrists, at least in the United States, weren't especially interested in diagnosing patients according to any classification system for about thirty years, from 1950 to 1980. That was because diagnosing different conditions based on symptoms didn't have a clear value since the treatments then available (various psychotherapies for the most part) were the same for different groups of patients.

That situation has changed—dramatically.

But to understand how much it has changed, and why a classification system for depressive illness has now been so widely accepted, it's necessary first to set the scene by taking a look back.

## Defining the Major Types of Depressive Illness

The idea that depression is a disease isn't new. The great doctors Hippocrates (c. 460–370 B.C.) and Galen (c. A.D. 130–200), as well as some of their predecessors, recognized that at least some forms of depression (especially what they called melancholia) had a basis in the patient's physical constitution. What changed over time was the notion of the disease itself. From Galen's era until the late eighteenth century, the meaning of "disease" could be defined by separating the two syllables *dis* and *ease*. It meant a change for the worse in one's sense of well-being and was thought to represent the interaction between a person's constitutional makeup and circumstances. A physician, it was believed, could make a reasonably good assessment of a patient's constitutional makeup, once temperament or personality style was understood. This was because temperament was considered a reflection of the balance among the body's four fluids or "humors." Too much blood made for a sanguine temperament, while too much phlegm made a phlegmatic person, and too much yellow bile resulted in a choleric person. Finally, too much black bile meant a melancholic temperament (literally, *melanin* for black and *cholia* for bile). A melancholic, in other words, was a depressed person. This is not what we mean when we talk about disease today, of course. But it's important to note that in this ancient idea was a recognition that patients with extreme melancholia or elated states should be treated as ill patients and that their problems derived from the interaction of their bodily constitution and the environment.

By the Middle Ages, however, the physiological ideas of Hippocrates and Galen as they pertained to psychiatric and other medical maladies were reinterpreted with a religious or moralistic slant. People who were mentally ill were thought to be possessed by the devil or to be sinners. Later, the idea that certain people were damned in this way was ascribed to a tendency toward degeneration, which was supposedly passed down, becoming worse from generation to generation. (For more on this, take a look at the chapter on genetics.) Immorality in one generation led to nervousness in the next, insanity in the third, and imbecility in the fourth. In these circumstances, people with melancholia and mania were stigmatized and either locked up in madhouses or else banished from the community. Eventually, doctors in the Enlightenment period started to change this situation for the better. In the eighteenth century several physicians—the best known were the two French psychiatrists Jean Esquirol and Philippe Pinel—campaigned to liberate the mentally ill from their shackles. They promoted the view that people who were psychiatrically ill should be treated in asylums (literally, places of safety) located in the countryside. This was a novel idea, but also a more benign one than earlier approaches to care for the mentally ill, since it was based on the idea that patients needed to be safeguarded from the abuses and corruption of the cities.

By the nineteenth century, patients with disabling severe depressions or melancholias were recognized as requiring either hospitalization or special care from their families and friends to get them safely through periods of illness. Abraham Lincoln, for example, suffered bouts of depression as a young man and on two occasions was sent to stay with relatives in the Kentucky countryside to recuperate. Knowing about his condition, his relatives were careful to watch him and keep him away from a nearby riverbank so that he wouldn't jump into the river.

At the turn of the twentieth century, psychiatrist Emil Kraepelin provided a coherent and comprehensive description of melancholia and mania. In his view, melancholia and mania constituted two parts of a single bodily disease, or as he called it, "a single morbid process." But he readily acknowledged that he had no particularly effective treatments for the condition and that he could find nothing wrong in the brains of deceased patients whom he autopsied. His theories met with skepticism from some prominent psychiatrists of his day but were widely accepted by most European psychiatrists and have come to form the basis for the classification system in psychiatry that is still in use today.

Among the most persuasive objectors to Kraepelin's theory was Sigmund Freud, whose treatment of mentally ill patients relied on psychoanalysis. Freud believed the depressive symptoms were rooted in unconscious conflicts and that the key to effective treatment was to help the patient become consciously aware of the hidden inner conflict. Freud regarded melancholia as a condition resembling grief or mourning; the patient, he said, had lost something vital to his or her inner life, such as the trust of a friend who, perhaps, had become a surrogate parent. In this sense, the loss was symbolic and not apparent to the patient. In Freud's opinion the patient was angry but the only way to express animosity toward the friend—symbolically—was by directing the anger inwardly. Thus, the psychoanalytic theory interpreted depression as anger turned inward onto oneself.

Psychoanalysis has largely gone out of fashion, even though it hasn't been disproved as a theory. Psychoanalysis has been abandoned by most clinicians and therapists (and most psychoanalysts as well) as a credible treatment for clinical depression and bipolar disorder. Therapists have recognized that medical and other psychological treatments are beneficial and less expensive. Psychoanalysis is still a powerful idea that continues to influence our culture and was the ideological basis for the briefer forms of psychotherapy, among them cognitive and interpersonal. Its influence, though, continues to be as hotly debated as the therapy itself was before it.

## How the Modern Classification System Developed

The introduction of lithium as an effective drug treatment for mania (1949), the use of electroconvulsive therapy, or ECT, for depression (1940), and the first antidepressant drugs (late 1950s) led slowly but inevitably to the conclusion that severe depressions and manias must be true diseases. While researchers still don't know why these different treatments work, their experiments in controlled clinical trials convinced them that medications were effective in restoring to normal many manic or depressed patients. This "proof" underlined Kraepelin's earlier assertion that these disorders were physical in origin. Today, the Kraepelinian viewpoint that severe forms of depression and mania are diseases caused by bodily dysfunction is not much in question, at least among psychiatrists. I'll go further into the scientific and practical support for this view in a later chapters because it is the essence of what we know about the condition beyond our patients' experience.

Kraepelin's view that all depressive disorders are "a single morbid process," with variations in the pattern of symptoms and course of illness, is not accepted by the majority of psychiatrists today. Specialists in these disorders now divide depressive illnesses into the purely depressive type (unipolar) and the type with manic and depressive relapses (bipolar disorder). The classification system now in use can be found in the "bible" of the psychiatric community, the *Diagnostic and Statistical Manual*, or *DSM*. Now in their fourth edition, these manuals reflect the conventions developed by committees of experts from the American Psychiatric Association. The first and second editions were each used for several decades. Since the publication of *DSM III* in 1980 there have been revisions in 1987 *(DSM IIIR)* and again in 1994 *(DSM IV)*.

The *DSM* also recognizes both a severe unipolar condition—major depressive disorder, recurrent type—and a milder form of pure depression called dysthymia, which is not so episodic as it is chronic. Similarly, the *DSM* recognizes a more severe form of manic depression (Bipolar I) and a milder form (Bipolar II). For our purpose in this book, I will focus on the major classes of affective or mood disorders taken from the fourth and latest edition of the *DSM IV*: Major Depressive Disorder (single and recurrent), Dysthymia, and Bipolar I and Bipolar II Disorders. The *DSM IV* also describes schizoaffective disorders which I will define and briefly discuss.

These four widely agreed upon categories among the "mood" or affective disorders are defined in the following way:

1. Major Depressive Disorder (Unipolar disorder) characteristically features parallel changes in mood (sadness, anxiety, apathy, or numbness, separately or in combination), vitality (energy, concentration, interest, activity level and speed), and self-regarding feelings (guilty feelings, feelings of uselessness, unreasonable pessimism, or even suicidal impulses). In addition, the illness is sometimes marked by changes of sleep as well as appetite and weight. Major depression, especially severe major depressive disorder, tends to be episodic. In other words, when you are ill you are very ill and when well you are well, for the most part.

2. Dysthymia milder in the number and symptomatic severity of its symptoms compared to those seen in major depressive disorder. The set of symptoms in the *DSM* list are similar to those for a major depressive episode but for dysthymia to be diagnosed the symptoms have to persist for two years or more.

### Table 1. American Psychiatric Association
### Diagnostic Criteria for Major Depressive Episode

A. At least five of the following symptoms have been present during the same two-week period and represent a change from previous functioning.

  1. depressed mood
  2. diminished interest or pleasure in activities
  3. significant appetite/weight loss or gain
  4. insomnia or hypersomnia
  5. feelings of worthlessness or excessive guilt
  6. diminished ability to think or concentrate
  7. recurrent thoughts of death or suicide

B. Not due to general medical condition, drugs, or bereavement.

From *American Psychiatric Association Diagnostic and Statistical Manual of Mental Disorders*, 4th ed. (Washington, D.C.: American Psychiatric Association, 1994).

In addition to feeling low or apathetic in mood, patients with dysthymia often feel inadequate and overburdened. They may feel that they're to blame, or else are blamed by others, for the problems in their family. This is different only in degree from major depression, whose victims will often feel abjectly hopeless and worthless. Patients of mine whose depression fits into the dysthymia category object (without good reason) if I say it is a "mild" condition for two very good reasons. For one thing, they point out that feeling "a little" hopeless is not a small problem even if the feeling lasts only for a week. To have this condition for two years or more affects every aspect of life in a negative way. People with dysthymia don't appear to have changed. Thus their families and friends see this state as a part of their loved one's personality, not as an illness. People with this disorder often work extremely hard both to accomplish what they have to get done and to keep appearances up. Another feature of dysthymia should be noted: Most patients who have this pattern of chronic depressive symptoms also have episodes of major depressions from time to time, but (especially if they are not getting effective treatment) they don't recover as fully as patients do who have major depression alone.

  3. *Bipolar I* disorder is a condition characterized by the occurrence of severe manias and usually major depressions as well. For purposes of classification, mania is the defining element because people who have had mania but haven't had a depres-

## Table 2.  American Psychiatric Association
## Diagnostic Criteria for Dysthymia

A. Depressed mood for at least two years.
B. Presence while depressed of at least two of the following:

   1. poor appetite or overeating
   2. insomnia or hypersomnia
   3. low energy or fatigue
   4. low self-esteem
   5. poor concentration or difficulty making decisions
   6. feelings of hopelessness

C. During the two-year period of the disturbance, never without the symptoms for more than two months at a time.
D. Not better accounted for by chronic depressive disorder or major depression in partial remission.
E. Never manic or clearly hypomanic.
F. Not due to chronic schizophrenia.
G. Not due to direct physiologic effects of drugs (prescribed or abused) or general medical condition.
H. The symptoms cause significant distress or impairment in important areas of functioning.

Adapted from *American Psychiatric Association: Diagnostic and Statistical Manual of Mental Disorders, 4th ed.*

sion are still called Bipolar I. Bipolar I is defined by the presence of at least one full manic syndrome with or without a depressive syndrome. In defining what an episode means, the *DSM* criteria require four or more of the mania symptoms shown in Table 3. The severity of full manic syndrome results in severe impairments in every aspect of functioning. It is also associated with delusions (and sometimes hallucinations) and lead to markedly poor decision making. Patients talk so much and so fast that it makes conversation almost impossible.

4. *Bipolar II* disorder is characterized by much less severe but still notable hypomanias (mild manias) associated with major depressive episodes. A *DSM IV* diagnosis of hypomania requires the presence of three or four manic symptoms. (See Table 3.) Only three symptoms are required to make the diagnosis if the patient has a clearly euphoric mood. If the mood is just irritable the *DSM* requires four manic symptoms to make a confident diagnosis of hypomania. Of critical importance is that while the change in the patient's functioning should be enough to be noticeable by others, it is not as marked as in the mania

syndrome. By definition (i.e., the *DSM IV* definition) no delusions or hallucinations occur in hypomania. Their presence would be sufficient to reclassify the episodic as a mania. Similarly, if there is a marked impairment in social and occupational functioning, e.g., if a hospitalization is necessitated, the episode would be a mania.

In Bipolar II patients, the depressions usually far outnumber and outlast the hypomanias. In addition to major depressive episodes, many patients with Bipolar II have long periods of low mood. Although this constitutes an important part of the course of their illness, the current DSM rules do not permit the diagnosis of dysthymia

### Table 3. American Psychiatric Association Diagnostic Criteria for a Manic Episode

A. A distinct period of abnormally and persistently elevated expansive or irritable mood lasting at least one week of necessitating hospitalization; for hypomania lasting at least four days.

B. At least three of the following symptoms if mood is euphoric (four symptoms if mood is only irritable).

    1. inflated self-esteem or grandiosity
    2. decreased need for sleep
    3. more talkative than usual
    4. flight of ideas or subjective experience that thoughts are racing
    5. distractibility
    6. increased activity
    7. excessive involvement in pleasurable activities which have a high potential for painful consequences

C.  1. For mania: Symptoms sufficiently severe to cause marked impairment in function at work or in relationships or to necessitate hospitalization or psychotic symptoms are present.
    2. For hypomania: Symptoms change from usual behavior noticeable by others but not sufficient to meet criteria for mania.

D. Not due to drugs or general medical conditions.

E. (For mania only) Does not meet criteria for mixed episode.

Bipolar I is defined by the presence of even one full manic episode with or without a depressive syndrome.
Bipolar II is defined in *DSM IV* as hypomania associated with one or more major depressive episodes.

From *American Psychiatric Association Diagnostic and Statistical Manual of Mental Disorders, 4th ed.*

## Table 4. American Psychiatric Association Diagnostic Criteria for a Mixed Episode

A. The criteria are met both for a Manic Episode and for a Major Depressive Episode (except for duration) nearly every day during at least a one-week period.

B. The mood disturbance is sufficiently severe to cause marked impairment in occupational functioning or in usual social activities or relationships with others, or to necessitate hospitalization to prevent harm to self or others, or there are psychotic features.

C. They symptoms are not due to the direct physiological effects of a substance (e.g., drug abuse, a medication, or other treatment) or a general medical condition (e.g., hyperthyroidism).

in the presence of Bipolar I or II. Also, when a mania or hypomania is directly due to the physiological effects of medication (including an antidepressant, drug abuse, or medical conditions), it isn't classified as mania or hypomania. This is a departure from earlier editions in which manic episodes caused by cocaine or other drugs of abuse wouldn't "count" as a classifiable mania but, if taking antidepressants brought them on, were considered the same as spontaneous manic or hypomanic episodes. Whether this change was wise or not is the subject of some research and some debate.

# Schizoaffective Disorder

I will briefly discuss one final *DSM* category that causes a lot of confusion for patients and families who speak with me. It is called schizoaffective disorder and according to *DSM IV,* it comes as either the bipolar type (if a manic or mixed episode has occurred) or the depressive type (if only depressions have occurred), depending on the mood syndromes in an illness that would in other ways resemble schizophrenia. That is the schizoaffective patients have two of the five criterion symptoms of schizophrenia for at least one month: 1. delusions; 2. hallucinations; 3. disorganized speech; 4. grossly disorganized behavior or catatonia; and 5. "negative symptoms" (blunting of personality or affect and blunting of drive or will). The *DSM* also requires that the time when the patients were having mania, mixed states, and/or depressive syndromes must be brief relative to the duration of active illness.

First, let me tell those confused parents and families that many clinical psychiatrists, including myself, also find this a dubious and confusing category. Second, psychiatrists who are involved in research note that good diagnostic agreement (called reliability) cannot be achieved with this definition. The current conventional wisdom in the literature is that the patients who fit into this category, using the current diagnostic criteria, have a mixture of conditions, mostly bipolar disorder and schizophrenia. There is a debate about whether there might be also a third sub-grouping of patients who fit into this category who have something unrelated to either schizophrenia or bipolar disorder. That would be a third type of psychotic illness that is as yet unrecognized. In Europe, there has been some sympathy for the idea, however, the concept of Cycloid psychosis (originally a German concept of Dr. Karl Leonhard), is a distinctly episodic disorder rather than a chronic condition as necessitated for *DSM IV* Schizoaffective disorder.

My conclusion is that for the most part Schizoaffective disorder is not very helpful for patients, families, or doctors. For the patients who (in my opinion) have bipolar I disorder, I think the information content of the diagnosis is usually that the disorder has features that are atypical for bipolar disorder, either delusions and hallucinations that are not easy to relate to the mood disorders (i.e., grandiose content for mania and blaming hopeless content for depression) or that the illness has been unremitting or chronically deteriorating rather than episodic. These, of course, are not happy messages as they imply a worse prognosis . . . but we never say die in this business and the next research discovery, like the discovery of ECT in the late 1930s, might be preferentially beneficial for very severe conditions.

# A Critique of *DSM IV*

The reemergence of scientific studies of severe psychiatric disorders in the last forty years has been guided by Kraepelin's general classification of schizophrenia (Dementia Praecox was his term) and manic depressive illness (which for him included severe depressive states as well as bipolar disorder) as disease states despite the absence of clear brain abnormalities (i.e., neuropathology) to validate them. The *DSM III* in 1980 was an important step forward in that it provided a mechanism for making reliable or reproducible diagnoses for clinicians and researchers who would attempt to make good the assumption of a brain disease underlying severe disorders of mental function. However, what began as a manageable classification system that helped clarify that symptoms mattered has grown exponentially without obvious breakthroughs to justify the rapid expansion of categories. This threatens to make the field more confusing to all of us and in that way to become less useful as a guide to what is important in treatment and research.

A common element of both unipolar and bipolar conditions is that they have less and more severe forms. Intuitively, this suggests that the outcomes of these illnesses will be related to the severity of symptoms. However, this isn't the way it always plays out in real life. Most patients with the very severe forms of unipolar and bipolar disorder who are correctly diagnosed and who stay with appropriate types of treatment actually do very well (think of Art Buchwald). Even some people who are never treated but have only a few episodes in their life return to normal function (remember Abraham Lincoln and Winston Churchill). By contrast, many patients with the so-called milder forms, bipolar II and dsythymia, may not be recognized as ill but are perceived as moody and impulsive or pessimistic. As a result these "milder" patients often receive inadequate care or none at all.

## Diagnosing Depression

Why is it still so hard at times even for experienced professionals, to recognize depression when it might seem easier now?

One of the principal reasons that it can be hard is that depression by its nature is insidious in that it occurs in the context of a person's life. Since life is always emerging, it can deceive doctors and patients alike by camouflaging symptoms as the natural turns and twists of life or as any one of several well-defined medical conditions. Let's start with the medical conditions and their relationship to depression.

When a patient has a worsening medical condition, which may have been stable for years, it is natural for a doctor to assume that the exacerbation of the condition is due to aggravating factors—a change in diet, for instance. One aggravating factor especially for migraine headaches and irritable bowel syndrome, or IBS, can be depression. Both disorders or syndromes are often set off by dietary changes or stressful events. Most people who have these conditions adapt to them by regulating diet, sleep, exercise, and judicious use of symptomatic medications. When patients have bad migraines and the migraine headaches that were occurring perhaps once a month suddenly become intense and relentless daily events, patients know something is wrong. And what is wrong seems obvious.

A worsening medical condition in such cases often turns out to be a sign, you'll find a "presenting" depression (a person comes in with complaints that point to a certain illness or with signs of the illness on exam). Some of the most vexing are themselves clinical syndromes without definitive diagnostic tests to confirm them or to rule them out. They vary and include chronic fatigue syndrome, fibromyalgia, irritable bowel syndrome, and migraine headaches.

I have had several patients like the one I'll call Mr. Sprule, a forty-five-year-old stockbroker who'd had a well-controlled irritable bowel syndrome since he was a teenager. If he ate too much, or had food that was too spicy, or was under a lot of stress, he would suffer severe abdominal cramps and have to run to the toilet. Before he'd come to see me his IBS had suddenly flared up seemingly as a result of recent difficulties at work, where he had been unhappy for a few years. He had become consumed with how he would meet the mortgage payments on his new home if he had to change jobs when his IBS became worse than ever, with continuous diarrhea. The medicine that usually worked for a flare-up did no good at all. After two weeks he was too disabled to go to work, he'd lost twenty pounds, and was so dehydrated that he needed to be hospitalized and given IV fluids. Even in the hospital his doctor wasn't able to bring his cramping and diarrhea under control. I was called in to see him because his doctor suspected that Mr. Sprule might have depression.

When I spoke to him he said he was "not opposed" to the diagnosis, but it just didn't really make any sense to him. He was scared, he said, not sad. He certainly had good reason to be scared; he was terrified that something was terribly wrong with his colon; and he had considerable evidence that this was, in fact, the case. The tests on his colon showed nothing abnormal.

He was in such a state of worry, he said, that he couldn't concentrate on reading and of course he felt "worn out" most of the time. Significant to me, he also had a mother and a brother, both of whom had been treated for severe depression. When I questioned him further, he told me that he had left college in his freshman year because of fatigue and poor concentration lasting for six months. He had felt he was sure to flunk out and had not left his dorm room for days at a time. He didn't have diarrhea then, nor any other medical explanation for it. I concluded that Mr. Sprule did have a major depression, but I wasn't sure whether the IBS had set off the depression or whether the depression had set off the IBS. Whatever the case, once he was given an antidepressant, paroxetine (Paxil) in this case, he showed a dramatic improvement. Within two weeks diarrhea stopped. A month later was back at work concentrating well.

## Masqueraders: When Fatigue and Muscle Aches Point to Depression

Sometimes depression masquerades as syndromes that are poorly understood and not easily defined. Yet these syndromes have many adherents, both people who believe that they suffer from them (and they do suffer) and doctors who believe that they can treat them. Consider, for example, chronic fatigue and fibromyalgia. Maybe you're familiar with chronic fatigue syndrome (CFS) because of all the attention it has received in the media in the last several years. Typically, the condition is associated with fatigue and malaise. It can persist for years, which is why it's called chronic, and in the severest cases can prove so crippling that it robs people with it of the ability to maintain a job or a normal relationship. Less well known is fibromyalgia, a syndrome characterized by a pattern of severe muscular aches and pains. The problem with both of these disorders is that we don't really know what causes them. Only recently have some doctors considered them as specific conditions while others are skeptical. Even those doctors who are "believers" use different criteria to diagnose them. These conditions like depressive disorders have not been fully validated by a pathology or a diagnostic test. We can't see any disease-causing agent under a microscope that might account for most cases, nor can we run a blood test that would offer us proof that something is there or not.

With further research, scientists will eventually identify the source of what we call chronic fatigue syndrome and fibromyalgia. Clinicians see that for many patients with such constellations of symptoms one of the driving forces in their presentation is depression, albeit disguised as happened with IBS.

One of my patients, for example, had a clear history of three depressive periods, each lasting several months. But about six months after stopping her antidepressant medications, she started feeling tired and lethargic. At the same time, she also started having particularly painful muscle aches in her shoulders, thighs, and calves. She would wince in pain whenever she was touched at her "trigger points" by a doctor during an examination. She'd never experienced anything like this prior to her depression and she didn't think that her condition was due to her depression. She reasoned that, when she was depressed she slept all the time, and now she couldn't stay asleep. She also was convinced that her feelings of hopelessness, irritability, and fatigue were all due to her muscle pains. However, once we were able to get her back on medication and adjust the dose so that she could get a good night's sleep again, the muscle pains vanished and her condition resolved within four weeks.

## How Do You Know If Depression Is the Correct Diagnosis?

How can I prove to a skeptical patient that a diagnosis of depression is correct and a diagnosis of another syndrome such as fibromyalgia is incomplete or even incorrect? I can't, at least not today. Therefore, it is important for patients to know *how* I have come to a diagnostic conclusion as it is to know what that conclusion is. Let's take the example of fibromyalgia. In addition to recommending standard rehabilitative therapies for muscle aches and pains, including exercise that often alleviates aches and pains, doctors specializing in fibromyalgia will also give their patients antidepressants, particularly the popular serotonin reuptake inhibitors such as Prozac and Zoloft. Although psychiatrists who see these patients tend to regard them as having depression, I don't think fibromyalgia clinics are necessarily wrong in either diagnosing or treating fibromyalgia. Their diagnosis of fibromyalgia is based on a set of particular signs and symptoms: pains and aches at a number of widespread musculoskeletal sites and frequent sleep problems. The treatments include treating the sleep problem carefully, exercise, and frequently prescribing antidepressants. Most people who have depressive symptoms do not have classic fibroymalgia, but many depressed patients do meet all the criteria for fibromyalgia. At times during their treatment many patients with both depression and fibromyalgia tend to see them as somewhat separate. All the same, many people who are diagnosed with fibromyalgia have depression. But debating the existence of one condition or another is not the best solution for either the doctor especially when treatments work together well.

We see the same dilemma when it comes to identifying chronic fatigue syndrome in someone. You'll find that clinics specializing in this syndrome have different criteria to diagnose the disorder. But the same signs that doctors look for in patients with chronic fatigue syndrome are also typical in depression. About 90 percent of patients with clear-cut treatable depression will complain of the symptoms of fatigue. Because of its stigma and the fact that some people do not recognize clinical depression as a bodily disease, many patients and doctors would naturally prefer a physical explanation. (In addition, they like to designate it by a term that sounds like it has no relation to a psychological problem.) Some patients diagnosed with CFS have clear-cut signs like fevers and enlarged lymph nodes that indicate the presence of an underlying inflammatory or infectious pathology, but only a minority of people said to have chronic fatigue syndrome have them. If the definition of CFS is narrow enough, we can pretty easily distinguish it from clinical depression. What causes the symptoms? There has been speculation for two decades that the syndrome is caused by the Epstein-Barr virus (EBV), a common virus that is usually dormant in most adults. So far, though, scientists have been unable to establish EBV or any other viruses as the cause even in patients with enlarged lymph nodes. Blood samples often detect prior exposure to the virus but that is not surprising and doesn't show us a current cause for symptoms.

As of today, we need a solution that is effective, compassionate, and practical. We can say that there does appear to be a valid syndrome called chronic fatigue syndrome. A high percentage of people with chronic fatigue symptoms have had one or more instances of major depression in their lives when they didn't have chronic fatigue syndrome. So we shall try to ensure that making this diagnosis doesn't become a way to prevent or discourage people from getting the best treatment for depression.

Because the medical-sounding terminology of chronic fatigue syndrome and the tests, some patients may give more credibility to treatment programs that will delay the treatment they need for depression. What is needed for the patient is an open discussion between doctors and patients about all these issues so that patients understand what we do know and don't know about all of these syndromes. This will allow them to get answers, advice and make an informed decision about getting treatment.

## Is It Depression or Is It Attention Deficit Disorder?

In contrast to disorders like fibromyalgia and chronic fatigue that are so ambiguous and disputed, we have good evidence proving the existence of other disorders that are getting a great deal of attention these days: Attention Deficit Disorder (ADD), and Attention Deficit Hyperactivity Disorder (ADHD). What ADD has in common with the two other disorders is that, at least in some cases, it is a mask behind which depression may be lurking. Estimates of those who have ADD or ADHD range from very low rates to two out of every one hundred young people. ADD is most often diagnosed in children between the ages of six and nine, with boys outnumbering girls by about three to one. About fifty years ago pediatricians referred to young boys with normal IQ scores but learning problems as having "minimal brain damage." These children had poor reading skills and inattentiveness and tended to be hyperactive. Subsequently, reading disability was separated and appreciated as an identity all of its own—dyslexia, about which we now know a lot more than we used to. The other "half" of the syndrome—ADD (or ADHD)—is harder to define. Severe cases appear to run in families more than they used to and appear to be associated with genes in the dopamine neurotransmitter receptor system. In addition, children with this disorder tend to respond well to stimulants and (to a lesser extent) to antidepressants. In the vast majority of cases, these stimulants improve attention without inducing euphoria or hyperactivity. The proof that these medications work is easily seen in the classroom: Kids who were fidgety and couldn't pay attention before they were put on medication generally perform better when they take their medication. The majority of physicians agree that, in severe cases, something is clearly wrong with these children, and most doctors agree about the importance of prescribing the medication, at least for a trial period. However, particular approaches to teaching and learning are just as important to their educational achievement as medication is. New brain studies of young boys with ADD focusing on the region controlling movement and attention suggest that it is structurally different from the same region in boys without this condition.

Things get much more problematic when the disorder is diagnosed for the first time in older adolescents or adults. Some researchers estimate that the disorder declines sharply to affect only two adults in every one thousand by age thirty. On the other hand, many adults who have had the disorder as children report that they have the same difficulty with attention, but have managed to adjust to it better. So we debate whether there really is such a thing as adult ADD at all. It isn't listed yet in the latest version of the *Diagnostic and Statistical Manual (DSM IV)*. But I want to be clear about what we do know and what we don't. For severely affected youngsters whose condition began by the age of seven, it makes good sense to realize that this diagnosis and treatment can make their "job" in life (to get a good education and to get along with peers) a successful experience. Only a modest proportion of patients diagnosed with adult ADD that I have examined had symptoms of ADD as children. That is why it's important to make sure whether a syndrome like adult ADD isn't depression or some other condition in disguise. For patients with a clear-cut episode of depression or a form of manic depression at any age, the lack of ability to concentrate is also a common and key symptom of depression. Many adult patients are more aware of their problems with concentration than the change in their moods because they are less aware of moods than of effectiveness at work. Stimulants will help them concentrate better whatever the cause and will do this much more quickly than antidepressants will, but it's not the best antidepressant. We can use stimulants as add-on treatment for depression when regular antidepressants fail to work.

I worry about the large number of patients today who are diagnosing themselves and are asking their doctors to treat them for adult ADHD. Long-term use of stimulant medication, especially by people who have a "mild" form of manic depression, may have adverse effects. They run the risks of becoming dependent on the stimulants (alone or especially in combination with other mood-elevating drugs) or precipitating manias.

In short, there is not enough new knowledge today to justify the creation of a new condition for the diagnostic manuals. We need to be open-minded about these possible syndromes, but ultimately what you want from your doctor is recognition of the problem you or your child has and help to manage it better, regardless of what name we choose to give the problem today or tomorrow.

# CHAPTER 5

∞

# Stressful Events:
# When People Get Depressed

Most people who suffer from severe depression are not depressed all the time. They have long periods when they are free from illness for years. Then something happens and they have a relapse, but what is that something? It is natural to look for a precipitating event or the stressful situation that is culpable and it is just as natural to find the stress or trigger. But this exercise begs the question: What exactly is the relationship between stress and depressive illness?

There are two ways of looking at the question. One is to look at the timing of the event and the onset of the depressive or manic condition. If you get hit by a piano that's fallen out of a tenth-floor apartment and are instantly killed, then we can rightly say you died from the event. But if you got up and walked away apparently uninjured and died twenty months later while walking home in the hot Florida sun, it would be reasonable to look for some other cause. The piano that struck you might have contributed to your sudden death in ways that we could imagine (maybe a heart injury or a chronic subdural hematoma that left you vulnerable to overexertion), but it would require considerable detective work to prove it. The closer the event and the outcome are to each other in time, the easier it is to see a cause and effect relationship between the two. When it comes to depression, however, this natural way of looking at things creates more confusion than almost anything else for patients, families, and their health professionals.

"Depression is when your dog dies and you feel sad." That was how one of my patients sarcastically put it. Well, he's wrong, but he's also right! When you lose a loved one, whether it's a close family member, a good friend, or a pet, it's natural to grieve. But some people, probably because of their genetic makeup, can become clinically depressed when they lose a loved one. On the other hand, I have also seen more than twenty patients who became manic after a grievous loss. What we are talking about here are precipitating factors. I use the word *precipitate* to refer to factors that seem to determine when someone will get depressed or manic, as opposed to factors that determine whom is most likely to have depressions or manias in their lifetime. Precipitating events or "stressful" life events can lead to depression in some people and discouragement in others. One is an illness, the other is a natural response to misfortune.

The reality is that families with depression and more life events are also a population of more vulnerable people. That's to say that people who experience a great deal of turmoil and upheaval in their lives also have a greater chance of having depressive illness. Do these people get depressed because they're genetically related or because they're responding to life events that occur in their family? Well, they have both a genetic predisposition and they have more life events. How do you know which one is causing the illness, or whether both are? To answer these questions we have to think about how the brain responds to environmental influences, something about which we still need to learn much more.

## What Is a Stressful Event, Anyway?

In this discussion about depression I'm referring to *stressful* life events. You would think these events are, by definition, unwelcome ones. But that's not always true. Say you are given a promotion at work. That's good, but it may also have a downside. You may have many more responsibilities in your new position that you don't think you can handle, or you may have to uproot yourself and your family and move to another part of the country. Or it could be such a great opportunity that it puts you under a lot of pressure. You don't want to let down your boss or yourself. You're afraid that if you mess up your dreams for career advancement will go up in smoke. Your promotion could be a stressful life event in spite of its positive aspect. Before we go any further, maybe we should step back a moment and think what we actually mean by stress in the first place.

To most people, stress means that an upsetting event has occurred or that difficult demands are being placed on them. Medical researchers following the teaching of the great physiologist Walter B. Cannon have a different take on the word. By stress, they mean the nervous systems, hormonal (rapid production of noradrenaline and cortisol hormones), and behavioral ("flight or fight") response to intensively unpleasant conditions. When researchers study stress response and stress response systems they look at how animals and humans respond to stimuli to acute injuries. Many of my patients will tell me, "Dr. DePaulo, I'm not depressed, I've just been stressed out lately." That's their way of saying they don't feel well. However, in saying this, they have shifted their focus away from their illness and placed it on what they perceive, rightly or wrongly, as the cause of their problem. It may be their way of avoiding dealing with what's wrong so they don't have to give their attention to what I want them to focus on, which is *what* is it that you are experiencing that is different in your reaction now compared to your usual reaction to an upsetting event.

I use the word *stress* in both the layperson's and the medical sense of the word. If I refer to the stress response, I mean the body's physical and behavioral response to the event. If, on the other hand, I talk to a patient about a stressful event, then I am referring to an event or circumstance that he or she finds very upsetting.

Stressful events are not all random. They can even be the result of depression as much as depression can be the result of an earlier precipitating event. For example, a patient might already be depressed and not know it, and because of the depression will have excessive anxiety about not doing a good job. In this situation the individual might well give the impression that he or she doesn't know what to do and he might become withdrawn or more irritable than normal if subjected to even mild criticism at work. Some of my patients have been fired from their jobs because their illness wasn't recognized, either by themselves or by their employers. Later when considering whether anything seemed to bring on the depression, the patient might say in all honesty, "Losing my job was the stressful event that brought me down into depression."

And to repeat the point I made earlier, the stressful event that sets off a depression or manic episode can be a good thing (even winning the lottery or getting a big promotion at work) just as easily as it can be a bad thing.

Finally—and this is important to bear in mind—*stress is not all bad.* Stress is a part of life. The most stress-free life is one in which nothing happens. Not that I'm recommending the life of a daredevil, but I remember the words of a great man with manic-depressive illness, Sir Winston Churchill, who said, "There is nothing more exhilarating than being shot at and missed."

So even though stressful events seem to happen in clusters prior to a clinical depression, I don't encourage my patients to lead stress-free lives. That would be impossible anyway. My goal rather is for them to be able to live normal lives and, to the extent possible, to pick and choose their stresses or risks. In some instances, I would even suggest that they embrace them. After all, nothing that improves your life comes without its accompanying risks and stresses. You could avoid getting married, having children, changing jobs when the opportunity is a good one, or competing for a promotion or striving toward a goal that you might not reach, but what kind of life would that be?

## How Stress Can Precipitate Depression

There are almost as many environmental theories to account for depression as there are people who have depression. It would be a major breakthrough if we understood how events in the world around us interact with the internal functioning in our brains.

How do we begin to understand the interaction of the internal and external development of depression and still fit it all together with the evidence that severe depression is a medical disease like cancer or diabetes? Genes play as important a role in asthma as they do in depression. But if you have asthma, you know that you must be careful about letting your bedroom get dusty. You also have to be careful with exercise, especially running outside in cold weather, and you have to take extra precautions during allergy season. The genes for asthma seem to affect the function of the lungs and immune systems. But most episodes of asthma follow a "stressful" occurrence, such as being exposed to pollens. Even a psychological stress can bring on an asthma attack in many patients. On the other hand, if someone who did not have asthma had to go into a dusty attic and in the process stirred up a lot of dust, he or she would cough and have difficulty breathing for several minutes but would not get asthma. So for practical and for research reasons, it would be good to know which "stresses" can lead to depression episodes and how they do so.

Labored breathing is not asthma and feeling sad is not clinical depression. An excessively dusty room can bring on labored breathing in anyone and asthma in some, just as stressful life events can bring on sadness and discouragement in anyone, but clinical depression only in some. It is not your fault if stress brings on clinical depression any more than it would be if you had asthma and dust precipitated an asthmatic attack.

A great deal of research is now being done on how stress affects the brain, especially how repeated stresses affect those parts of the brain involved in depression. While we still have more questions than answers, it does seem pretty clear that repeated severe stresses and persistently elevated "stress hormone" levels compromise the function of brain cells in some critical brain regions possibly linked to depressive illness. (I'll talk more about the brain-depression connection in chapter 6.)

Are there places or situations that you should try to avoid in order to minimize the risk of a manic or depressive episode? Better yet, are there things you can do that will prevent depression or at least decrease its severity? The short answer is that we only know a few of the precipitating and protective factors. But at least we've gone past simply theorizing about the problem. We actually have some good ideas today and many more to test in the future.

Certainly I recommend regularity of sleep, eating, and exercise, all of which seem to moderate the effects of stress, although I couldn't prove that if I had to. In particular, I feel that what you do to counteract or moderate the effects of stress is also important. When to choose certain stresses and when to avoid them is as important as what the stresses are. First, avoid things that you find stressful if you are already having anxiety or even mild depressive symptoms. Timing is crucial. For instance, going off on a vacation may seem like a wonderful idea in theory, but it might turn out to be a bad time to take off from work, increasing the stress you'd feel once you were actually on vacation. In many cases, however, you're better off experiencing stresses than trying to avoid them because they may act as warning signs. The more you are aware that you are experiencing stressful events, the more you should ask yourself (or your doctor) whether you are already into a depression.

Are there things that you should avoid for the rest of your life if you are at risk for depressive illness? Are there events or circumstances that always precipitate clinical depressions or manias? The answer is no, not that we know of.

Well, you might want to know whether there are events, that have been clearly associated with worsening depression (aside from abusing illicit drugs and alcohol) once you already have an episode. The best-known and best-studied stressor is the death of a spouse. But the death of a child or the death of any loved one from suicide are widely believed to be even worse stressors. Today, many people would say that childhood traumas, especially traumatic abuse—sexual or physical—is one of the "causes" or aggravations of depression. This assertion is both true and false in important ways. It's true because the evidence suggests that childhood traumas are associated with increase the risk for depression; but it's false in that the same can be said for almost every psychiatric condition. To put it simply, wiping out the best-known stressful events would be desirable for many reasons, but their role in causing depression is not the only, or even the most important, reason to do so.

Several years ago, CBS commentator Mike Wallace was on trial for libel over a story he'd done. For weeks he sat in a drafty federal courthouse in New York City while the prosecution denounced him as a liar and a fraud. So naturally, he thought, he would be feeling down. Who wouldn't in such a situation? "I'm pessimistic by nature and so it didn't occur to me when I began to feel badly when I was on trial for libel," he recounted at an annual gathering of DRADA, the support group for patients and their families, at Johns Hopkins. "I felt lower than a snake's belly. I used to speak to my own physician and we'd known each other for ten or fifteen years. He said, 'You're strong, you're talking yourself into something.' 'No, I'm not,' I told him. Finally I wound up collapsing and going into Lenox Hill Hospital."

Although Wallace was ultimately vindicated, the ordeal was so agonizing for him—his professional reputation was on the line—that you might assume that the court battle was in some way responsible for "causing" the depression. It certainly appears to have been a precipitating factor. So you could say that this case of depression was essentially externally influenced.

However, when Wallace next suffered an episode of depressive illness several years later, the only significant development that preceded it was a fall while playing tennis that resulted in a broken wrist. It certainly isn't in the same ballpark with being sued for $120 million for libel. A broken wrist may be cause for some demoralization—you aren't going to be able to play tennis or piano for some time—but on its own would hardly seem to account for a depression that requires hospitalization. What we can safely conclude is that environmental influences are important in both depression and demoralization, but they do not provide a sufficient explanation for major depressive illness or manic depression even in the direst circumstances.

## Seasonal Changes Can Turn Depression On and Off

Maybe the simplest and perhaps the most selective of precipitating factors that we have identified is the effect of the seasons and light on depression and mania. I notice the effect on me the first April evening when daylight saving time goes into effect and the weekend in late October when we set the clock back an hour. For the first few mornings after the change in April, I hate waking up in the dark. As it grows lighter with the passing weeks it gradually becomes easier. The reverse happens in October. I love that extra hour of sleep but a few days later I'm having more trouble waking up and getting going in the dark. It is even gloomier when it gets dark so much earlier in the evening.

Hardly anyone I know looks forward to having fewer hours of daylight in winter, but some people actually become clinically depressed every fall. We call this phenomenon seasonal affective disorder, or SAD.

SAD is fairly easily treated. This pattern of depression was first recognized by a group of psychiatrists at the National Institute of Mental Health. They showed that the patients' depressive symptoms were relieved if patients with SAD were exposed to very bright lights for a set period of time each day. The doctor devised a small bank of very broad-spectrum fluorescent lights. When the patients sat in front of them with their eyes open for two to three hours a day, they seemed to get better after three to five days. If they stopped, though, they quickly got worse again. The simplicity of this therapy makes me appreciate how ingeniously, and subtly, human beings influence the environment generally. (To learn more about how bright lights work, see chapter 16.) It's one thing to consider how the invention of artificial light has changed humankind's relationship to leisure, sleep, and so on, but it also makes you wonder how its widespread use also might be having an important effect on our brains and our behavior. Of course, it's hard for any of us to imagine life today without bright lights.

Seasonal change seems to have another effect, too, aside from incidence of SAD. The numbers of psychiatric hospitalizations and suicides reach peak levels each year in November and May. The bigger peak occurs in November in the northern hemisphere and May (the beginning of winter) in the southern hemisphere. What drives these seasonal effects and whether all of them depend just on the hours of sunlight each day is something we don't know.

Until now I've talked mostly about the epidemiology of depressive disorders: who is more prone to get these disorders, what kind of forms and disguises these disorders assume, and what kind of environmental influences may cause those people who are genetically susceptible to become ill. These influences, as I've said, can range from seasonal changes to disruptive family lives. Because depression is such a complicated illness involving so many factors, scientists have been pursuing several avenues of research in addition to epidemiology in an effort to understand it. Epidemiology is only one of what I call the four sciences of depression, which I believe will provide the best explanation for clinical depression and manic depression. Now that we've explored what goes on outside (in the environment) that can contribute to depression, it's time to turn inward and take a look at what goes on inside ourselves that may bring about these disorders, which is where the next three sciences of depression come into play.

# PART TWO

∞

# Unraveling the Secrets

In the last few chapters I frequently referred to people who are "genetically susceptible" or "genetically prone" to developing depressive illness. So it follows that like epidemiology, genetics is one of the four sciences of depression. The other two sciences are neuropharmacology and brain imaging.

Of the four, the second science—genetics—is commanding the lion's share of attention these days and no wonder. For several years geneticists have been identifying genes that govern different types of structures, biochemical processes, and behavior. A large number of disease-related genes have now been discovered. The success scientists have had in completing the sequence of the entire human genome (almost all of our DNA), consisting of approximately 30,000 genes, holds the promise of identifying yet more disease-causing genes. Genetics has already given us remarkable insights into the role genes play in contributing to several mysterious brain diseases such as Huntington's disease and Alzheimer's disease. We now have the basic tools to discover how some genes may predispose certain individuals to depression and possibly show how other genes offer protection against it.

The third science of depression is neuropharmacology, which is the study of the effect various neurotransmitters, brain cell receptors, and drugs (for example, medications like antidepressants) have on the brain systems. Brain imaging constitutes the fourth science of depression; advances in technology over the last few years have made it possible for researchers to visualize the structures better than before and to some extent the functional (biochemical) activity of the brain. The advanced brain imaging methods include structural MRI, functional MRI, and PET scans.

We're poised on the brink of some remarkable discoveries about depressive illness. That's because of the genetic technology and advanced brain imaging techniques that will allow us to understand brain structure and function in ways we could only dream about even in the late eighties, when many of these innovations still didn't exist. Even with this new technology, however, achieving the breakthroughs we hope for will not be an easy task. It will require the same commitment to research that has been made in the past for cancer and heart disease. Practically speaking, our objective is to speed up the time it takes to make an accurate diagnosis (compared to today's average of a ten-year delay for bipolar disorder, for example) and to be able to predict which patients will respond best to which treatments. If we are to do this, though, the country will need to make a sizable investment, not only in money but also in talent. We would like to recruit our brightest young medical professionals and scientists to participate in the effort, but this can only happen if they have sufficient incentive. That means that society has to make the conquest of depressive illness an imperative.

In brain research we are trying to trace various routes through the brain, connecting one region to another. Each of these regions has different structures and functions. We believe that some of these routes, or pathways, once understood, will account for the development of depression and manic depression. The medical terms doctors use for these pathways are the pathogenesis (path to the start) or pathophysiology (path to the action) of diseases. It amounts to knowing which specific changes in the working of the brain make the difference between being well and going into a depressive or a manic state. We already have inklings about what we're likely to find. For instance, we have good evidence showing that several genes acting in the brain are among the critical causes of these illnesses. When we are able to identify three or four of these genes, then I expect that we will be much closer to understanding the biochemical processes in the brain that create these conditions. My optimism is based on a current precedent. Researchers during the last decade have discovered five genes related to Alzheimer's disease. Even though the first gene they found accounted for only about 1 percent of the cases of Alzheimer's, its discovery nonetheless represented a breakthrough. The gene they had identified turned out to be responsible for one of the most significant features of the illness, the abnormal amyloid deposits in the brain. Neuroscientists had long known about amyloid deposits; what they didn't know was how they came to be there. It was believed that these deposits might represent a response of the brain to trauma. But once scientists realized that a gene related to amyloid was the guilty party for some Alzheimer's cases, their entire conception of this much-feared disease underwent a profound change. It gave them a new path along which they could search for additional clues.

Over the last several years, other mutated genes have been discovered that reveal a great deal more about how the disease occurs. By following the Alzheimer's pathway, scientists are able to trace how cells in the brain are methodically killed off in a step-by-step fashion. It appears that a cascade of biochemical events occur that produces too much of one form of a protein that precipitates rather than remaining dissolved or more liquid in the brain cells. As soon as the implications of these discoveries were understood (only weeks), molecular scientists and clinicians around the world were conducting studies using this experimental knowledge in the hope that they could prevent, destroy, or render harmless the precipitation of the proteins that was gumming up the brain cells. Scientists have put these mutated genes into mice and observed them as they developed brain deposits characteristic of Alzheimer's. The mice's normal ability to learn how to navigate mazes became massively impaired. They then gave a group of mice with these genes a treatment designed to soak up the product of this abnormal cascade of chemicals. The treatment reduced these deposits in the mouse brain and improved navigation too.

Because of these remarkable discoveries, scientists now have an unprecedented opportunity to develop strategies to intervene at logical places in the pathway of Alzheimer's in order to stop or slow the progress of the disease in humans. This is exactly what we are hoping for in the case of depression and manic depression. But we must develop the same kind of understanding of the depression and bipolar processes in the brain that we now have in Alzheimer's.

In the chapters that follow, I will tell you how research in genetics, neuropharmacology, and brain imaging—separately and together— will help to unravel the secrets of depressive illness. I will try to be clear about what we've learned from these sciences to date and what we are likely to learn in the future. But I want to be clear about what we don't know and the challenge ahead. The bottom line is, when we understand how nature creates this illness it will become clear what we can do to treat it rationally.

∞

# CHAPTER 6

# What Do We Know About the Brain?

"There is no way an unassisted human brain, which is nothing more than a dog's breakfast, three and a half pounds of blood-soaked sponge, could have written 'Stardust,' let alone Beethoven's 'Ninth Symphony.'" That's how the novelist Kurt Vonnegut put it. Well, one of the "sponges" did produce "Stardust" and another did the "Ninth Symphony." All of Mr. Vonnegut's satirical novels came from a really different sponge. But he is onto something; even now the brain is still largely unexplored territory, a precisely wired mechanism of 100 billion neurons and at least one trillion supporting cells. Whether viewed as a supercomputer or a sponge, the brain has neuroscientists, psychologists, philosophers, and experts on artificial intelligence off balance. They are all scrambling and speaking different (technological) languages as they conduct experiments to probe its secrets.

The brain is our most important and mysterious organ. When it comes to trying to understand how depression develops, the brain is where scientists have naturally concentrated most of their attention. Yet until relatively recently so little was known about the structure and function of the brain that very little progress in this direction was possible. In 1950, for instance, we didn't really know that neurons used chemical messengers—neurotransmitters—to communicate with one another. We didn't know about neurotransmitter receptors or how they worked. So the notion that we would one day develop drugs that could treat depression, mania, and schizophrenia by altering the neurotransmitter system was inconceivable. Neuroscientists have made progress unraveling some of the mysteries of the brain; enough to have won a Nobel Prize (shared by three outstanding scientists). However, most drugs we use to treat depression, mania, and schizophrenia were not born out of basic neuroscience research. Rather, they have been discovered by happy accidents, as you will later review when you reach the discussion of pharmacological treatments. The Nobel awards, in this instance, are a strongly supported recognition of what has been made possible, rather than a celebration of the conquering of brain diseases.

Like most doctors who deal with patients' everyday problems, we have just enough knowledge of abnormalities in brain structure and chemistry in patients with depression and with bipolar disorder to feel confident that we will eventually prove that these conditions are brain diseases. We do have effective treatments, after all (even if we do not understand how they work), so why should we worry about what's actually going on in the patients' brains?

How does the brain produce depression and mania? We must know how the abnormal brain works if we are to improve our diagnosis and treatment of patients in a dramatic way. Why? Because we must be able to identify people who are at risk of depression, we must know after a first emergency visit, not after their third hospital stay, what is wrong. We must provide them a treatment that we know will work for them; and we must persuade them (and healthcare officers and insurers) that these are diseases that need treatment in a way that is as clear as we have done for cancer and for AIDS, so that no insurer and very few patients would deny the help that is available to them.

## How Does the Brain Work?

First, a few basics. Brain cells or neurons carry out basic processes such as synthesis, metabolism, packaging, and transport of molecules. These are required for the health of the cell and are remarkably similar across species from single-celled yeast to humans. They are also directed to carry out the neurons' specialized functions: Some neurons are devoted to vision, some to hearing, some to motor function, and so on.

Just as the neurons respond to signals from other neurons, they also respond to stimuli from the external world through the sensory organs. At the least it is a two-way process. How is all this vital information communicated so that all 100 million neurons are kept abreast of what is going on within and outside of the body? It turns out that the transmission system involves chemical messages moving into the small gap separating one neuron from another, which is called a *synapse*. These chemicals are the neurotransmitters I referred to earlier.

These neurotransmitters are accepted by the next neuron at a specialized site called a *receptor*. Receptors are composed of protein structures on nerve cells that are specifically designed to recognize and bind to a particular neurotransmitter (see Figure 1, Synapse).

These functions are carried out in the context of an overall set of purposes. This is then an orchestrated, coordinated program of activity in which neurons particularly in the brain send messages to other neurons, initiating goal-directed plans using the motor, sensory, intellectual, and affective capacities of the brain. Some neurons are precise conduits of specific pieces of information that must be accurately transmitted. For example, if I reach under a couch looking for my keys I can tell even without seeing whether I have come across a coin, a key, or a ring of keys, and I can also sense whether they are wet or dry, etc. This information connects one neuron to another in a single file, if you will. A different set of neuronal relationships is

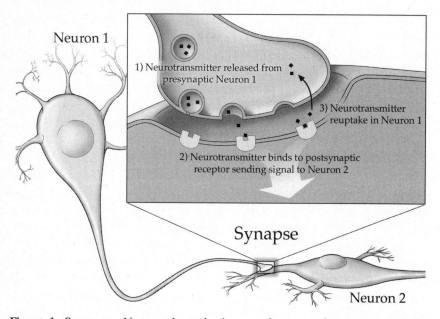

**Figure 1. Synapse.** Neuron 1 synthesizes, packages, and transports neurotransmitter to presynaptic cell wall, where it releases the neurotransmitter into the synaptic space. On Neuron 2 specialized receptor molecules (in white) recognize a single specific neurotransmitter. When the postsynaptic receptor is occupied in this way it usually opens a channel for an ion exchange or it activates a signaling mechanism inside the cell. In either case the "information" carried by the neurotransmitter is received since Neuron 2's actions are changed in this process. The action is slowed or stopped primarily by the reuptake of the neurotransmitter back into Neuron 1.

needed to fit this activity into the context of purpose. For example, one aspect of context has to do with the priority of a particular activity. I might be relaxed and looking for the keys while still watching or half-watching a baseball game on TV. Alternately, I might be in a race with time as I reach under the couch for the keys realizing that my pregnant wife is having strong contractions every three minutes and I have to drive her seven miles to the hospital *now*. This kind of information is best carried by a specialized set of neurons that "speak" to all the other neurons at once; perhaps the way a captain might speak to all the navy enlistees standing in neat rows at a formal gathering, or with a siren blast and the ship's loud speaker in an emergency. Do we need all hands on deck and now, or do we need just a few? Do we need them right now any way that they can get there or do they make sure that the medals are pinned on their shirt in the right sequence before arriving?

We know as much as we do about neurotransmitters because of drug studies done in humans as well as in animals, usually rats or mice. There are many neurotransmitters operating in the brain. Each one has multiple receptor types. For example, there are many serotonin (5HT) receptor types in the brain. One or maybe two of these are related to depression. The 5HT system is organized so that most of the neurons that release serotonin originate in a group of neurons in the midbrain. This group is called the Raphe (pronounced *rah-fay*) Nucleus. A second important neurotransmitter is norepinephrine, which is recognized by at least four specific receptor types. The nerve cells that release norepinephrine originate in a midbrain area called the Locus Coeruleus (pronounced *sir-rule-eus*).

The neurons that release these two neurotransmitters are small in number but have long axons (a single long arm) that take messages from the cell body out to the neurons that are to receive the messages. In the case of these neurons they have many branches coming off the main trunk of the axon reaching many neurons throughout the cerebral cortex. These pass up from the midbrain into the frontal lobes of the cortex and then sweep back to the rest of the brain (parietal, temporal, and occipital lobes). This enables them to influence *all* parts of the brain at the same time. The way in which they are organized suggests that the neurons distributing these neurotransmitters are involved in communication of information such as moods, emotions, and appetites that would influence many brain activities in a coordinated way (e.g., sensing danger, making decisions quickly, and preparing simultaneously for flight and fight activities).

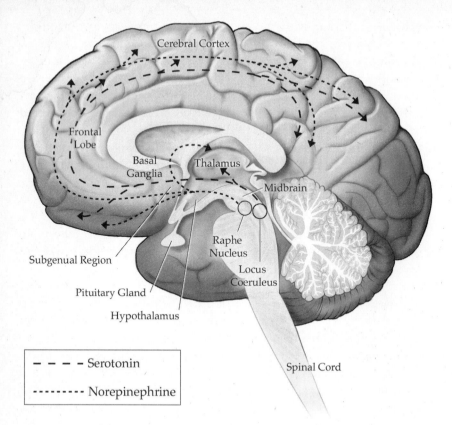

**Figure 2. The Brain.** Some of the brain structures involved in mood and affective changes are indicated above. Note that most are below the cerebral cortex and contain neurons that are organized to communicate to many cells at one time.

## Searching for Depression in the Brain

Major advances in research that have occurred in the last several years have given us much greater insight into brain structure and function enough to reenergize direct studies of the brains of patients with depression and bipolar disorder. Neuropathologists and anatomists have dissected brains for several centuries. The psychiatrist and neuropatholigist Kraepelin surmised a century ago that when all was said and done the major causes of depression and manic depression would turn out to be genetic and vascular.

Most of what we have learned in the eighty years since Kraepelin's death would seem to bolster his views. The cautionary note is that we need to keep the whole person in mind—personality and circumstances—when we are planning a treatment program. In other words, we are not just treating a disease but an individual with a disease.

## Brain Imaging Methods

One of the greatest advances in revealing brain structure and function in living human beings has come about because of improved brain imaging techniques, the best of which currently is the Magnetic Resonance Imaging (MRI) method. You don't need to know how a magnetic field can produce a detailed picture of our brains to appreciate the greater detail obtained from an MRI head scan compared to the earlier Computer Assisted Tomographic scan. With the use of powerful computers we can now use the MRI method to study some rapid biochemical actions that are evoked in response to some stimuli (something the patient looks at or thinks about). This is called a functional MRI. We have also learned a lot through studies of humans with precisely defined brain injuries, which has allowed us to discover some of the functions associated with particular regions or pathways in the brain. It's from using both these methods—imaging techniques and examining what happens if a part of the body or its function is impaired—that we've come to know so much about memory, learning, language function, perception, and fear response (in animals). These same methods, we believe, will enable us to understand depressed and manic syndromes, too. Recent studies showing wonderful pictures of brain changes are associated with drug craving and the good feelings that follow ingestion of addicting drugs. But we will need much more information before we are able to fill in many of the gaps in our knowledge.

## The Catecholamine Hypothesis: The Big Idea Behind Antidepressants

Julius Axelrod, who won a Nobel Prize for work carried out in the 1960s on norepinephrine, offered scientists a new direction in which to look for causes of depression. Axelord learned how noradrenaline was normally synthesized and operated in the brain and peripheral nervous systems. He also showed how these physiological pathways might explain some aspects of depressive illness, especially how some medications reversed it and others precipitated it. His framework of ideas, called the catecholamine hypothesis, continues (in modified forms) to be the most potent driving force behind the development of antidepressants today. His ideas have also served as the basis for new ways to "boost" or speed up standard antidepressants, by using a drug with both stimulating and blocking effects at one type of epinephrine receptor.

The first and simplest catecholamine hypothesis was that depression resulted when a depletion of *norepinephrine* occurred in the brain cells. If that were true then it would follow that restoring or elevating norepinephrine might help lift the mood. Several years ago physicians reported a disturbing trend among patients being treated for high blood pressure. Many of them had been given a drug called reserpine, which depletes norepinephrine. An alarming number of these patients were committing suicide. Why would a lack of norepinephrine cause a person to become so despondent be driven to suicide? The culprit seemed to be a low level of the neurotransmitter. The fact that the first two types of known antidepressant medications—tricyclics and monoamine oxidase (MAO) inhibitors—each seemed to increase norepinephrine activity strongly supported this idea.

The first major update to the catecholamine theory was the addition of other compounds, particularly *serotonin*, to the picture. Subsequently some theorists added *dopamine*. Another major revision, which is still evolving, was the finding that the neurotransmitters work by binding to neurotransmitter receptors. What Axelrod and his students found was that there are multiple types of receptors for each different neurotransmitter. These receptors are specifically made to link up with particular neurotransmitters.

## From Neurotransmitters to Antidepressants

When we describe how a message is conveyed we need to refer to a sender, a recipient, *and* a means of transmission. The message is probably going to be different if it is spoken or written, whether it's transmitted by U.S. mail or e-mail, over copper wires or fiber-optic cable, than whether it is received by a computer, or a cellular phone.

The receptors are complex proteins which are located within the neuronal cell wall where they can receive the transmitter molecules from a neighboring neuron. The receptor activates an internal signaling system within the cell, which is what makes the cellular machinery alter or change what it is doing. Now each neurotransmitter also has multiple receptors that it talks to. Some are present in order to keep the right amount of the transmitter where it's needed and when. The others are types that are distributed on different cell types, and in different tracks in the brain. This means that the same neurotransmitter can have different influences in different parts of the brain. It also means that if a gene mutation causes an error in construction of a shared element of several receptors for a single neurotransmitter, it could have several different effects on brain function. As a result, you have a receptor with somewhat different actions based on variations in each subunit. If there are two subunits per receptor and three types of each subunit, there will be a total of nine possible structures for the fully functional receptor related to one (yes, just one) neurotransmitter. That means that the same neurotransmitter could give several messages or create multiple influences with "a single shot." It also means that if a gene mutation causes a small error in construction of one subunit, it could have several different effects on brain function.

What are the practical results of these discoveries? Well, for one thing, it has made it possible to develop new drugs targeted to specific receptors (5HT2A, for instance, or 5HT3). There are even a few designed to hit a particular subunit trying to influence one, rather than all, of the receptor's activities. Currently neuroscientific "engineers" are attempting to make more and more precise medicines that do just what we want them to but nothing else.

Neurotransmitters perform rather modest functions at one level. They say to the cells with whom they connect via synapses: "Do more" or "Do less of whatever you are doing!" Norepinephrine is a classic inhibitory neurotransmitter. It says, "Slow down!" So, when there's a deficiency of norepinephrine, some part of the brain cannot put on the brakes fast. If it were a car it would crash.

## The Discovery of Antidepressants and Brain Theories for Depression

Fifty years ago, when internists specializing in infectious diseases were beginning to treat TB patients, they noticed that a certain antituberculosis drug made some of their patients become very cheerful, even hypomanic. It was discovered that besides inhibiting TB bacteria, this drug was blocking the enzyme responsible for the breakdown of one of the brain's neurotransmitters, namely norepinephrine. Norepinephrine is a catecholamine monoamine compound related to other neurotransmitters such as epinephrine, dopamine, and to a lesser extent serotonin. The development of a new family of antidepressant medications known as the monoamine oxidase inhibitors (MAOIs) followed this accidental, but happy, discovery and was an early contributor to the chemical theory of depression known as the catecholamine theory. In the brain, the net effect of using an MAOI to inhibit the monoamine oxidases was an increase in the amount of active norepinephrine in the synapse, so the catecholamine theory was that depression was caused by not having enough norepinephrine active in the synapses of the brain.

Serendipity also played a major role in the discovery of the tricyclic antidepressant drugs, which scientists discovered inadvertently when they were looking for a more effective form of chlorpromazine (Thorazine). It was the first drug used to calm agitated patients and to reduce hallucinations and delusions in schizophrenics and manic patients. A small change in the structure of chlorpromazine was made in order to create a more effective drug with fewer side effects, but something went wrong. The result was a new drug called imipramine, which, while it didn't help patients with schizophrenia, and was discarded until they discovery that it worked very well as an antidepressant. How does imipramine work? It blocks the reuptake of catecholamines such as norepinephrine by the presynaptic neuron (see Figure 1, The Synapse). That is, it prevented norepinephrine from being sucked back up by the neuron that released it. This reuptake system turns out to be the major system for shutting off the norepinephrine effect in the brain. By blocking this mechanism the tricyclic drugs sustain higher levels of more norepinephrine circulating through the brain. It is the primary means the neurons use to stop the neurotransmitter activity. It is more rapid and effective than the MAO enzyme in decreasing the amount of norepinephrine in the synapse. So two different drug families—MAOs and tricyclic—increase the brain's supply of norepinephrine, and thus we thought that's how they improve depressive illness.

So we were almost ready to believe that we had the keys to the kingdom, but then we discovered that the lack of norepinephrine alone could not account for all or even most depression.

While neurochemists were trying to sort out the riddle of norepinephrine, some scientists were turning their attention to another neurotransmitter serotonin, whose major function in the body was then thought to be related to blood flow and intestinal activity. It was also learned that MAO inhibitors and tricyclics either inhibited the metabolism of serotonin and blocked its reuptake respectively and so the serotonin hypothesis was added to depression theories. A team of researchers at Yale University conducted a series of experiments in which they tried to directly manipulate this system in depressed patients. In fact, they caused a brief relapse to occur in patients who had partially recovered with antidepressants from depression. They did this by changing their diets in a way that essentially eliminated most of the serotonin precursors from their systems in a matter of hours. Two-thirds of the partially impaired patients immediately had a relapse. The results were pretty dramatic; one patient began to talk about her husband's death that had occurred many years earlier and lamented that she had no male children to carry on the family name. She insisted that she was a failure and couldn't see a future for herself. Another patient, when asked why she was crying, admitted that she didn't know but wasn't able to stop. All it took these patients to recover, interestingly, was a meal rich in tryptophane, a compound that is a building block in the production of serotonin. However, patients who had gotten fully well did not relapse. Why not? I don't know either.

Serotonin was involved in an experiment by Swedish scientists examining the spinal fluid of severely depressed patients. They found that the patients, who had very low levels of a serotonin compound called 5HT, were more likely to commit suicide than patients with normal levels.

Based on these suggestive findings about serotonin and norepinephrine, scientists hypothesized, severe depressions might be seen as either serotonin- or norepinephrine-deficiency depressions. Some people who were depressed had low norepineprhine levels while others became depressed because of low serotonin levels. That spurred pharmaceutical companies including Eli Lilly in the United States to find drugs that would block only the reuptake of serotonin. The search for a serotonin blocker yielded the most widely written-about antidepressant so far, fluoxetine or Prozac. Its commercial success as an antidepressant with relatively few side effects refueled the conviction among doctors and pharmaceutical companies that serotonin was the key to understanding the mechanism of depression. But again, serotonin isn't the whole story.

Thus we close our short tour of two long-standing theories of depression. There is some credible evidence that supports the theory that both norepinephrine and serotonin systems have important roles in depression, but we don't think that we can make them into a comprehensive explanation by themselves. These are our current neuromythologies, neither true nor false, based on what we know today—like old ballads that tell a sad story in a brief but compelling way with a moral at the end. Ballads are not always based on specific true stories but they give a sense of direction about the big truths down the road. Even if we learn that catecholamines aren't the key actors in the story, they are certainly a part of it. How could we get an idea of the other actors? Since these messengers are working all over the brain it would help us if we got some ideas about what are the important parts of the brain involved in depression.

## Why Some Stroke Victims Become Depressed and Others Do Not

Over the last century we have learned much about which brain regions control our normal functions by studying patients with brain injuries. And probably no injury of the brain has been as extensively studied as stroke. Dr. Bob Robinson, now professor and chairman of Psychiatry at University of Iowa has been observing for twenty-five years that 30 to 40 percent of the stroke patients he examines develop severe clinical depression. Although this came as a surprise to many doctors then, eighty years ago the great Swiss psychiatrist Eugen Bleuler (who coined the term *schizophrenia*) had been reporting similar findings. Many doctors thought that some type of depression would be an expected psychological response to a devastating illness like stroke. Perhaps that is why so few people who do suffer from strokes (about four hundred thousand Americans every year) are treated for depressive disorders. But it is important to take note that most stroke victims do not become clinically depressed at all. Even after only two days following a bad stroke, many patients assure me that they are seeing "improvement" already and that they are grateful for the wonderful nursing care they receive at our hospital. These were obviously patients who are doing well in terms of their rehabilitation and their mood. I have seen other stroke patients who have had such severe physical and intellectual changes that I am unable to tell whether they are depressed, especially if they are unable to talk. Then I have observed a third group of patients who have not had such physically devastating strokes. These patients are clearly quite depressed but they often focus their unhappiness on the stroke. They report that they feel devastated, hopeless, and even feel a bit of a failure or blame worthy. But they don't see their low moods as an illness any more than most patients do. Finally, some stroke patients develop other affective syndromes. Mania is uncommon following stroke and "emotional incontinence" (episodic uncontrolled of laughing or crying) is rare. With these patients I was unable to tell whether they were depressed, especially because they were unable to talk. Then I observed some patients who were not doing poorly physically but who were clearly quite depressed. It is clear however that not all patients respond to stroke, regardless of how severe, in the same way. Why this difference? That was something Dr. Robinson wanted to find out.

Dr. Robinson asked whether a stroke in one particular area of the brain was more likely to be associated with depression than strokes in other regions. The clinical reason to ask the question is obvious: If we can predict who is most at risk for clinical depression after stroke we will diagnose and provide treatment more quickly to them. Scientifically, Dr. Robinson was looking for the anatomy of depression, the brain problem that might be causing depression in cases without brain injury. By studying the brain MRI scans of stroke patients he saw that the biggest risk was associated with the left-sided strokes in the front of the brain: the frontal lobe. To test whether this observation would hold, Dr. Robinson decided to induce right frontal lobe strokes in rats. The result was a depletion of norepinephrine and a period of abnormal activity that lasted about ten days and then went away. Bob and his team pretreated some rats with tricyclic antidepressants and observed neither the chemical changes nor the behavioral changes that had occurred before.

In humans Dr. Robinson found that a stroke on the left frontal lobe caused immediate depression and a stroke on the right side did not. Other groups pointed out that some, perhaps just as many, patients with depressive illnesses became depressed sometime after having a stroke on their right side. Dr. Robinson suggests that it is possible there are two kinds of depression after a stroke. The onset of the depression occurs rapidly and more severely in patients with left frontal stroke, while it might develop more slowly and is less severe in patients who've had a stroke on the right side. Dr. John Lipsey at Johns Hopkins and Dr. Robinson, however, have found that severe depression after stroke responds well to tricyclic antidepressants (nortriptyline) but not to serotonin reuptake inhibitors. There is more to learn about strokes and mood disorders of many types.

However, stroke is by no means the only brain injury that is strongly linked to depression. Two conditions usually considered to be "movement disorders"—Parkinson's disease and Huntington's disease, which is inherited as a simple genetically dominant condition—also affect some of the same regions close to the left frontal cortex that strokes do. In addition, almost half of Cushing's disease (adenoma of the pituitary gland) and multiple sclerosis patients develop depression or manic depression.

There is a relationship between Parkinson's disease and depression which has been dramatically illustrated by a recent report in the *Lancet*. The Parkinson's patient whose case was the subject of the article was a sixty-five-year-old woman who had a thirty-year history of marked rigidity and moderate tremors. She had no history of any psychiatric disorder or depression, even after the onset of Parkinson's. Because her tremors were very bad, doctors attempted to relieve her symptoms by stimulating deep structures in her left frontal lobe, the region of the brain targeted by Parkinson's. This has been successful for a number of Parkinson's patients. This one region that is associated with depression in Dr. Robinson's studies. Under stimulation, using electrodes, the patient suddenly started to cry. She said she had feelings of sadness, hopelessness, and guilt. "I'm falling down in my head," she complained. "I no longer wish to live, to see anything, hear anything, feel anything." Asked why she was crying, she replied, "I'm fed up with life, I've had enough! I don't want to live anymore. Everything is useless, always feeling worthless. I'm scared of the world." When asked why she was feeling so sad, she said, "I'm tired. I want to hide in a corner. I'm crying over myself, of course. I'm hopeless. Why am I bothering you?" She never experienced any pain or had any hallucinations. Nor was there any change in her symptoms of Parkinson's.

The doctors stopped the stimulation and as soon as they did the depression disappeared, in fewer than ninety seconds! In the next few minutes her mood actually became a little hypomanic. She started laughing and joking with the examiner, playfully pulling his tie. She had no trouble recalling the entire episode. Significantly, researchers were unable to evoke similar depressive symptoms when they stimulated the right side of her brain.

If the full constellation of depressive symptoms can be evoked by electrical stimulation of a minute region of the brain in a person with no history of depression, does that indicate that depression may be "hard-wired" in the brain? Can symptoms of manic depression be evoked by deep stimulation of a different region of the brain? We could postulate that something is wrong with the structure of the brain in many unipolar and bipolar patients, yet many people with the same kind of changes in brain structure do not have obvious cases of depression or bipolar disorder.

There are a few other brain studies suggesting decreased size of the left basal ganglia nucleus (caudate nucleus) in depression and a decreased volume of another structure known as the *subgenual nucleus* that occurs in depressed patients in families with bipolar disorder. Many studies have also noted other changes in frontal brain structures and in the metabolism on both sides. But simply observing these changes is not sufficient for our purposes. We will also want to know *how* a change or pattern of changes in the brain leads to the clinical changes in mood, self-regard, and vitality. Today we know something is askew in the brain and that the changes are clustered in the deep frontal structures. It is still quite conceivable that the primary abnormality could be somewhere else in the body, but as the organ of mental life, the brain, we assume, must be the critical step in the pathway from the primary problem (wherever that is) to the clinical syndromes. Whether the primary cause is in the brain itself or in the hormonal, nutritional, genetic, or vascular system, the brain will continue to be the main focus of research on depression and bipolar disorder for many years to come.

# CHAPTER 7

∞

# Genes and Depression: The Fateful Inheritance

Long before the advent of the science of genetics, most people were aware that depression and manic depression ran in some families. What was not known was how these illnesses were transmitted from one generation to the next. That knowledge would come about only through a series of groundbreaking discoveries that began at the end of the nineteenth century, with the work of a monk named Gregor Mendel. The father of modern heredity, Mendel worked in the gardens of the monastery. He had been the first to observe how various traits in pea plants, tallness and shortness, for example, were passed along from parent to progeny. He observed that the results of cross breeding a particular type (species) of pea—those with wrinkled coats—with others—those with smooth coats—regularly produced hybrid peas with a simple and predictable ratio of wrinkled versus smooth coats. From these and similar experiments he proposed that inherited characteristics—eye color, height, and sex, for instance— were due to paired elements, now known as genes, one derived from the male parent and one from the female parent. In humans we can't conduct experiments like this. We can, however, conduct studies of twins and adopted children to see whether depressive disorders have been inherited and, if so, to what extent. Many twin studies and a few adoption studies support the theory that the risk of depression and bipolar disorder is genetically linked.

In her book *Touched with Fire,* my colleague Dr. Kay Jamison has put together the family trees of great artists and scientists dating back for centuries. The point of her exercise was to highlight the association of artistic prowess with depression or manic depression as these conditions reappeared from generation to generation in several families. Among her studies was the forebearers and relatives of the renowned author Edgar Allan Poe. Poe suffered from severe depressions and remarked in a letter, "Some curse hangs over me and mine." Alfred, Lord Tennyson, who had five brothers, two sisters, a father, and a grandfather with the clinical manifestations of depression or bipolar disorder, called it a "taint of blood." The idea that nothing could be done for patients with genetic disorders (since the problem was built in) held sway in people's minds for a long time. As a result of the discovery of DNA structure and deciphering of the DNA code, it has been clear that we could, at least in theory, use genetic information to design treatments.

From these discoveries, we learned that there were four letters in the alphabet of the genetic code: A for adenine, G for guanine, C for cytosine, and T for thymine. We also learned that a sequence of three consecutive letters (e.g. CCG or ATA), which are within a gene, form a word in the genetic code (called a *codon*). Each word is an instruction that guides one step in the construction of a particular protein for which the gene has sole responsibility. The string of codons in the gene can be thought of as a sentence in the genetic code. In other words, examining the DNA sequence—converting each successive set of three base pairs into the corresponding codons—will spell out the exact sequence of amino acids which make up the protein and the order in which they appear in the protein's structure.

Now that we are at the beginning of the twenty-first century we have in our hands for the first time virtually the whole map of the human genome, a "parts manual," as it's been called, consisting of 30,000 or so genes (fewer than the 100,000 scientists expected to find before the publication of the sequence of the genome in February 2001). Because we have only twice as many genes as the primitive roundworm (which has all of 302 nerve cells, as opposed to 100 billion brain cells in humans), it's obvious that the genes and their parts combined and interacted in more complex ways than we previously realized. Understanding how these processes are regulated is expected to occupy scientists' time for many years to come. From this research, though, we hope to learn two basic things about depressive illness: the genes for the illness, and how they interact with one another and with the environment to cause depressive and bipolar conditions.

## What Do We Know about Depressive Illness and Genes?

The fact that depression and manic depression run in families does not prove that it is caused by genetics. Languages and religion run in families, too, and they are not genetic. However, Poe and Tennyson were probably right when they said that it was something in the family aside from culture that had brought out the disease. We know this because of the consistent results of twin studies and adoption studies begun in the 1930s and continuing to the present. In the twin studies, psychiatrists find individuals with unipolar or bipolar disorder and then get permission to examine the other twin. The studies have found that genetically identical twins are more than twice as likely to share these diseases (unipolar or bipolar) than are genetically fraternal or nonidentical twins: 50 to 96 percent of identical twins compared to 0 to 40 percent of nonidentical twins (see Table 5). A sibling or offspring of a patient with a major depression or manic depression has a 10 percent chance of developing the disorder compared to the general population which has about a 5 to 10 percent risk of major depression and a 1 to 2 percent risk of manic depression or bipolar disorder. The conclusion that inherited genes are one of the causes of these illnesses is further supported by adoption studies. These studies showed that even when the children of a unipolar or bipolar biological parent is adopted in the first weeks or months of life they still have a greater risk of developing depression or manic depression than do the biological children of the parents who have adopted them. And they also have a greater risk than children with no depressed parents who are adopted very early in life.

Given the fact that we still don't have the depressive genes identified, what can we say *today* about the genetics of depression and bipolar disorder or manic depression? It turns out that we've learned more about bipolar disorder, the less common form of clinical depression, than unipolar depression. We know, for instance, that even bipolar manic depressive disorder is not a single genetic disorder, or even a combination of different disorders caused by different single genes. Bipolar disorder turns out to be a set of genetic disorders resulting from the interactions of two or more genes. Important nongenetic factors that we have already described (involving the environment, for one) also play a part as well as others we will learn about once we find these genes.

Although no genes for depression or bipolar disorder have been identified and isolated yet, there are at least four and as many as eight regions on chromosomes that have been identified that are likely to contain genes related to unipolar and bipolar depression. These areas are being scoured now to find genes that we can hope will transform Poe's and Tennyson's belief in a hereditary basis to these illnesses into specific knowledge about their nature. Even without the genes, though, recent genetic studies lead us to conclude that multiple genes acting together are the original causes in these illnesses.

## Progress in Genetic Mechanism

Scientists have discovered forms of inheritance that don't look like anything Mendel predicted. Several of them are of great interest to researchers studying depression and manic-depressive illness.

## Imprinting

One type of inheritance that produces very different patterns is called imprinting. Imprinting has two meanings in biology. Behavioral scientists apply the term imprinting to young offspring, for example, ducklings who identify almost any adult duck as their mother and then follow her anywhere she goes. Genetic imprinting refers to the observation that some genes are "marked" in either the sperm or the egg, and that this mark alters their actions so that the effect in children depends on whether they come from the father and the mother. What is the "mark" in genetic imprinting? The mechanism we know about is a type of chemical sleeve that covers the gene and blocks its ability to make its protein. This would "silence" the gene when you get it from the parent who "marks" it. There may be other mechanisms, too, but they are unknown today.

Imprinting of some genes is normal, so how can we say that it could cause diseases? Well if imprinting silences a gene, then a gene mutation that could cause a disease by making an abnormal protein would be silenced when inherited from the parent who puts the mark on it. In this way imprinting prevents the disease. This would affect the pattern of illness in a large family so that only mothers or only fathers could pass the gene to their children.

Imprinting could have a role in the inheritance of depression or manic depression. My colleagues at Johns Hopkins have found evidence suggesting that for some families a gene on chromosone 18 increases the risk of manic depression on the father's side but not the mother's. Whether imprinting is involved in manic depression is unknown but this possibility exemplifies both the frustrations and the joys of research. To learn the genetic rules of depression we might have to rewrite the rules of genetics. There are more rules or exceptions to them in this story.

# Triplet Repeats

Typically, you inherit one copy of each gene from your mother and one from your father. Your parents' copies come from your maternal or paternal grandparents. Thus, there are four copies of the genes that you can inherit. We used to think that they are inherited as exact copies of one of the four possible genes in play. We have recently learned that sometimes genes contain long runs of the same DNA sequence in which three letters (base pairs) of the genetic code are repeated many times in a row. The most frequently studied sequences so far are CAG (cytosine-adenine-guanine) repeats. You will recall also that each set of three letters in a gene is a codon or genetic "word" that directs the addition of an amino acid to a protein. When a long run of three repeating base pairs (a triplet repeat) occurs, the child of a parent who has twenty-five copies of one repeat sequence, for instance, might get forty to sixty repeats of that sequence instead of twenty-five. These long repeats are much more likely to expand than to shrink. As the number of repeats increase they can disrupt the normal function of the gene altogether so that no gene product (protein) is made. Several triplet repeat disorders are now known, including an important psychiatric disorder of children called the Fragile X Syndrome which causes mental retardation and some distinctive facial features we can observe. For seventy years it has been observed that some inherited diseases occur earlier and are more severe in each succeeding generation in families. But it was only in 1991 when the Fragile X gene was discovered that we learned more about triplet repeats. We do not know yet whether triplet repeat genes are involved in manic depression, but we have observed some families where younger generations have the disease earlier in life.

# Mitochondrial DNA and Bipolar Disorder

There's yet another unusual genetic explanation for the clustering of depression and bipolar disorder in families. In the last twenty years, researchers have learned that some genes (i.e. mitochondrial genes) are inherited only from the mother. Mitochondria are found in the cytoplasm. (Cytoplasm is everything in the cell except the cell wall and the nucleus.)

Since sperm cells have no cytoplasm, babies get their mitochondrial genes from their mothers. Although they are small in number, the mitochondrial genes are very important as they are basically the energy or power packs of the cells. These genes are especially important in sugar metabolism and in muscle and nerve cell functions.

Like any other kind of DNA, mitochondrial DNA is subject to mutation. Mitochondrial mutations also lead to diseases. A combination of factors, including aging, environmental elements, and mutated genes located on chromosomes (called nuclear genes) can cause damage to nerve or muscle cells and alter insulin production. Studies, still in their early stages, indicate that mood disorders can occur in persons with known mitochondrial DNA defects. Since there are many families where the manic depressive disorder is transmitted from the father, mitochondrial genes couldn't explain all instances of genetically transmitted mood disorders. It could, however, account for some families in which the illness appears to be passed exclusively from the mother to the offspring.

## What Do We Do If We Find the Genes?

Finally, the most important question is what exactly will psychiatrists do with the genes for depression and manic depression when we find them? Three possibilities suggest themselves to me:

1. The DNA sequences from the mutated genes that cause the depression or manic depression could be used to create a simple but useful blood test. This could be used to confirm the diagnosis of these conditions. In addition different combinations of mutations could determine why one treatment works beautifully for one patient and not at all for another patient. So the DNA or mutation sets could make a blood test to give us guidance on which of our current treatments work best for which patients.
2. Once we have a gene or several genes in a bottle, scientists could do many manipulations to see how these genes and their proteins change the affected person's brain cells. This is a critical step in trying to understand the pathways to disease, the Holy Grail of our field. In other words, how does the brain create depression and manic depression?
3. Once we have identified the genes for the illness, researchers specializing in depression and manic depression (together with scientists in other brain sciences) will be in a position to uncover or to create new treatments aimed at the disease

pathway itself. It is possible that we will cure or possibly even prevent brain changes that cause the disease. Some answers could be a change in diet or corrective sunlight exposure. New drug development, on the other hand, usually takes quite a long time (ten or more years) to be fully developed.

4. If we are successful in determining how depression and manic depression are produced we will be in a better place than ever before creating treatments and we will also have made it easier in the long run for many more people to be treated. That's because an understanding of the biology and chemistry of these diseases will erase much of the stigma that inhibits people from getting help. Once the causes of depressive illness are no longer mysteries, as they are now, I believe people will be much more inclined to recognize them as they do cancer or diabetes, as diseases rather than as personal failings or weakness.

Some other interesting things will come to pass when we develop a deeper understanding of depression and bipolar disorder. The history of medical science is filled with countless examples of how research into a particular disease often leads to greater knowledge of normal bodily functions. This happened in the case of diabetes mellitus. To make any headway against diabetes, researchers had to become experts in the normal production and regulation of blood glucose or sugar. Then they had to become experts in energy management by the body. Conclusion: When I look at what is possible with brain science and genetics as partners in research for psychiatry, the first thing I think about is the great intellectual talent and technological resources that could be put into this endeavor. How long will it take, ten, twenty, or even fifty years, before we have a physiological understanding of depression and bipolar disorders and logical treatment choices for all of our patients?

# CHAPTER 8

Hormones, Headaches, and Heart Attacks

By now you realize that the depression story is pretty complex, with surprisingly strange twists and turns. In this chapter I'll be talking about some complicated but fascinating research and then I'll get to a category that we might call Not Knowing Which End Is Up. The culprits in causing depression and manic depression are not limited to genes or brain chemistry. Other unwelcome disorders ranging from migraine headaches to heart disease are also connected to these illnesses. Even the experience of pain appears to have a link to depression. The pain you get when you sustain a physical injury seems to contribute to the "pain" you get when you are hit with depression.

One of my most unusual, but cherished, consultations involved a first-grade teacher who came to my office with her husband. The question they put to me was: Should they try again to have a baby after two previous failures? They then proceeded to tell me a harrowing story. From what they said it sounded as though the patient had a life-threatening toxic reaction to being pregnant. She would no sooner find out that she was pregnant, which was her lifetime dream, than she would be plunged into a nightmare. She started throwing up uncontrollably. She would become so violently ill that she couldn't keep anything in her stomach, not even water. Her situation got so critical that she was admitted to the hospital and had to be put on intravenous fluids. Her doctors were unable to stabilize her enough to wean her off the IV fluids and permit her to go home. Yet, even though she wasn't taking anything in by mouth, she still continued

to vomit. After weeks went on like this she and her husband reluc-
tantly came to the conclusion that to spare her from irreparable harm
she had no alternative but to undergo a therapeutic abortion.

Three years later, she became pregnant again, and again the same
thing happened. She vomited continuously, required hospitalization,
and finally had to resign herself to having an abortion to save her life.
Remarkably, both times she had the abortion the vomiting and nausea stopped as quickly as they had started. And while she would feel
emotionally drained she went on to make an uneventful recovery.
That she'd gotten pregnant twice with the same terrible results had
persuaded the doctors and nurses who'd cared for her that she
should stop trying. But she remained unconvinced by their arguments. And that was why she came to see me. Although it might
sound crazy, one of her doctors suspected that the true cause of her
violent physical reaction might have been depression. That was by no
means the consensus among her treating staff. One staff member
with a Freudian bent suggested that she might have some kind of
inner conflict—perhaps she unconsciously didn't want to have a
child—and that this was why she couldn't eat or maintain her health
in pregnancy.

What was clear to me, however, was that this was a woman who
loved children; that was why she'd gone into teaching in the first
place. After listening to what both she and her husband had to say I
had no doubts. They clearly wanted to have children of their own.
Whatever else was giving her problems, she was not suffering from
any inner conflict that was manifesting itself in terms of physical
symptoms. I told them that they should try again.

Several months went by without any contact from her. Then one
day she called and said, "Dr. DePaulo, it's happening again." As
before, she was vomiting uncontrollably but she insisted that she
wasn't pregnant; she'd just had her period. I advised her to come in
and see me. I immediately had her tested to be sure. Despite her firm
belief that she couldn't possibly be pregnant, she was pregnant.

This time I was on the alert for depressive symptoms. All the signs
were there: the lethargy, the feelings of guilt and worthlessness, and
so on. So I began her on a course of antidepressants. Even though
the vomiting abated, she still needed to be hospitalized. Then, as the
due date approached, I decided to take her off the medication as a
precaution; I didn't want the fetus to be overly exposed to the drug
so close to birth. Almost immediately after she stopped her medication, she had a relapse and began to vomit again. We put her back on
the antidepressant, and, fortunately, she gave birth to a healthy baby

boy. And what was almost as gratifying to me is that every year, on his birthday, the parents come back to visit me with their child.

What does this case say about the causes of depressive illness? This story has many morals, but the reason I relate it here is to point out how powerful hormonal influences can be on mood. In this case the hormonal system acted in two ways: it triggered not only the vomiting but it also the classical symptoms of clinical depression. Hormones are powerful but the same hormones often affect moods in either direction—up and down.

## Hormones, Stress, and Depression

The endocrine system, like the brain and the heart, is one of the control systems of the body. It's made up of a set of glandular organs, among them the pituitary, the thyroid, and the adrenal glands, and the ovaries or testes. The endocrine glands, working with the brain, keep the internal environment of the body synchronized with a variety of changing circumstances. They produce the chemicals that we know as hormones and secrete them into the bloodstream in order to regulate other organs throughout the body. They regulate the rate of our metabolism, telling the cell to speed up or slow down. In addition, an amazingly intricate feedback mechanism works in the opposite direction by when the organ system affected sends its signals back to the endocrine glands to regulate how much hormone it produces at any given time. The most critical and centralized endocrine regulatory centers are in the brain.

The coordinated mechanism between the brain and the endocrine system allows the body to respond to external stresses as well as to malfunction within the organs themselves. The brain centers that regulate the endocrine glands have prominent connections to the emotional tracks in the frontal lobe and midbrain.

When we are under great stress whether psychological or physical, the brain centers such as the hypothalamus and the pituitary gland signal to the adrenal glands to produce more cortisol, often referred to as the body's stress hormone. Cortisol has several effects. It reduces inflammation and swelling after injuries (useful if, for instance, you had to ignore a painful injury in order to run a mile to save your life). So, cortisol is the hormone to think of when you hear stories of superhuman strength or endurance which are displayed in crisis situations. The famous examples are of a mother lifting a car off her child's leg or a soldier continuing to fight in battle oblivious to his serious wounds. In modest amounts, it makes most people feel more confident. Cortisol's activity can also be manufactured in several forms of medications called steroids, which some athletes have abused to promote muscle development and to make themselves more aggressive on the field. Cortisol and its sister hormone, epinephrine, are released in the well-known "fight or flight" response in critically stressful situations. In addition to blocking inflammation, cortisol shunts blood flow away from the gut to the muscles and it also has major affects on moods—and that is where we meet another depression theory.

## Stress and Mood

This theory comes from the actual experience of people who fall ill when problems develop in the endocrine system. The endocrine glands can malfunction in the production, storage, or secretion of their hormones. The best-known disease in which mood changes occur is called Cushing's disease, named after the neurosurgeon Harvey Cushing, who first identified it. This condition is caused by the growth of a small benign tumor or overgrowth of functioning pituitary gland cells.

Pituitary cells produce a hormone called ACTH that signals the adrenal gland to make more cortisol. Along with several physical changes, about half of patients with Cushing's disease become clinically depressed while 15 percent become manic. Why some patients become clinically depressed and others manic even though they both have the same hormonal changes is a mystery to me.

Patients who are given large doses of steroid medications made to treat other conditions also may become clinically depressed or manic.

The depression-cortisol equation to some extent works in the other direction. Many studies show that a substantial fraction of patients with severe forms of depression overproduce cortisol. When researchers look at individual patients over time, they see cortisol levels go up as the patients become more depressed and reduced when they get well (or became manic), only to display elevated levels again when they cycle back into depression.

This occurs in a majority of severely depressed inpatients and a minority of depressed outpatients and brings us to the cause or effect question: Does the stress system go haywire and cause depression or does depression set off the stress alarm in our bodies thereby causing the high cortisol levels? We do know that people with depression and bipolar disorder have a high level of risk for relapse if they have to take steroid medications.

Several lines of research are being pursued to explore these observations. Much of the research on basic brain and hormonal systems is being carried out in the hope that we will learn something that will illuminate the pathway to depression and manic depression. One promising avenue of research is intended to test drugs that block a brain compound called CRF, which sends the original signal to the pituitary gland to start the stress response systems. Some researchers think these drugs might be antidepressants or mood stabilizers.

## Pain and Depression

Patients with conditions causing chronic pain have very high rates of major depression and treating the depression is an important part of helping these depressed patients get back on their feet. As significant as is the relationship between the stress hormone system and depressive disorders, the relationship between pain and these disorders is just as substantial and as complicated. First, it is not easy to measure pain. The best way we have of assessing pain in people is to ask them where and how much it hurts. However, when patients suffer from chronic pain and the loss of functioning is in reaction to their pain, subjective reporting is more difficult to interpret. This is because of many factors, not the least of which is the sometimes unfairly skeptical attitude of medical professions. That said, we know more about the neuroanatomy and neurochemistry of pain than we do about depression. Several new findings in the area of pain provide us with new ways of thinking about what we might look for in depressed patients to explain how pain and depression go together.

First, we have discovered that several pain treatments—especially the newer (nonnarcotic) ones—are also treatments for epilepsy and manic depression or depression. We have also known for years that most antidepressants have some useful antipain properties. Studies of spinal cord and brain structure after the occurrence of chronically painful injuries suggest a number of intriguing ideas that could help us. When someone with a back injury is in chronic pain for weeks or longer, cells that make them sensitive to touch seem to migrate from the part of the spinal cord they usually occupy to a region with a concentration of pain fibers. That suggests that cells previously dedicated to touch over time may start producing impulses that are experienced as painful. What was perceived as a light touch might later be felt as intense pain. Pain, it seems, produces a predisposition to feel more pain. Or to put it in broader terms: What you experience, and how you react to it, can actually change your nervous system!

The next part of the pain story may seem familiar. We've long known that sensory nerve cells connect the brain down into the spinal cord. Pain tracks are connected to one that use the neurotransmitters most involved in depression, norepinephrine and serotonin. The second part of the story is that the nerve cells carrying the sensory signals up to the brain split into two tracts, one of which leads to the midbrain, which has a multitude of connections to the basal ganglia and/or limbic system. We believe that this is the part of the brain that responds to these signals by telling you that pain is a *bad* feeling. The second tract leads to the outer layers or cortex of the brain where each body is represented. This is the part of the brain that tells you *where* it hurts. *It's your right hand, stupid; move it!*

The main lessons here are that pain and depression very often go together and that the depression is brought on by "real" pain, not imagined pain. Moreover, depression is often missed or not adequately treated, which makes it very hard to reactivate or mobilize patients who are debilitated by pain and restore them to their normal levels of energy and vitality.

## Migraine Headaches and Depression

The pain condition with the most unique connection to depression is the migraine headache. Migraines are not just ordinary headaches. They represent a distinct phenomenon in their own right. In their classic form, they are preceded by the appearance of sparkling dots floating in front of the eyes. The onset of the headache itself follows, starting off as a dull ache but fairly quickly becoming focused in the left or right temple. The pain intensifies, changing from dull to throbbing. The afflicted person feels nauseated and becomes so sensitive to stimuli that he or she will avoid lights and noises. Symptoms of yawning and frequent urination occur in some migraine sufferers. Some people with migraines experience neurological impairments—difficulty in speaking correctly, loss of vision in half of the visual field or even loss of control over one side of the body. The headache can persist for up to two or three days, but usually lasts at least several hours. What I have described is the full-blown migraine. Many migraine sufferers have this classic headache only four to six times a year but develop milder headaches much more often.

A critical feature of migraines is that they are episodic. Why should this matter? Aren't all headaches episodic? The answer is yes, but not all headaches are precipitated by the peculiar set of triggers that migraines are. Migraines often occur following a period of stress. People with stressful jobs, for instance, will be stuck in bed with a severe migraine on Saturday mornings after the week's work is done. Sometimes, a cycle of headaches may get set into motion, with each type of headache occurring more and more frequently, even every day. In this state patients are likely to feel that their headaches are getting out of control—and they are.

One of the changes associated with the onset or worsening of migraines is depression. Migraines certainly don't help moods, but most people with migraines don't have clinical depression. Some scientific evidence suggests that depression is linked to the occurrence of migraines. Dr. Kathleen Merikangas at Yale, Dr. Naomi Breslau at Henry Ford Hospital, and Dr. Karen Swartz at Johns Hopkins University have studied large populations of people suffering from migraines and shown that these individuals have higher rates of depression and panic disorder. Migraine sufferers are three times more likely to suffer from major depression than nonmigraine sufferers. However, the major practical importance of this finding is that when depression is what set the migraine into motion, doctors should recognize the true cause and treat the depression.

The intensity of migraines is related to the tension in the walls of the arteries and abnormal relaxation of these walls. The actual pain is produced by the nerves that detect the widening of the artery following each passing pulsation of blood through the dilated or stretched area. Tiny nerves with serotonin receptors regulate the degree of relaxation or contraction. Acute treatments for migraines affect serotonin receptors but they are not the same ones that seem most active in depression. The SSRIs and the antimanic agent called Depakote are among the effective treatments for migraines. Even the "old" tricyclic antidepressants (which don't specifically act on serotonin) are quite effective as prophylactic agents to prevent or reduce migraine recurrences.

Based on what we've learned so far, we believe that future studies of migraine and the other pain mechanisms might tell us much more about the mechanisms underlying clinical depression and its triggers, but in the meantime remember when migraines do go out of control or you experience any painful chronic condition, you should always check for depression.

# Heart Attacks and Depression

While I've said that the brain plays a crucial role in depressive illness, I've also mentioned that depression is involved with systems and organs *outside* the brain. But one of the most important organs in our body that's associated with depression is the heart.

The heart, as everyone knows, is the center of the circulatory system. To understand the heart's function, 90 percent of what you need to know concerns pumps, pipes, and valves. The major difference between the heart and mechanical plumbing is that the heart's pumps, pipes, and valves are carefully regulated by a nerve network with extensive connection to and from the brain. The system is regulated (or misregulated in disease states) by hormonal systems, which respond to the external environment. As we are all aware, the environment places demands on the body, especially the heart

The intricate connection between the hormonal system, the nerve networks, and/or the brain suggests that a change in one system will cause a change in another. So a dramatic change—for instance, in the perception of the world, which is what happens in depression—is likely to have an effect on the heart as well. Essentially, the heart will be living in a new environment. These changes may occur even if the perception by the brain is inaccurate or the response by the hormones to the external environment is inappropriate.

Studies have shown that people who have episodes of depression are two to four times more likely to have a heart attack over a thirteen-year period than people who have never had a depression. This calculation factors out all other known risk factors for heart attacks such as smoking, cholesterol levels, estrogen status, and medications. We don't know why depression increases the risk for a heart attack, but the existence of this link seems solidly based since it comes from three or four completely different studies and is very consistent from one study to another.

Is this an important connection? It appears to be very important. In one of the earliest studies, the data suggested that the link between the risk of a heart attack and depression was as strong as the link between cigarette smoking and risk of heart attack. In addition, people who have a heart attack while they are depressed are much more likely to die from the heart attack than those who are not depressed even when the heart attack is of the same severity.

Right now there are three basic theories to account for this phenomenon:

1. The nerves that help regulate the heart rate and output may malfunction in depression and thus cause more instability in heart rate or more arrhythmias.
2. The blood clotting mechanisms, especially the "stickiness" of platelets (small blood elements that help the clotting of blood), may become overactive in depression and cause too many clots to form within the blood vessels creating blocked arteries.
3. A higher activation of the adrenal gland in depressed patients creates more stress hormone (cortisol). This could contribute to heart attacks in several ways: It might cause higher blood pressure and impair glucose regulation as in diabetes. An over-supply of cortisol and/or norepinephrine in their own right can also have an adverse effect on the body. This area of research is literally just getting started and the answers, what-ever they turn out to be, will have a major public health impact.

What we can say with fairly good assurance, based on the studies we have, is that heart attacks do not appear to cause depression. Would treatment of depression help moderate the severity of a heart attack? We don't know because no one has studied the question yet. But there are studies that show that treatment of depression may lessen the risk of getting a heart attack in the future.

So where do all these diverse and often ambiguous studies and findings leave us? Clearly hormones and pain are among the stronger and (for now) the most confusing influences on depression and bipo-lar disorder. In earlier chapters you may recall that the hormonal shifts of puberty seem to set off a large increase in rates of depres-sion, especially in females. Pregnancy is often a time of well-being while the postpartum period is often a higher risk time for depres-sion. But we have numerous examples in which the reverse situation applies as in postpartum mania, pregnancy-related depression, and stress hormone mood changes that are completely unpredictable.

What's important to keep in mind is that no one system, organ, or other factor is responsible for depression—not one steroid, not one gene, not one neurotransmitter, and not a lesion on one side of the brain or the other. What we seem to have is a mixture, a stew with lots of different and exotic ingredients.

# PART THREE

∞

# Depression and Mania and Destructive Effects on the Whole Person

In the last twenty years, policy making institutions in the United States and elsewhere in the developed world have begun to pay much closer attention to the rising costs and socioeconomic impact of clinical depression and manic depression. And no wonder: These illnesses are exacting a very high price because so many people who are in need of help are going untreated. But in the three chapters that follow I want to focus on the enormous personal costs that these twin terrors impose on patients and their families. One of the major reasons why the cost is so great is because all too often people don't know that they're ill. And even if they do they might never get treatment because of the perceived stigma.

Ask anyone whose spouse or child has depression or bipolar disorder, and you will learn about the emotional drain and the constant crises that the illness has brought into their lives. When one spouse has even a modest depression most couples have a hard time thinking positively about themselves or each other. "Why is she so unhappy? Is she mad at me? What did I do? Why won't she tell me what I did rather than go around acting so irritable and withdrawn?" As it gets worse . . . well, you get the picture.

Persuading a reluctant adult to go for treatment is actually tougher than getting a child in for treatment. In some instances it can take years. Often the depressed spouse, who has low self-esteem to begin with, reacts angrily to any suggestion that a psychiatric evaluation or treatment might be warranted, taking it as an accusation. If the marriage does survive under these circumstances, the damage can still be considerable and very difficult to repair.

The impact of a manic state hits faster and more chaotically than clinical depression, but it can be just as devastating. Like an earthquake, it can produce aftershocks that affect the patient's family and friends for months or years even when the episode has long been cleared up. If you haven't lived through it, you can only imagine how hopeless families feel as they scramble to get help for someone who seems so out of control.

One measure of the difficulty families go through in trying to find help is that it can actually take up to ten years from the onset of symptoms before a patient obtains an accurate diagnosis of bipolar disorder. Sometimes even professionals can miss the diagnosis entirely. What the family goes through until the "system" gets it right can be torture.

Not all patients can wait so long to get a diagnosis and treatment. Some people need it urgently and when they don't receive it, the results can be tragic. The most reliable estimates we have available indicate that three-quarters of the suicides in the United States are caused, directly or indirectly, by depressive illness. Many people with depression may not commit suicide, but some will continue to make attempts, not all of them intended to be lethal. Nonetheless, the impact of attempted suicide on families is still awful, creating fearfulness and anger, which are probably the two emotions most immobilizing. "If I say this and he runs out the door, it will be my fault!" or "How could he do this to himself . . . to me?" If, of course, someone actually does go on to take his or her own life the consequences are far worse because the act is so final, so irrevocable. Perhaps it's true that there is no "good" way to die. Losing your parent, spouse, sibling, or child is almost unbearable under any circumstances. But it does help families if they know that they have done everything they can to help and if they have had a chance to say good-bye. Suicide eliminates both of these opportunities. No one has a chance to say good-bye. It leaves families and friends with questions but no answers. In the chapters that follow I will raise many questions, but I will also try to provide some helpful answers, too.

# CHAPTER 9

∞

# Depression, Manic Depression, and Relationships

In the past, both clinicians and researchers placed too much emphasis on how families might cause or aggravate depression, but they didn't pay enough attention to the damage that depressive illness does *to* the family. There is a saying that a parent can only be as happy as his or her unhappiest child, but the same is probably true when we consider how unhappy a depressed spouse or partner or close friend can become when their loved one is in a clinical depression. More than almost any other illness, depression is a family disease, in two ways. On the one hand, it is often genetic. But in addition, if one person is depressed other close family members will feel put off, shut out, and often guilty. Friends and members of the family may feel that they have done something to cause unhappiness or isolation or irritability that they sense in a loved one who is depressed.

Patients are now benefiting because we have more knowledge about the medical origins of severe depression and mania and more effective medications to treat their illnesses. It's ironic then, but undeniable, that while things may be looking up for the patients there is less support for their families. And as private and public institutions are discharging severely depressed patients with ever greater speed, it is their families who are bearing the greater medical and social burden with less support.

Insurers and HMOs often don't recognize what the patient needs in terms of care or the level of care the patient needs. And most states want to get out of the mental health world altogether. They no longer see the care of the severely mentally ill as one of their fundamental responsibilities. This represents a significant change in social priorities over the last several years. Perhaps what we need is another social crusader like Dorothea Dix (1802–1887), whose passion and powers of persuasion were critical in getting twenty states to build safe asylums for the care of the mentally ill in the mid-nineteenth century. Even outpatient care, now that we have the tools to do it effectively for most patients, can be difficult to obtain and sustain.

The importance of the role of the family in the care of major psychiatric illness has become increasingly recognized over the last twenty years. Patients with major psychiatric illnesses are spending more time with their families because of shorter hospital stays for acute episodes and deinstitutionalization policies. Many patients will fail to respond to drugs, especially as early as we would wish, and need rehabilitative care. Depressive illness seems to be associated with more family distress and impairment than are other illnesses. Depression, it has been found, has a much greater impact on marital life than rheumatoid arthritis or cardiac illness. One study found that only severe forms of cancer affected a family as adversely as depression or bipolar disorder.

Just how much distress depression can cause in a marriage—or any close relationship for that matter—is brought home to me by my patients. When couples marry they take vows to remain faithful to their mates in sickness and in health. When it's in sickness all the time, however, the marriage will probably suffer. Ironically, this is less true when the illness is physical. In fact, from my experience with patients, it appears that a physical illness is more likely to bring a couple closer, even in cases of terminal cancer, because both partners view the disease as the common enemy. In depression, though, sometimes it's hard for either partner to determine who or what the enemy actually is.

## How Depression Affects Families and How Families Affect Depression

There is no reason to assume a single linear relationship between depression and family functioning. It seems more likely that there's a relationship between how vulnerable the depressed person is and the stability of the family. If the family is beset by problems (remember what we said about "life events") and also have other people in the family who suffer from serious illness (mental or physical), the depression is likely to worsen or take longer to lift. So the effect is one of a negative feedback loop, where the patient's vulnerability and the family's problems are reinforcing each other.

Families have varying degrees of adaptability; some cope well even in difficult situations, some have great problems in these situations. The degree of ability to adapt is influenced by a variety of factors: their socioeconomic resources, family composition, availability of social support, presence or absence of other psychiatric and/or medical illnesses, and the family's current situation (life events). If the family is able to respond effectively the depressive illness may persist for only a relatively short time and then go into remission. If, on the other hand, the family is unable to respond adequately, the depressive episode may be prolonged and relapses are likely to occur more frequently, further impairing the family's competence to cope and setting off a vicious cycle.

The impact of the depression on the family can be dramatic. One study indicated that 40 percent of adults living with a depressed person were experiencing or had experienced depression themselves. Would they have been depressed if their spouse wasn't depressed? Can you "catch" depression the way you can catch a cold? Not exactly. It appears that individuals prone to depressive disorders are more likely to be attracted to and marry one another. (We'll learn more about this unusual phenomenon, called assortative mating, in our final chapter.)

How someone will respond to a spouse's depression varies, depending on any number of factors, including the nature of the relationship before the depression occurred. Many depressed partners are able to sustain good marriages in spite of everything; the values, commitment, and communication skills of the depressed person and the spouse, rather than the illness itself, may play a more important role in maintaining marital status in the face of depression. It is also possible that marital distress may affect the severity of depression. Up to 70 percent of depressed patients reported that they had stressful marriages before the onset of depression. Whether these reports are factual or whether the depression makes people think that their marriages were always shaky is hard to say.

In most marriages, women are more often the caregivers for whomever gets ill, no matter what kind of illness it is. When the wife is depressed, though, men often do not see it. But if they do, they tend to expect that their wives will take up the full burden of their dual role—as worker and homemaker—as soon as they show signs of becoming even a little better.

The family situation can undergo a change later in life when both spouses are ready for retirement. They may suddenly find that they have to confront problems at home they may have managed to ignore for years because they'd thrown themselves into their work. What happens when they are not getting much reinforcement from doing a good job at work? In that event, husbands and wives can become severely depressed.

## What Happens to a Family When Depression Hits?

What exactly happens to a family when someone becomes ill with depression? If someone in your family falls ill with cancer or diabetes, all things being equal, it wouldn't take long before you'd begin to realize something was wrong. Sooner or later most serious illnesses are going to make themselves known by presenting any number of physical symptoms that a doctor can diagnose and treat. What's different about depression?

Well, for one thing, you might think that your spouse is simply in a funk and that sooner or later he or she will snap out of it. Or you might think that the problem is in the marriage or at work. In many cases the person with depression doesn't realize that he or she has an illness at all. So when the family is plunged into turmoil its true cause will often go unrecognized. The most difficult situation of all arises when neither the depressed person nor the partner recognizes that one of them has depression. So the healthy spouse might wonder why his or her partner is being so negativistic, withdrawn, and irritable.

Meanwhile, if you're the person who's depressed, it's all you can do to get through the day. You're thinking too much about what you've done wrong. You're pretty sure your spouse thinks you're awful and you're basically waiting for him or her to get mad at you. So if a spouse claims to be baffled or upset because you're so pessimistic and unapproachable, it's hard not to withdraw further because it seems to confirm your worst fears.

The depressed patient often has a difficult time accepting support from the healthy spouse. That's because if you're the depressed partner you're likely to believe that your spouse is just telling you things you want to hear, not what he or she truly thinks. When you're depressed you don't believe that you're worthy of receiving love. It doesn't help when your spouse assures you that you are loved and appreciated. *Why is he saying this? Either he's being polite or he's putting me on, trying to con me. If he really sees me as the terrible person I am, then he'll want to get as far away from me as possible.* And what if your spouse manages to convince you that he or she is being sincere? Well, then you'll most likely decide that person has very bad judgment and must be deeply flawed in ways you never suspected before. It's a double whammy. The depressed person is thinking too much about what he or she has done wrong five hours or five days ago and imagining what will go wrong in the next five hours or five days. And the partner is baffled and upset by the sudden distance the disease has put between them, since he or she is unable to comprehend the reasons for it. With depression, the skills and ability to relate to other human beings are significantly diminished and the perception of the relationship is warped. Researchers found the depressed person's fatigue, feelings of hopelessness, constant worrying, and lack of interest in social life to be especially disruptive to the stability of a relationship.

Curiously, sadness isn't one of the things that you see as interfering in relationships where one or more people are depressed. In fact, you see sadness only in about half the cases. In the other half, anxiousness and apathy dominate. Depressed people will often become overly anxious about their health or grow obsessed about their finances. On the other hand, the person might not feel anything really—either positive or negative—and just doesn't care. Such people watch passively, as if from a distance, as the relationship implodes before their eyes.

When the couple at least knows that depression is involved, it can definitely be helpful. Knowing the source doesn't mean that it will change the direction of the relationship; the disease is still going to have an adverse effect. Even when you've been through a depression before and can recognize the symptoms, it's still difficult to deal with how your depression (or your spouse's depression) affects the two of you. Researchers have found that even when spouses are aware that their partners do have a real illness they still have no idea what to do in a practical sense to deal with the mood disturbance. But at least the recognition that the depressed person isn't himself or herself at the moment offers some consolation to the partner.

## How Depression Impairs Confiding and Communicating

As you can see, when we talk about how depression affects a family we have to talk about how each member involved perceives what is going on. Suddenly someone who may ordinarily be cheerful and self-confident is more irritable or withdrawn or more pessimistic about things. That makes the person more critical about how things are at home. Spouses of depressed partners frequently receive the impression that they are being held responsible for their partner's depressed state without being given any idea of how they could modify the behavior to make things any better.

Depressed people often don't have the ability to concentrate on a relationship and they feel stupid even though they're not. They're not as articulate as they would ordinarily be, so they are unable adequately to express their wishes or needs. They may feel that they're doing even worse than they actually are. This means that depressed people aren't very available in confiding relationships. Depression is also destructive to the relationship because it robs the couple of their closeness so that they become more distant and more two-dimensional almost out of necessity. Instead of being based on friendship and mutual partnership, these relationships are transformed into one in which the healthy spouse becomes the caretaker.

People who are depressed will be embarrassed to say how they feel, often fearing it will make them sound crazy or bad. If you're depressed you may feel guilty about imposing your depression on your partner and may become more withdrawn on that account. As a result, communication within the family becomes particularly problematic, especially where self-disclosure by the depressed person is concerned. And when the healthy spouse denies that there's friction in the marriage, the depressed partner may only become angrier, especially when the partner is aware of the illness. This kind of response can lead to further depression or a manic outburst on the depressed person's part. The anger may be turned inward, too. It's possible that in certain respects, healthy spouses are simply better at coping more effectively in the handling of anger than ill partners. A conflict with an ill partner may be more difficult to acknowledge and express.

## How Children Are Affected by a Parent's Depression

It's hard to be the best parent you can be when you are depressed. That's why, in my experience, I believe it's so important for a parent even with a milder form of depression to get good treatment. Obtaining treatment is especially crucial if one of the parents is manic or severely depressed. Ironically, though, it actually may prove easier for a family to cope with severe depression or mania in its midst, so long as the parent receives a good diagnosis and treatment. That's because the severely depressed or manic parent is more clearly ill, making it more likely that he or she will seek medical attention. In milder cases, the parents may just try to soldier on without receiving the help they need. But their children and spouses are still going to suffer the effects of the illness, without having the benefit of understanding what is causing their distress.

So what should you do if you are a depressed or manic parent? The first priority is to get well. But you shouldn't be afraid to tell your children what's going on. Be straightforward with them. Tell them what they want to know but also make sure that you tell them what they *need* to know. You don't have to go into elaborate detail. All that's necessary is something on the order of "I'm sad because I have an illness but I'm getting good care for it and I'll be better soon."

Children tend to notice irritability and withdrawal. The parent who has the most contact with the children (this is usually the mother) will also have more opportunities to be irritable. One mother told me, "When I wake up in a depression and pull myself out of bed, I often think I'll be okay today so long as no one looks at me cross-eyed." But then if you have active children, they won't just look at you cross-eyed! In such situations it really helps to have a supportive, confiding spouse to console you . . . or to help dress and feed the children.

## How Recovery Affects Relationships

What happens when the person with depression is treated and begins on the road to recovery? Once again, it depends. Although family function improves when the patient's condition improves, the family will still have more difficulty than normal families. Once the disease is treated aggressively, psychotherapy can help alleviate some of the lingering problems that might have been caused or exacerbated by the depression. Marital disputes can actually increase after the depressive symptoms improve, if the healthy spouse expects an instant return to normal or usual social functioning. It could take months before the symptoms improve enough to get back to normal. (You'll learn more about recovery and rehabilitation in Chapter 17.)

Even though I don't recommend it as a therapeutic exercise, a depression can actually have a positive effect on relationships after it's gone. A number of people, especially men, it seems, come out of their shell after recovering from depression. Many men who've recovered from depression actually show a positive change in sensitivity in their relations with their wives. (I have even had a few wives ask me to leave their husbands a little bit depressed because they felt more needed by their spouses when they were depressed than when they were "normal"!) Once you've looked into the abyss and experienced loneliness in such a painful way, you're in a better position to focus on what counts in life and recognize who really cares about you. I can't tell you how many patients have told me that their spouse emerged from depression a more sensitive and sympathetic person. Again, I wouldn't suggest going through a depression in order to become a better husband or wife, and the positive effect doesn't always persist, but it's worth pointing out that depressive illness doesn't have to do lasting damage to a relationship, as long as you and your partner get the help you need and understand what is at stake. This continues, at least for a while, although with complete recovery there is a tendency for some men (and a few women) to return to business as usual.

## How Well Do Families Recognize Hypomania or Mania?

Even more than clinical depression, mania can be extremely disruptive to close relationships. But because mania is marked by its own unique symptoms that are almost opposite to those seen in depression, the type of damage done can be very different. In depression the healthy partner may end up being frozen out of the relationship by a withdrawn and uncommunicative spouse, while in mania the healthy partner may end up being consumed by the fire of someone who has gotten completely out of control. The result in both cases is that the relationship is thrown into turmoil and possibly destroyed, but the threat of severe mania is more directly physical, functional, and social.

If you've ever had a child who wandered off and got lost you undoubtedly remember just how frantic and panicked you were. Once your child is back safely in your arms your first reaction was relief. *Thank God, you're okay and nothing happened to you.* But then the relief soon turns to anger. *How could you have put me through this? Do you know how upset you made me by getting lost?* The dynamic in families with manic depression in them can be much the same. The healthy spouse carries a big burden in the manic episodes, becoming more controlling and fearful as a result.

For example, when Mrs. Phillips becomes hypomanic, it's not immediately apparent. She isn't visibly speeded up in her activity and she doesn't exhibit the rapid pressured speech that's typical of manias. She's a bright, attractive woman in her late forties who is normally happy in her marriage and proud of her two daughters, both in their early twenties. Even as she becomes manic she appears dignified and rational. Most acquaintances wouldn't realize that there's anything wrong at first. But her family has seen her go through full manic cycles enough times to recognize the symptoms. And by now I have no trouble detecting the recurrence of mania as soon as she sits down in my office and begins talking. It's then I realize that I am hearing the hypomania of Mrs. Abigail Phillips.

When she is on her way up (to hypomania) our sessions sound like a broken record. I no sooner ask her how she's feeling than she begins to talk about her husband. "Oh, Dr. DePaulo, Jerry is at it again!" Before I can ask what she means, she reels off a catalog of his faults. He's controlling her, he's keeping her from doing what she wants, he doesn't really love her. The more she talks the more she finds to blame him for. Now I've met Jerry and I know that he's actually a nice guy who bends over backward to please her. Her daughters had to go through the wind tunnel of her manias a few times before they understood what their mother meant by Jerry's "problem." It seemed that Jerry was so "presumptuous" that he dared to question her (gently) about her shopping binges and her habit of making long-distance calls at three or four in the morning.

If we're lucky, her manic phase may end after only a few days. If we're not, it may go on for weeks. But however long it lasts, if a mania occurs in someone you love, it throws everything out of kilter. Abigail Phillips' daughters can't help but feel upset by her behavior and the dismissive attitude she displays whenever they venture an opinion. On the other hand, they know that if they rebuke her for yelling at their dad or point out that maybe she shouldn't be calling relatives in the middle of the night, they'll just irritate her more . . . and be adding fuel to the fire! They are also concerned that even after she's recovered, she might resent them for having criticized her.

Abigail's manias had her family confused for many years. Jerry and his daughters didn't know what to do and they felt like they should have been better at coping with the situations created by her condition. Yet they should feel some satisfaction at having succeeded in persuading her to see me and agree to go back on her medication (lithium). Even then they have a lot to handle since it takes a few weeks for the medicines to really work and for her to begin to return to normal. Even after she's better her illness still affects her family. While they're certainly relieved to see that she's recovered and no longer blaming them for imagined slights, at the same time they also wonder why she put them through such hell in the first place. Why did she stop her medicines? They can't help feeling angry at her. They're even apt to hold her doctor responsible for her manic behavior. I don't think Abigail will stop taking her medication again, but I wish that I could guarantee it. For all the trouble that she has put her family through during the episodes, they've actually escaped relatively unscathed compared to other families that have been thrown into turmoil because of uncontrolled manias.

## How Manic Depression Affects Families

Many patients have driven their family into debt or they have exhibited embarrassing behavior that may take the form of boasting, showing off in public, or risking violent confrontations with strangers. During an episode, those in the throes of manias may challenge, taunt, belittle, and humiliate the people they love the most. Such behavior may not be seen as an illness but as willful belligerence. That's what happened, at least to a degree, in the case of Mrs. Phillips and her daughters. The uncharacteristic sexual or violent behavior that people engage in when they're in their manic states often results in lasting humiliation, lost jobs, ruptured marriages, and reputations ruined forever. Then, once the episode is over, my patients and their families have to deal with the devastation mania has left in its wake: the debt accumulated, the rifts created, the relationships injured. Worse, the patient must now determine how to resurrect relationships with family members and close friends that have been frayed or almost destroyed by their behavior during the illness. It works the other way around, too. The family members have to pick up the pieces, make restitution on the debts, explain (or try to find excuses for) the embarrassing incidents, and try to put some order back in their lives. They sometimes may feel that their loved one doesn't realize the extent of the damage that they have done. It's no fun to have to clean up other people's messes. As with unipolar depression, family members cope better with symptoms that they clearly view as arising from illness than they do when they have no idea what is happening. And the healthy spouse often learns to get the checkbook out of sight. Not surprisingly, financial difficulties and getting fired from a job are among the most devastating effects of the illness.

You can see then that manic depression has an impact on relationships that, while similar to severe unipolar depression, is also marked by some significant differences because of the nature of the disease. While the lows of manic depression have the same tendency toward withdrawal, irritability, diminished self-esteem, and lack of engagement with people, the highs or manic episodes are something entirely different. According to many of my patients, they feel a sense of helplessness and alarm during an episode because they lack all control over the occurrence of severe mood swings.

## How Families React to Mania

Where mania is present, the dynamic of relationships within families can also undergo dramatic changes. Someone who is ordinarily independent may become extraordinarily dependent, for example. If the manic spouse is in a particularly volatile state and apt to fly off the handle and do who knows what, the partner may think: *I can't let her out of my sight, she's got to stay with me or else she'll get in trouble.*

The spouse bears the burden of the manic episodes and as a result the relationship with the ill person becomes controlling and fearful. But you should be aware that the response to manic depression, like unipolar depression, differs depending on the family involved. In some cases, the condition may be viewed with less concern, especially where the manic condition is relatively mild and where it has led to high productivity and success. As an example, think of a highly charged executive who never seems to slow down for an instant. This individual may actually be suffering from a mild mania or hypomania, but because he or she is raking in lots of money and enjoying the esteem of colleagues and family, no one would ever think to call the person ill.

## How Couples with Depressive Illness Stay Together

After all this you might be asking yourself how anyone could go through such anguish and turmoil. Could anyone want to remain married to someone who suffers from severe manias or depressive illness? It's a testimony to the courage and resilience of most of my patients that they are able to sustain good marriages in spite of their illness. When researchers ask these couples about being with a manic spouse they are quick to express their fears and frustrations but at the same time assert that they remain committed to their marriages. The vast majority of people in these relationships insist that they will stay with their spouses, no matter how ill they are. When asked why they stayed married, most healthy spouses cited the moral convictions and their years of married life that they have enjoyed. Most will wait for the spouse to return when the episode is over.

In one study, half the well spouses said that they'd experienced a sense of loss, as if their spouses had died. In the same study, half the spouses reported that they were kept going by the hope that their spouses would one day be cured. And while 88 percent said they wanted to stay with the patient in spite of the changes, nearly half felt that the patient had become like a child to them. About three-quarters reported that their hopes and dreams for the marriage remained unfulfilled because of the patient's illness but few reacted bitterly when they know what was wrong. Grief, guilt, and sorrow were common reactions. It is important for the well spouse to understand the ill spouse's withdrawal and change in temper is not a choice.

Studies of spouses of manic-depressive patients show that they are more likely to consider marital separation than spouses of unipolar depressive patients. This reflects the ravage of mania and its lack of inhibitions.

When people with mania are exhibiting inappropriate behavior, families should heed the warning signs and get help quickly. Several steps need to be taken to optimize the chances for recovery:

- Find professional treatment.
- Get the patient on medication (usually lithium, though others are helpful).
- Educate yourself about the illness.
- Join support groups.

Love can overcome a lot of obstacles, to be sure, but the disruption that manias can cause to a family can last for decades or longer. The healthy members of the family feel isolated, and not just because of their uncertain relationship. They usually have no friends in whom they can confide or who will truly understand what they're going through.

In spite of all the chaos and misery that depressive illnesses cause, studies have found that most healthy partners say they want to stick with the relationship. Nonetheless, they also will admit to feelings of loss, as if their partner had died, and so all they can do is to pray for a cure and hope that one day their loved one is restored to them.

## How Depression Affects Work

When we talk about relationships we also have to talk about function at home and at work. One way to measure severity is on the basis of how the patient is able to maintain day-to-day functioning at home and on the job. Psychiatrists speak of two types of day-to-day functioning. There's affective functioning, which describes how you relate to other people, and function on the job. Depression impairs both types of functioning to one degree or another, but it has a more negative impact on affective functioning. If you have a job that you can do without interacting very much with fellow workers you can generally keep doing it even when you're depressed, unless the illness is so debilitating that you can't get out of bed. The real problem arises when you have to get involved with other people at work. You may have to make a sales call or ask critical questions at a meeting or maintain a positive relationship with a client. That kind of interaction requires emotional energy which is something in very short supply during depression. If you're left alone to push papers or assemble a machine all day long you can probably do it. In that case it's more like occupational therapy where just the satisfaction of performing your job may provide a life to your mood. But executives and salespeople are under much more of a strain to carry out their work when they get depressed. So people in positions such as these will tend to hide out, doing their best to avoid calls or meetings. They usually feel terribly guilty about ducking out on their responsibilities, but sapped of will, stamina, and enthusiasm, they believe that they simply aren't up to the challenge.

Even though many people lose energy when they're depressed they don't want to stop working because work, especially when it involves impersonal and more mechanical tasks, can distract them from their depression during the day. Then they can collapse when they get home unless it's their turn to prepare dinner, in which case their spouse might wonder why dinner is not being prepared. If one spouse's job doesn't happen to be financially critical, the other spouse will say, "Look, if you say you're only operating at half speed, why don't you skip work and save some of that extra energy for us?" In fact, the suggestion that a depressed spouse should drop out of a job to conserve their physical and emotional resources doesn't work very well. That's because it is the day job and the opportunity to perform mechanical tasks (as opposed to being personally involved) that gives the depressed person relief, not life at home. I have had to give several lectures to misguided spouses about this issue.

We know that depression on the job exacts an enormous toll in lost productivity. The direct cost of depression to the United States in terms of lost time at work is estimated at 172 million days yearly. And because depression is more prevalent in people younger than sixty-five, more employees are at risk.

Even when you feel better, you will notice when you return to work that your ability to concentrate isn't fully recovered. You may believe that everyone else in the office must have noticed your sub par performance as well especially if you just came out of the hospital. You wouldn't be alone. Practically everyone in this situation becomes convinced that they're about to be fired or found out. And because the disorder skews perception, you might really end up judging your performance more harshly than either your bosses or coworkers do. In these situations the negative attitude only feeds on itself, creating yet more anxiety and poorer performance.

Despite the problems people with depression face on the job, they're usually still better off going to work if they can. The ability to maintain some day-to-day functioning, especially outside of the home, is helpful. For one thing, it gives them a reason to get out of bed in the morning, one of the hardest things to do when depressed. Work also provides a good distraction from the illness for most patients. And completing even simple tasks means that the patient accomplished something that others value.

If a person can somehow muddle through when they're depressed, they still can't do their best, because they don't have it in themselves to perform efficiently. A person ends up "leaning into the wind," as I like to put it. If you've ever tried to brave a gale-force wind you know what I'm talking about; you can't stand up straight, you have to keep hunched over and struggle to make any progress at all. Well, that's what a depressed person is doing in the absence of treatment. If you know the person well, you can sometimes see this literally: in their posture and in the way they begin to look ill. Colleagues may begin to wonder what's wrong and point out to them that they look tired and drained all the time. If that happens to you, you know it's time to find treatment.

# CHAPTER 10

⚭

# Destructive Behavior

Nothing makes the job of a psychiatrist treating depression and manic depression harder than alcohol and drugs. The most difficult treatment situations that I have ever seen patients and families confront, since I started my training in psychiatry twenty-seven years ago, occur when the patients' illnesses are complicated by what we call addictive behaviors. While I have seen many successful outcomes, none were easy to achieve.

Let me be precise about what I mean by the word *behavior*. Depression and manic depression are diseases, not behaviors. They are, however, *associated* with certain types of behaviors. We'd say that seeking help is a good behavior and that the most destructive behavior of all associated with depressive illness is suicide. Alcohol abuse and dependence, drug dependence, anorexia nervosa, pathological gambling, and repetitive self-injury are all negative behaviors. That is, they are activities defined in terms of their goals or their consequences. Addictive behavior, we would say, is "abnormally" driven.

Depressive illness sometimes seems to make some people more prone to destructive behaviors; at the same time destructive behaviors generally tend to make depression and manic depression worse. Let me give you an example. I had a patient many years ago who ordinarily didn't like to drink alcohol. She rarely drank even when the social situation encouraged it. Although she didn't know what to call it, she developed a chronic lethargic form of major depression. For a period of three years, she had almost no energy or interest in anything, especially in the first half of the day. It was tough for her to get out of bed in the morning. After months of mornings spent lying in bed, she began to feel desperate. For unclear reasons, she thought that drinking whiskey might make a difference in her mood and attitude. And somewhat to her surprise it actually did. Then she began to keep an eight-ounce tumbler and a bottle of whisky at her bedside. As soon as she woke up she would drink a full glass while still in bed. It took about fifteen minutes for her to feel it "kick in," and then she'd get right up and start into her chores with a real sense of purpose. After several months, she realized that this was a strange situation and she wanted to find out what was going on. She came in for an appointment and explained what had been happening. Then she admitted that she feared she was becoming an alcoholic. Her real problem, I told her, wasn't alcoholism at all. So she was actually gratified to learn that she had a clinical depression. She was very happy to have antidepressants as replacement for her alcohol, which she gave up with apparent ease.

I hesitated to use this patient's case as an example because she is not typical of most patients who resort to alcohol or drugs to relieve symptoms of depression. For one thing, she seldom drank before her illness. And when she realized she was getting into trouble with alcohol she quickly sought an evaluation. Even though she didn't recognize that she had a clinical depression, she knew that something must be wrong with her, seeing that alcohol seemed to "cure" it even if it was only for a few hours at a time. I do not think her case is representative for another reason: *alcohol is not generally used by people with depression as self-medication.* A small minority of them may begin drinking seriously to medicate themselves, but once they become dependent on it, it is the alcohol (or other addiction) that comes to enslave the person. Getting alcohol becomes the principal goal, overriding other considerations. (As it is with people who are dependent on alcohol but not depressed.) By the same token, being deprived of alcohol becomes a much more driving force than the desire for relief of depressive symptoms. So, you may wonder, why did I highlight this case at all? Well, I wanted to make the point that there's a greater risk of abusing alcohol or drugs by people who have depression of moderate severity than for patients whose depression is quite severe. People with illness of moderate severity, after all, can still move around. As a result, they still have enough strength and initiative to seek out a number of "remedies" that actually make their depression worse and more difficult to treat. To compound the situation further, the remedies can become very big problems in their own right.

A number of such depressive-related destructive behaviors, when combined with depressive illness, can wreak havoc. Some of this behavior, like the example I just cited, probably would never have occurred if the person hadn't been depressed at the time. But many patterns of behaviors as they relate to depression and to mania are common and do involve choices, at least when they start. While they are linked to the illness, they are not integral to it. That is to say, only the patient can stop them.

The affected person makes this difficult decision and if things go well—he or she gets support like from Alcoholics Anonymous (AA), and treatment—the person becomes sober and is well at least "one day at a time." By taking responsibility for his or her own recovery, the individual with depression can level the playing field. That leaves only the depression demon to face down, which is hard enough. Ironically, the most severe depressions can actually stop someone's drinking because he or she lacks the energy or the drive for anything. That's one of the few positive things in the relationship between depression and alcohol. Unfortunately, the effect is often temporary since many of these people often go back to drinking when they recover. As I said, there are also many different kinds of destructive behaviors that can come into play and make treating the depression difficult: smoking, gambling, anorexia or bulimia nervosa. But there is no question that the most common destructive behavior affecting depressed patients, barring suicide, is alcohol or any substance abuse.

## Dependence and Abuse: What's the Difference?

Today we use the terms *abuse* and *dependence*. Even if a person drinks only once a month but each of those times is slapped with a DWI or gets into fights, then we would say that this is a person who is abusing alcohol. While a person like this may not be dependent at this point, that's no guarantee that he or she won't go on to develop dependence. In any case, the individual obviously has a major problem. Dependence is actually easier to define than abuse in that it is progressive and not so episodic and is based on the pattern of drinking (or substance-using behavior). One slightly facetious definition of an alcoholic is someone who can take it or leave it, and so he or she takes it. Alcoholic dependency certainly includes regular use, but it is also characterized by psychological experiences and physiological changes that occur over time. Dependence or addiction is a brain-based but also a self-induced pattern. As your brain gets used to the regular supply of a substance (like alcohol or cocaine), you experience a craving for it. Once a dependent person is deprived of the drug that used to be in plentiful supply, he or she can become ill and go into withdrawal. Withdrawal symptoms may at first be intermittent and mild but when the picture is fully developed, the person may experience shakiness, nausea, profuse sweating, and hallucinations.

Dependent behavior may often be difficult for an outsider to spot because it is generally progressive: it takes place over time and it is usually so gradual that going from one gradation of severity to the next is almost imperceptible. We do know that the progression of the behavior is marked by a narrowing of the repertoire as the person sinks deeper into dependence. Ordinarily there's a social regulation of eating, drinking, even gambling and other behaviors. Each culture has a normal set of rituals people are expected to follow, and what is accepted in one culture (social drinking, for instance, in the Western world) may be anathema in another (drinking is forbidden in strict Muslim countries). But whatever the culture, normal and acceptable behavior cannot be maintained if full dependency sets in. The dependent person will begin to drink with the same frequency whether it's a workday, a weekend, or a holiday. If an alcoholic realizes that there won't be an opportunity for a drink for the next four hours, for example, he or she may seek fortification by having a few quick belts ahead of time.

A spouse's scolding or a child's concern, which once might have had some effect, no longer carries much weight. The alcoholic may apologize or argue but the substances are in charge. If people who are drinking (or abusing a substance like marijuana or cocaine) are also clinically depressed, they might not have any idea how dependent they are unless they have been sober for several months.

Although it may sound strange, these dependent individuals actually find abstinence surprisingly easy to maintain for brief periods of time if they are in a hospital ward and are deprived of any access to alcohol or illicit drugs. They often stop to prove that they are not addicted, although they will then go back to the habit. They are not exposed to the same social environmental cues that trigger their craving and it's relatively easy to remain sober so long as they know they will soon be discharged.

# Overcoming Dependence: Why the Stakes Are So High

As clinicians, we are very concerned about the high relapse rate to drugs and alcohol, particularly when it occurs along with depression and mania. Those patients who drink or abuse drugs are far more likely to suffer a relapse and in less time than patients who managed to abstain for long periods or did not drink to begin with. I can't emphasize how powerful dependence is, or how enduring its impact. And this isn't an observation that comes out of my experience with patients alone. Research in the labs has established what happens in the brain when dependence takes hold. For instance, in one experiment, scientists made cocaine addicts out of a population of rats. Then they took the drug away from the rodents and kept them drug-free for a year, which for a rat is practically a lifetime. To see how the previously addicted rats would respond to the drugs after prolonged abstinence, the researchers exposed the animals to water with the drug in it. Even after a year without cocaine, the rats eagerly consumed the water and became addicted all over again. They had developed such a craving for it that they only had to taste the drug to become hooked in spite of the passage of so much time. It appears that over time the addiction can actually "rewire" the brain so that the individual (person or rat) is far more susceptible to the addictive substance than before the addiction started. That's why I believe organizations like AA have it right. For people who have a history of severe dependence, there's a physiologic reason that makes it nearly impossible to resume drinking at moderate levels and in a socially acceptable way. This is especially true for patients with depression and manic depression because the stakes are so high.

Some form of substance dependence and/or abuse is found in as many as 32 percent of individuals with any affective disorder. People with manic depression are particularly at risk. One study suggests that perhaps 60 percent of those people with Bipolar I, the more severe form, have substance or alcohol problems at some time in their life. The same study indicated that the probability of having alcohol or drug dependence and/or abuse is several times greater in people with manic depression than in the population at large, while the risk is about two times greater in unipolar depressed patients compared to the general population.

## How Drugs and Alcohol Affect Treatment

Alcohol and drugs exert a pernicious influence on depressive illness in other ways, too. It can take up to two years for the patient to recover fully from the effects of substantial alcohol and/or drug abuse related to the pattern of illness. People with unipolar depression and manic depression clearly have more frequent relapses while they are abusing alcohol and/or drugs as well as for a while after they stop. But the problem isn't limited to long-term effects. The impact of alcohol and drug abuse makes itself felt during treatment as well. For one thing, there is a danger of chemical interactions. Alcohol reacts with some medications more strongly than others. Some of the antidepressants, mood stabilizers, and neuroleptics that patients are prescribed act as central nervous system depressants and tend to induce drowsiness, at least when given in large doses. When these medications are taken together with alcohol, the effect is amplified. So if you were on one of these medications and were drinking, and then were foolish enough to get behind the wheel of a car, you'd have a good chance of dozing off before you reached your destination. Fewer problematic interactions occur between alcohol (if consumed in small amounts) and antidepressants with nonsedative effects, notably the SSRIs such as Prozac and Zoloft, and bupropion. Illicit drugs with stimulating properties, such as cocaine or MDMA (Ecstasy), can be much more dangerous if they interact with antidepressants; these interactions may cause psychotic manias and in a few cases they can cause an alarming elevation in blood pressure.

Another good reason to be wary of alcohol and drugs while on medication is that alcohol loosens inhibitions (as do many drugs, such as MDMA and cocaine), which gets in the way of thinking clearly and acting carefully. A patient who drinks excessively may forget to take medications or decide they aren't worth the trouble. This can contribute to relapses or to a worsening of the condition.

The general rule is that most illicit drugs are dangerous enough by themselves but are especially so if you are prone to depression. MDMA, for instance, depletes the brain of serotonin and taking it seems risky for any patient who might be prone to depression or have the illness. (A depletion of serotonin in the brain, as you may recall from Chapter 6 on the brain, can increase the chances of developing depression in someone with the illness.) Some drugs, including MDMA and cocaine, can cause death in their own right at lower doses than would be the case with the same amount of alcohol.

Alcohol and illicit drugs such as marijuana, cocaine or MDMA also make suicide more likely in patients with depression. A report published in 1990 states that between 20 and 35% of suicide victims had a history of alcohol abuse or were drinking shortly before their suicides.

## The Link Between Smoking and Depression

So far, the drugs I have cited are illegal. But of all the drugs that you can become dependent on, probably the hardest to give up is legal. I mean, of course, cigarettes. Cigarettes are very effective vehicles for administering an addictive drug (nicotine). And it appears that, as in the case of other addictive drugs, cigarette dependence has some relationship to depression. The link between cigarettes and depression had received little attention until the late 1990s, when researchers at Columbia University embarked upon a study of a medication that they thought would help patients stop smoking. Bear in mind that they weren't looking at depression in this study. They tried to recruit only the most addicted smokers, those who had failed at least three prior attempts to achieve abstinence supervised by health professionals. As part of the study the smokers first underwent a standard psychological exam. It turned out that an astonishing 60 percent of them had at least one episode of major depression compared to about 10 percent in the general population. To make certain that this wasn't some aberration, other researchers carried out follow-up studies, which also found the same phenomenon.

I sit at the other end of the telescope in a clinic specializing in depression and manic depression. We can see that patients who smoke usually smoke more when they are depressed (unless they are so fatigued and depressed that they give cigarettes up temporarily). On the other hand, relatives of several of my patients go into full-blown depression only when they *stop* smoking. Several of these family members couldn't tolerate the two- to three-week wait for antidepressants to work and so return to the cigarettes and get "well" in less than a week. One of my patients repeated this pattern of behavior three times in as many years.

What these findings suggest is that the extremely addicted groups of smokers are probably different from a random sample of smokers and that major depression might make it easier to become addicted and harder to stop. That has broader implications for all addictive substances since the study suggests that there is a sort of winnowing out process, so that people who keep coming back for treatment for addiction (of whatever kind) are more likely to be depressed than those who don't have an addiction.

## The Link Between Eating Disorders and Depression

I think that there is a similar link between depression and eating disorders like bulimia and anorexia. Forty percent of young women in this country will experiment with abnormal eating behaviors at some time or another, by restricting, bingeing, or purging, or some combination of the three. These behaviors are the reverse of alcoholism and substance abuse in gender ratios since only 10 percent with eating disorders are male.

For most of these women the disorder doesn't last long, while for some the disorder gets worse and worse over time. As in the case of substance abuse, young women hospitalized with eating disorders have very high rates of depression, especially for the chronic forms of depression and manic depression. I don't think their depression causes the eating disorder or vice versa. In families loaded with depression and manic depression, we find very few families members with eating disorders. In our studies we have found only ten cases in over 200 families. The depression may provide a more powerful reinforcing mechanism so that women who experiment with eating disorder behaviors become more easily addicted to them. In other words, as with smoking, an eating disorder behavior is much more difficult to stop when a patient is depressed and being both depressed and having an eating disorder will make it more likely that the patient will need inpatient care. These patients often see the depression as part of their eating disorder. Once we treat for the eating disorder we are depriving them of one way they have to control their symptoms and, temporarily at least, they often feel worse.

## The Link Between Gambling or Shoplifting and Depression

We also see a relatively small number of patients who will develop destructive behavior like pathological gambling or shoplifting, which can become similarly habitual. The connection is suggested by the patients who gamble or shoplift only when they are depressed and at no other time. They find that the gambling or shoplifting makes them feel alive and not so "numb." When they gamble they don't do it to lose (though they most often do), they do it for the "rush," which feels just the opposite of depression. By the same token, when people with depression shoplift, the article they're stealing is of little consequence to them compared to the thrill of getting away with something, heightened by the fear that they might be caught.

## Stopping Destructive Behaviors

With any of these behaviors and addictions the same principle applies. There is a great need to make a personal commitment to stop the behavior despite the difficulty involved in doing so. Stopping these behaviors won't guarantee a cure of depression by any means, but it is an essential step. Let's put it this way: Making a decision to stop any destructive behavior, while not sufficient for recovery from depression alone, is absolutely necessary for a full recovery to take place. Abnormal behaviors don't just go away (as depressions do) unless the person resolves to put a stop to them and then follows up on that decision. From the doctor's point of view, eating disorders— or smoking or alcohol or drug dependence—are distinguished from disease states. They are not things you *have,* they are things you *do.* You may have a genetic predisposition for a particular behavior (evidence for which we have from twin studies), but we've also seen people who are addicted stop. A predisposition does not mean that a behavior is predetermined. There are teetotalers in families of alcoholics, after all.

Stopping a behavior, though, is obviously easier said than done. I once saw a woman in her late twenties who'd been treated unsuccessfully for an eating disorder several times. When I took a history and a mental status exam, I was able to tell that she also had an episodic depressive disorder, interspersed with occasional brief and mild manias. She had never been diagnosed with clinical depression or mania before. I told her that a successful treatment of her depression could make it easier for her to stop her eating disorder. Since she was already due to come into the hospital for two weeks for the eating disorder, I took the opportunity to start her on antidepressants. Her mood picked up considerably on medication. Even so, she still wasn't prepared to give up her eating disorder. So in this instance the depression was more treatable and the behavior more intractable. From this I have concluded that successful treatment of depression makes it *easier* for people to stop a coexistent abnormal behavior but it does not guarantee it. And easier doesn't mean easy. People who are free of depression enjoy life more and have more energy and self-esteem, so they are in a much better position to make positive changes in their lives. But behaviors are hard to change, especially when that behavior has become central to everyday life. All the more remarkable then, I have also seen the reverse situation: Patients whom I treated unsuccessfully for depression were, with the support of the staff, able to bring their eating disorders under control.

## Why "Delicate" Self-Injury Isn't So Delicate

No behavior is more destructive or more final than suicide. But we also see intentional, self-injurious behavior that is not lethal at all, and this too causes enormous problems in some depressed patients' lives; perhaps as a symbolic wish for suicide or an act of rehearsal for suicide. If we put suicide on one end of the scale of deliberate self-destruction, we would put a phenomenon sometimes called delicate self-injury on the other. Really this behavior is anything but delicate. People who practice this type of self-injury burn themselves with cig-arettes, scratch themselves with their fingernails, cut themselves with anything sharp, or hit their heads against the wall. So why would any-one do this? My patients offer me a number of explanations. They say they want to experience pain because otherwise they feel so numb. While it's clear that 99 percent of people with depression don't injure themselves in this way, we also know that a behavior that wouldn't occur habitually in the absence of some psychiatric condition like depression can sometimes take over a person. This kind of behavior can and does interfere with treatment, and when it's stopped, chances of recovery are greatly improved.

Some patients hide their behavior. Some will want to draw blood just to see it. Others find that by hitting or cutting themselves they manage to calm an agitated state. Often when they injure them-selves their family and friends will express concern and support. At first, they may try to remain nonjudgmental, but over time the behavior is likely to produce fear and anger. The person who engages in this kind of behavior appears simply to be trying to get attention. Families and friends will suspect that the person is faking. Their anger may spill over to the therapist or the doctor or anyone who might "wake up" to the danger that these repeated self-injuries seem to represent. The behavior also causes family members and friends to withdraw out of fear that they'll say something wrong to the person or trigger a catastrophe. They live in dread of the last blow being the fatal one. And those who engage in this behavior want to know that others around them care about them. Provoking family members to withdraw may actually be the farthest thing from their minds.

This behavior is not addictive in the physiological sense like alco-hol and substance abuse, though. Therefore it's very important that these individuals come to see that they're doing something detri-mental for their long-term prospects. I tell my patients that they need to be in a supportive environment to achieve full recovery. True recovery, I tell them, doesn't just mean the absence of symptoms. It means that they have to be able and eager to reengage with life, fam-ily, and friends. But reengagement is not possible if all the people you love want nothing more to do with you.

## What to Do about Suicide Threats

Threatening suicide is very much like self-injury. I had one patient who used to call me and say, "I'm calling to say thank you. You've been great to me, you've done everything possible, but I can't go on." You can imagine what it would be like to hear this. Usually I found a way to intervene in a situation like this and get hold of someone (in most cases a family member or friend) to help the person in danger to receive an emergency evaluation. Obviously, suicide is on this person's mind. But the effect of making suicide threats can wear down even the most loving and patient friend or family member. How many times can you go through this? Self-destructive behavior drives family and friends away and creates a sense of isolation not very different from the spiritual and emotional isolation that depression itself creates. And isolation is a risk factor for depression and for suicide. So quite unthinkingly, the person who frequently makes these threats can set up a vicious cycle.

Even psychotherapists and psychiatrists have difficulty in maintaining relationships with a patient who pursues this pattern of behavior over and over again. I once did a consultation for a doctor on a woman who exhibited such behavior. After examining her, I told her treating psychiatrist that I didn't think that it was a good idea for him to continue to be the patient's therapist and that we should find a replacement. The therapeutic relationship, I thought, was intruding on his life and it wasn't helping her. For one thing, she was getting angrier at him than she realized. He had agreed that she could call him at home but only on the condition that it was an emergency. But she took advantage of his offer and called him every night at home at seven on the dot. One night he had to run some errands at that hour and so she just let the phone ring. And as it rang she started taking pills. By the time he walked in and answered her words were so slurred that she was barely coherent. Fortunately, he managed to get her into the hospital in time. But it became increasingly obvious that the therapeutic relationship wasn't working. The patient's new doctor said he would agree to continue her psychotherapy but only if the family got involved. Once the family saw the new doctor at the hospital and more clearly understood the situation they were dealing with, they became more involved in her treatment. They assured the doctor that they would support the patient's treatment and assist her if she had to be admitted again. It took quite a while but the patient eventually did extremely well after nearly ten very bad years. The key to her recovery was the family's involvement. But she also needed a therapist who could take charge and make her—and her family—understand what harm her behavior was doing.

There's an old cliché that says that people who talk a lot about suicide aren't the ones who usually do it. A majority of those who do end their lives do, however, talk about it, but most people who talk about suicide thankfully don't complete the act. That's why suicide hotlines aren't very effective: While many of the callers are emotionally distraught, most of them do not commit suicide. On the other hand, many of those people who are most prone to taking their lives won't make use of the hotlines. As I'll explain when I say more about the causes of suicide, focusing on the suicidal threat itself runs the danger of missing the real problem—the depression.

Even we doctors and therapists are not able just to sit and listen to patients repeatedly threaten suicide forever. We, too, become fearful of losing the patient whom we care about and we also feel we are failing and will be blamed if the patient ever follows through on the threat. At the same time, doctors like parents will also feel angry at being put through such difficult and painful situations.

So what do I say to these patients and their family and friends? Basically, I tell families that I understand some of their feelings of fear and anger. I tell the patient this: *"When you injure (or threaten to injure) yourself, it causes anyone who cares for you to pull back. These are the people you need most in your recovery. Your parents can't live with the constant fear that they will find you dead the next time they come home. All of us, even your doctors, find this too painful."* Finally, I tell them this: *"Your family and your doctors have pledged not to give up on you. That's part of our responsibilities. Your responsibility, as a son or daughter (or father or mother), is to do everything you can to get well. This is your job—we can't really get you well without you doing your part. You expect me not to give up on you, well, I promise I won't, but then you can't give up either."*

# CHAPTER 11

⌀

# Facing up to Suicide

Depressive illness lies behind about two-thirds of the approximately 30,000 suicides annually in this country. Yet because depression so often goes unrecognized, and hence untreated, I am convinced that many (though not all) of these suicides could be prevented. A great number of people believe that suicide is understandable, but the reasons given for them—that a person is very ill or never recovered from the death of a parent—actually turn out not to be the real reason. I can think of no better example than the results of a recent study that looked at the cases where Dr. Jack Kervorkian was involved in doctor-assisted suicides. While the media reported that most people whose lives he helped end were terminally ill, autopsy results in Oakland County, Michigan, did not support this perception. Only a small fraction of these patients were terminally ill. I am concerned that most of the people who seek out someone like Kervorkian feel that their lives are devoid of hope. Given their perception that they are alone and terminally ill, it makes no sense to them to go on. In other words, depression might have a lot to do with their irrevocable decisions.

"It is legitimate and necessary to wonder whether life has a meaning," Nobel Prize–winning author Albert Camus wrote in his famous book *The Myth of Sisyphus*, "therefore it is legitimate to meet the problem of suicide face to face." In his view, even if life had no meaning, suicide was still an unacceptable choice. "In a man's attachment to life there is something stronger than all the ills in the world."

## The Impact of Suicide

Most people with depression do not commit suicide. Perhaps 6 percent of all people with major depression and about 15 percent of those treated for severe depression kill themselves. However, according to the World Health Organization study on the global burden of disease, suicide is the second-leading cause of death worldwide among females between the ages of 15 and 44. Among males ages 15 to 44, suicide ranks as the fourth leading cause of death after road accidents, TB, and violence. The same study estimates that in the coming decade depression will rank as the number two leading cause of death in the world; most of those deaths will be primarily in the form of suicide and secondly from coronary artery disease. The number of suicides in the United States has been holding fairly steady for ten years according to official estimates, running at about 30,000 annually. Between 1952 and 1995 the rate of suicide in persons under age twenty-five nearly tripled, though it now appears to be leveling off. Suicide is now the third-leading cause of death among 15- to 24-year-olds. Also of interest is the fact that the rate of suicide differs as a function of age. Elderly individuals have the highest rate of suicide. Studies have shown that suicide in the elderly is even more strongly associated with depression than any other risk factors (such as temperament or alcoholism) that are influential for younger individuals.

Suicide is a distinctly tragic phenomenon that we understand only in part, but we do know that biological and environmental ingredients must combine to break the bonds of attachment to life and we know a little about why. In this chapter I will describe some of these ingredients and talk about some of the consequences for those people close to a person who commits suicide. Suicide brings incalculable suffering in its aftermath that we must deal with. It's not an easy subject. But it's important to point out that though the relationship is sometimes confusing, suicide does have a strong connection to depression that we ignore only at our peril.

All too many people today still hold the belief that suicide somehow represents a rash but rational act committed by otherwise healthy persons. When someone takes his or her own life, the usual reactions are of shock and bewilderment. *How could she do such a thing? She never gave any sign that anything was wrong.* Or, *Why didn't he call me? I knew he lost his job . . . he and Janet split . . . but why this?* But suicide is not an act committed by an otherwise healthy and rational person. On the contrary, more often than not, the person who commits suicide is in the throes of a severe depression when taking his or her life. And in most cases the act is preceded by severe depression with increasing signs and symptoms of hopelessness and despair.

About two-thirds of the people who take their own lives suffer from major depression or bipolar disorder. Almost everyone else who commits suicide has depression, alcohol or substance abuse, or else has a delusional illness like schizophrenia. However, most people with depression—even men with severe depression (the highest risk group)—do not take their own lives.

# Parasuicide

It's understandable that we'd think about suicide in terms of all or nothing. Life and death are completely different states and certainly they seem to represent clearly different objectives. Death, we tend to assume, is the desired outcome of behaviors we call suicide and parasuicide (meaning like or similar to suicide). If we view behavior as representing a spectrum, we will find mostly people with severe forms of clinical depression at the lethal action end of it. At the other end, we find people who have clinical depression, and who harbor thoughts of engaging in nonlethal behaviors that involve self-injury. Put another way, some people will take their lives, some will act on suicidal feelings but not with lethal means, and others may think about suicide but never act on their ideas. Generally speaking the severity of depression plus personality traits, social background, and social circumstances all influence the risk of nonlethal self-injury.

I translate the prefix "para" to mean "like but not the same as." So parasuicide would mean like but not the same as suicide. The phenomenon of parasuicide is more common than suicide. Although parasuicide doesn't have the lethal consequences, we don't mean to imply that people are not at risk of suicide or suggest that their intention may not be suicidal. But there are some distinct differences between the population or groups of people who are more at risk for parasuicide and those who are at risk for suicide.

In Western countries, males are two to four times more likely than females to commit suicide. More women make parasuicidal attempts than men, tend to be younger (18–30), and come from somewhat lower than average socioeconomic backgrounds. About one third of parasuicide patients seen in an emergency room for nonlethal drug overdose or cut wrists have major depression, though not of the same extreme severity as those attempts that we would see as intended to be lethal, such as those made with guns. These patients are temperamentally more dependent, emotionally volatile, and are usually in the midst of a particularly stressful circumstance. It is extremely important to recognize that all these patients need good psychiatric evaluations and care, including the three-quarters of people at risk for this behavior who do not have major depression or manic depression. About one in four parasuicide patients will make repeat attempts within a year of the initial attempt, which may be due in part to the fact that very few of these individuals receive counseling or psychiatric care after their first emergency room visit. Although these (mostly male) patients represent only a small minority of those who come to the emergency room with overdoses or slashed wrists, they have the highest rate of return for repeat parasuicidal behavior. They are young men with impulsive behavior and what might be called unattached lifestyles. They have a clear idea of some gain they want to achieve from it when they commit these acts; they might mutilate a toe or finger to make another person feel guilty, for example. These patients also need therapy, but it can take years for them to understand how their behavior is actually interfering with their lives and chances for success.

Many years ago, when I was a first-year resident, I admitted a young woman to my ward with an overdose of pills after she'd had several rancorous arguments with her husband. I spent several hours with her in the emergency room taking her life history and learning about her troubled marriage. Her distress and demoralization were palpable to me. That was on a Friday. On Sunday a nurse called me at home to tell me that the patient had decided to leave the hospital against medical advice, and before we'd had a chance to meet together with her husband. I couldn't understand what would have prompted her to go home. I got on the phone with her. "Everything's fine now," she assured me, as if nothing had happened. "My husband agreed to paint the porch." That seemed to be all that was required to cause a reconciliation. Six months later, as a follow-up, I called all the patients who had left the hospital against medical advice. To my surprise and relief, I discovered that most of them, including this woman, were actually doing well.

I have no doubt that she was sincerely upset when she came to the hospital, at least on one level. But on another, deeper emotional level she had contrived a sort of plan. It wasn't a plan that she'd carefully or consciously hatched but her goal was clear all the same. She was looking for her husband to have a change of heart. She wasn't intending to die. Nor were most of the other patients who'd ignored medical advice and signed themselves out. I hasten to add that some of them do die in spite of their intentions, because they misjudge the dose of the drug or the time needed to be rushed to the hospital. Some of the patients with major depression who take nonlethal overdoses do so with more disregard for their safety than with intent to die. Those who do survive will tell me that they just wanted to sleep or to get a break from the pain that was overwhelming them. And although they realized that it was possible that they might never wake up, they took the risk anyway.

Parasuicide is not a strong predictor of suicide, but there's no guarantee that people who do engage in this behavior will not seriously injure or kill themselves in the future. People can repeatedly exhibit self-destructive behavior and never go on to commit suicide. At the same time, like self-injuries, parasuicide can be considered symbolic of suicide; as such, these behaviors are very destructive in the long term for relationships. For all the differences between suicide and parasuicide, there are many similarities as well, if not in intention, then certainly in some of the outcomes. All those who flirt with the idea of suicide or who make suicide attempts will create more troubled relationships with their families and friends and a number will experience untimely deaths.

## Assessing the Risk of Suicide

Thankfully, most people with severe depression don't kill themselves. But as we pointed out, depression is a major factor in two-thirds of the suicides in the United States and Western Europe. For people who are clinically depressed and who then go on to commit suicide, other risk factors have also been identified. What are the characteristic risk factors in assessing patients? The context is all-important in determining the seriousness of intent in an individual. When, for example, a patient suffering from clinical depression arrives for a consultation, an evaluation of suicide risk is an essential part of the consultation called for; especially if the patient is. We need to start a plan of treatment with a short-term emphasis on protecting the patient until the treatment has begun to work sufficiently for him or her to regain a sense of self-worth. So when someone says he or she doesn't want to live anymore and I am sure the person is suffering from major depression, how do I assess the risk that he or she will commit suicide? There are four big risk factors:

- The severity of the depression
- Depression with delusions
- The risk of even a brief relapse after treatment starts to make the patient feel better
- Impulsiveness and access to means of suicide

First, I assess the overall severity of the depressive illness. The more severe the depression is, the greater the risk. Delusions (fixed false judgment that is incorrigible and idosyncratic) that may accompany depression are also associated with a much higher risk of suicide. Anyone who is both depressed and is in the grip of a delusion is in far greater danger of acting irrationally. If you think that your house is on fire and you have to jump out the window, or if you believe that you are dying of AIDS or cancer, or if you are sure you are about to be arrested and that your family will be put on the street (and none of these things are actually happening), then you are at heightened risk for suicide. The pain and irrationality of delusional depression can be hard to understand if you haven't been through a delusional episode.

Ironically, if you are so depressed that you are completely sapped of energy, you may not have either the strength or the initiative to take your life. It also follows in such patients that they are in greater danger as they begin to gain back their energy. That's because their strength improves before their sense of self-esteem does. To put it another way, many patients will have regained the capacity and energy to take their own lives but have not regained the will to live. In general, we say that the risk of suicide goes up for a period of time either when the severe clinical depression either quickly gets better or suddenly becomes worse. The risk is especially high in the first thirty days of recovery for a depressed patient who is about to be discharged from a psychiatric hospital. That's because a patient who's recovering and suddenly has a transient drop in mood may take the blow especially hard possibly fearing sinking back to his or her lowest point and never getting any better. What the person doesn't realize is that he or she *is* getting better. It is hard for patients to realize that their condition is only in a fluctuation, which is to be expected as part of a normal course of recovery. The relapse represents a setback, not a return of full-blown depression.

Another risk factor we look for is access to the means of suicide. On the one hand, this sounds perfectly obvious; lethal means are necessary for a lethal end. Undoubtedly fewer police officers would commit suicide (more than twenty killed themselves in just one year in

New York City in the early 1990s) if they didn't have a gun immediately at hand when they felt the urge to put an end to their lives. But some aspects of this issue are still theoretical. One theory that has been advanced to explain why teenage males are prone to suicide, for instance, is that they have a much greater inclination to get hold of guns and illegal drugs. For one thing, these are much more available than they used to be a few decades ago and for adolescent males whose lives are in turmoil, such methods are perceived as solutions to complicated problems.

## Suicide Risk Factors

Suicides (in Western societies) are committed far more often by men than by women, notwithstanding the fact that women suffer depression, at least of moderate severity, far more than men do. In the United States, women account for approximately 16 percent of all suicides. We know that men drink more than women, tend to be more impulsive and more violent, and are more likely to reach for a gun when contemplating suicide. Women, by contrast, prefer to use pills to end their own lives. All things being equal, your chances of surviving a drug overdose are better than surviving a gunshot to the head or the heart. To take an example from one study, 111 drug overdoses all involving pregnant women were reported to a metropolitan poison control center over the course of four years. Although about half of these poisonings were life threatening, none of the fifty or so overdoses resulted in death in this particular sample. It is not that overdoses are safe, of course, or not lethally intended, it's just that our chances to pull through are better.

Is there something about maleness that causes the increased risk and is it immutable? I don't think we have any way to answer this question now. While men and women differ in terms of temperament and behavior, people of the same sex also differ in temperament and behavior. Intent, lethal or not, is also difficult to discern and is open to many interpretations. It is worth noting that psychiatrists in China report the highest suicide rates there are among young adult females.

We do know from studies, however, that social isolation adds to the risk, too; suicide becomes more likely if, in addition to having depression, you are unmarried, unemployed, and living alone. A person who has made an attempt on his or her live before is also more prone to suicide than those who have never made an attempt. However, among those who have committed suicide only half of them had made prior suicide attempts. This means that while prior attempts are an indicator of some increased risk, their absence should not be a reassuring sign that a depressed person is safe.

Twin studies have found a somewhat higher incidence of suicide among depressed co-twins of a twin who suicided compared to depressed twins who did not suicide. In a study of adoptees, researchers found that children from apparently normal parents adopted by families with a history of depression and suicides do not have elevated rates of suicide. This would suggest that the depression genes are part of the formula. It provides evidence that both the genetic and familial, possibly nongenetic, influences work together to increase the risk for suicidal behavior.

The most compelling evidence for a genetic effect, though, comes from studies done on twins with mood disorders. In one study of 149 pairs of twins, nine twins took their lives after their co-twins committed suicide. That's not much higher than you would expect to see in a population of severely depressed patients. This supports the idea that although there are genetic influences in the inheritance of a severe disorder there are also additional environmental influences.

Alcohol also plays what could be called a catalytic role in suicide. In fact, alcohol ranks second only to mood disorders as a risk factor for suicide. Alcoholic suicides also had a high level of divorce and widowhood (an independent small risk factor). In one study, one-third of alcoholic suicides had experienced the loss of a close interpersonal relationship within six weeks of their suicide. So in this respect they respond to the same kind of triggers that suicide victims do who are not alcoholic. Rates of completed suicide are 7–20 times greater among alcoholics than in the general population. Depending on which study you read, suicide has been implicated in 5–27 percent of all deaths of alcoholics. Or you can look at it another way: alcoholics commit 15–25 percent of all suicides in the United States. And as it turns out, alcoholics who commit suicide have more psychiatric symptoms (especially depression) than alcoholics who do not suicide. The interaction of alcohol and depression is very important.

Despite the dangers of drinking to excess, alcohol alone isn't the primary cause of suicide. The direct effect of alcohol—its effects on mood, reasoning, and personality—and preexisting mood disorders all play a role to the extent they are present. The psychiatric illness together with temperament may make a person prone to suicide but drinking acts as an additional risk by lowering inhibitions. Active alcoholism and/or drug abuse create a much higher risk of suicide to an even greater degree in combination with depression. This set of factors might explain why men are far more likely to commit suicide than females. Consider male tendencies toward impulsive behavior, temperament with more physical aggression, greater access to firearms, greater rates of heavy drinking and drug abuse. In combination with severe depression, which in its severest forms is equally frequent in men and women, the increase in risk is considerable. Finally let's not forget that alcohol literally makes depression worse over time.

## Looking for the Genetic Link

For researchers there could be few groups better to probe for a genetic link to suicide than the Amish, an isolated religious community in Pennsylvania that shuns many of the conveniences of modern life including the automobile. Here is a very tight-knit population having practically no intermarriage with anyone outside their community. That makes their genetic history fairly easy to trace over a period of several years. Suicide is very much frowned upon by the Amish. Nonetheless, a small number of suicides do occur.

Research genetics and psychiatrists studied all of the families (several hundred) in the Old Order Amish Community in southern Pennsylvania. They found that over a century only twenty-six persons were known to have committed suicide. Twenty-four of the twenty-six were judged to be suffering from major depression or manic depression. So the impact of this condition is clearly a large one. Interestingly, though almost 65 percent of those that did occur were all committed within just two families. This suggests that there was a separate genetic component (such as one affecting temperament) or a nongenetic family factor in the two families with fifteen suicides. The two families were both already known to have many family members with depression and manic depression, but there were also another sixty or so families with depression in several family members and only five of them had any suicides. What makes some people with clinical depression more likely to move from suicidal thoughts to lethal action? We know that depression has been strongly linked with genes. Naturally clinicians and researchers have wondered whether a particular depression gene might have a bigger role to play in suicides than other genes do. Two other theories also are being studied: First, the families with high suicide rates have depression, but they also have an inherited or genetic tendency to act too quickly or impulsively; or second, the example of depression in the family makes it psychologically easier to do it or harder to resist (a "contagion" theory). When Ernest Hemingway who suffered depression ended his life, was he mindful at some level that his father and brother had killed themselves? Since his suicide a son and a granddaughter have also taken their lives.

Genes are not destiny, however. They are relatively small factors in suicide per se, which is a relatively rare event compared to depression, a common event. The studies can help us find out where to focus our attention in formulating prevention strategies. They can also perhaps give us some sense of proportionality in what we can accomplish.

I want to emphasize that suicide isn't something that a person inherits. It's not fated that because you may have a father or a sister who committed suicide, you are condemned to do it as well. The risks from genetic factors are small and not immutable. The big genetic risks are for depression, which is treatable, and for substance abuse, which can be overcome.

## How Temperament Affects Risk

What can we do if our patient's temperament makes their depressions more lethal? We have learned the action of serotonin may play a role in temperament as well as in depression. In particular, there are several studies suggesting that people who have low levels of serotonin are more impulsive and action oriented. Some of the studies found low serotonin activity in the study participants were seen as rebellious and/or aggressive.

In the 1970s, researchers in Sweden examined brains from suicide victims and compared them to brain tissue from people who had died from other causes. They found that brains of suicide victims had lower levels of a serotonin metabolite called 5-HIAA than did brains of people who'd died from other causes. The same researchers observed among 119 hospitalized patients, those with low serotonin metabolites were more likely to have affectively ill relatives. Six of the seven patients who later committed suicide had lower serotonin metabolite levels compared to the average in all 119 hospitalized patients. So it appears that low serotonin levels may contribute to depression as well as to what is called "impulsiveness." And both might contribute to the risk of suicide.

## How Temperament Affects Risk

Thankfully, most patients with major depressive illness react to suicidal thoughts with fear. *"I shouldn't be thinking this way,"* or *"I don't want to die."* This fear is a healthy response and can motivate the person to seek help.

However, the risk may go up if the person who has suicidal thoughts is both depressed and acts on thoughts quickly or impulsively. This might be especially true if the person already has a plan and the necessary instruments at a crucial moment. Sadly, I have seen a mixture of planning and impulsiveness in suicidal behavior. The act may be sudden, undertaken in a moment of anger or frustration, but the depression and even a detailed plan may have been present for months.

One of my patients who was severely depressed told me the following story. While she was suffering from severe depression neither she nor her husband recognized what was wrong with her. For that matter, neither did her therapist. One day she went out and purchased a gun, which she carefully hid. However, she remained ambivalent about whether or not she should take her life as almost all suicidal patients do. Over the next few months she remained depressed and became extremely upset on a few occasions. Once she impulsively grabbed the gun and drove into the countryside. She realized that they, her husband, children, and other family, would be greatly hurt by her death but she felt desperate. She left the car and proceeded into the woods and began shooting at trees. She was both testing out her will and practicing she later said. After she'd carried out her test, she broke down and told her husband what she'd done, and he immediately got her into the hospital. After she got well, she, her family, and her therapist, rejoiced and she was prepared thereafter with the knowledge that she had an illness that could make her have the thoughts and some impulsiveness that could make the thoughts more dangerous.

## Adolescent Suicide

If you're like most people you probably remember your adolescence as an exciting but possibly tumultuous and sometimes painful period. Each year, from 2,000 to 2,500 adolescents in the United States commit suicide. Almost twice as many teenagers die from suicide as all natural causes combined including cancer, heart disease, AIDS, and birth defects. While about 1 percent of all suicides take place in the first fifteen years of life, the rate soars to 25 percent in the second fifteen years. Overall, the rate of adolescent suicides increased from 1965, reaching a peak in 1987, especially among males. (Rates among young black males, which traditionally have been lower than for whites, also went up for reasons that are still unclear.) In the decade spanning 1981 through 1990, suicide between the ages of ten and fourteen, while still quite low, doubled.

Several plausible explanations have been advanced to account for this rise. Adolescents now have considerably easier access to alcohol, drugs, and firearms than their parents and grandparents did. So they have the fuel to feed their rage and despair as well as the means to act on their urges. But other, more subtle factors may be involved. My former colleague Kay Redfield Jamison, in her groundbreaking 1999 book *Night Falls Fast,* suggests that the adolescent population today is more vulnerable to depression (and schizophrenia). Some thought should be given to the earlier onset of adolescence. American girls are having their first periods at an age earlier than ever before. This is largely due to better nutrition and possibly to other environmental factors that have yet to be identified and studied. We know that hormonal changes are linked to depression and the surge of hormones is characteristic of puberty. So it's possible that mood disorders are showing up at an earlier age than would ordinarily be the case because of this hormonal activity.

But since virtually every adolescent (not to mention virtually every adult) experiences difficulties and frustrations, we have to figure out why some adolescents will commit suicide and why others will not. While any adolescent who has made an attempt at suicide is certainly in need of a psychiatric evaluation, that doesn't necessarily mean that he or she will go on to commit suicide or indeed make another attempt.

When researchers looked at several adolescents who had committed suicide in the Northeast, they determined that 90 percent of them had a psychiatric illness at the time of death. In addition, most of them had experienced significant symptoms of depressive illness for two years before they'd taken their lives. So we've come around full circle; suicide, by and large, no matter what population is involved, can be considered a deadly consequence of depression.

The picture isn't that grim, however. In recent years, the adolescent suicide rate seems to have leveled off. No one is sure what can account for this leveling off. One theory holds that alcohol and substance abuse rates have been dropping. A second possibility is that better therapeutic treatments, notably the new generation of antidepressants like Prozac and Paxil, are having a positive impact. Prior to 1992, adolescents were rarely treated with the then, available antidepressants, the tricyclics, due to their side effects.

## Why Mixed States Increase the Danger

When it comes to putting people at risk for suicide, mixed states represent the worst combination of all. Remember we described mixed states as being a blend of blue and red; the person is constantly ratcheting between depression and manias. Rapid thinking, severe depression, and an agitated level of energy characterize the condition. These patients show extreme irritability, fitful sleep, and not infrequently will drink excessively and violently act out. We noted that people who are despondent because of their depression are frequently too lethargic to commit suicide. It takes too much energy. But someone in a mixed state, who is equally depressed, is unusually energetic and thus perhaps has a much higher risk for suicide. This is one of two reasons why bipolar disorder might be more strongly associated with suicide compared to unipolar disorder.

Up until this point I have mainly talked about the factors that make some people more suicide prone. But being predisposed to suicide doesn't mean that you'll actually go through with it. What tips a vulnerable person over the edge? And can anything be done to stop the person before it's too late? Those are some of the questions I'll attempt to answer next.

## What Triggers Suicide?

People respond to stress differently. Some people thrive under difficult circumstances, while others become traumatized. When you have a mood disorder, stressful events pose a special risk. The event might precipitate a depressive or manic episode or it might occur because the depression itself might cause additional stress. When researchers study suicide they look for triggers. Triggers release the forces that have been building up inside a person that can be the deciding factor in suicide. They're like the proverbial straw that broke the camel's back. They aren't by definition the most powerful cause of suicide. Usually the underlying depressive illness is the major cause. But without a trigger— a stressful event, for instance—the suicide is less likely to occur.

If your spouse walks out on you, it might trigger a relapse. But it's also possible that your spouse might decide to leave you if you already have depression, creating another stressful event in a loop that feeds on itself. Social stresses, particularly those affecting domestic life, increase suicide risk. Even the fact that you might have attempted suicide can create the situation in which you both lose a marriage and become more isolated at once.

But even in the absence of some precipitating event, my reading of the literature says that people commit suicide when they are severely depressed and when they are exposed to stressful events that bring about an acute and dangerous change in mood. These events usually occur in the hours or weeks leading up to the act. Such stress events include the loss of a loved one or the breakup of a close relationship, trouble with school or the law, or a particularly humiliating experience. Struggling with a serious physical illness can also cause a depressed person to consider suicide.

An undesired change in residence or in environmental conditions, especially for the elderly who resent any uprooting, can create an intolerable degree of stress. While some of these stressful events may come about as a result of chance, some may be a consequence of the person's depressive or bipolar illness. So there is likely to be a multiplicity of stress events in a depressed person's life.

Even changes in lifestyle and routine, which can be stressful events in their own right, may act as triggers. Sleep loss, whether from grief, jetlag, or insomnia, can shift some bipolar patients into mixed manic (agitated) states with high risks.

Researchers who conducted a famous study of suicide in the city of "Lundby" (an alias), Sweden, found that most victims experienced depressive or manic depressive illness when they killed themselves. But the researchers also found evidence for increasing rates due to recurrent job loss. They pointed out that the effect of the job loss was great enough to raise the whole suicide rate in the population. However, the effect was only seen in those persons with preexisting depressive illness. (That means that in the United States where about 10 percent of the population has or is prone to depression, there is a very large high risk group.) The risk also goes up if you're depressed and get arrested. In this case we are probably seeing how temperament (impulsive), behavior (substance abuse), and disease (depression) interact with a humiliating life experience and make the risk of suicide much greater, at least at that moment. This is especially worrisome when so many mentally ill persons who are detained by police, with the best intentions, or other peace officers in U.S. cities are put into jail. In the past they would have been sent to psychiatric hospitals, but today because of the shortage or lack of access to public hospital beds, putting these people in jail seems the only alternative to leaving them prey to their own illness and the dangerous streets.

Suicide itself can trigger more suicides. By that I mean that a suicide by one person can cause another to copy the act. In other words, suicide, like the flu, can be contagious or even epidemic. A highly visible sensational suicide makes it more likely that others who are at risk will follow the example. Outbreaks of suicide, or suicide clusters, have been recorded in Plano, Texas; Bucks County, Pennsylvania; Fairfield County, Virginia; South Boston; and suburban New Jersey, among other places. But outbreaks of suicide have also occurred in remote Eskimo villages, on Indian reservations, and on college campuses. Often the suicide victims know one another. Frequently it's an adolescent phenomenon. In one Texas community, for example, eight students at the same high school committed suicide within a fifteen-month period. When researchers studied another cluster— again in a suburb—they reported that in just six months two adolescents had committed suicide and five others had made attempts. Six of the youths had gone to the same high school, hung around with one another, and visited one another in the hospital. In nearly all instances the victims had a history of suicide attempts and threats at times unrelated to one another. Again these outbreaks occur primarily in those who are most vulnerable to begin with in that they are depressed and temperamentally vulnerable. These are the ones who are at risk from this form of contagion.

Natural events can also play a role that will affect the most vulnerable people. Evidence abounds that suicidal behavior is seasonal (as is depression.) More suicides also occur between four and seven A.M., when depression is often at its worst. While there is a decrease in suicides on major holidays and birthdays, more suicides occur on Monday. It's not called "blue" for nothing. And although you might think that more people would tend to commit suicide in the dark days of winter, in fact, the peak seasons for suicides happen to be early spring and early autumn. In the United States suicides for both men and women peak in April and May, while suicides in women alone show a rise in September and October. Why should there be such seasonal variation? Seasonal change in light cause many behavioral and physiological changes, including precipitating depression. (I've already mentioned SAD, or Seasonal Affective Disorder.) These changes have an impact on the levels of neurotransmitters like serotonin. They affect the sleep and temperature regulators of the body, the action of the endocrine and hormonal systems, and the production of testosterone and estrogen. Changes in these systems can play havoc with mood, particularly in a person with affective illness.

Protective social and cultural forces need to be taken into account as well in our consideration of suicidal influences. The general connectedness of people with their culture, although hard to measure, has been considered a major factor in suicide since Emile Durkham described "anome" in his book *On Suicide* (1874). Some societies have a strong taboo against suicide, such as the Amish, who still have a low rate. But most social and cultural forces are subject to change over time. Roman Catholics in the United States and Europe used to have lower rates of suicide but that is no longer so. In the Netherlands, for instance, physician-assisted suicide is legally sanctioned. In Japan the act of *seppuku,* or ritual suicide, has been considered an honorable tradition, though it is seldom practiced today. In a society in which suicide is taboo a person may be less likely to take such a drastic step than in a "modern" society, in which it is seen as an "understandable" response to a terrible situation.

Economic declines are also associated with higher suicide rates. In the Eastern European countries, suicide for men has been rising ever since the fall of the Soviet Union, as the economy has withered and unemployment has soared. This might also be related to the loss of the structure of the Communist system and the absence so far of strong institutions to replace it. In both world wars suicide rates in the United States went down. The young men who might have been thinking about suicide at home were off fighting in the trenches overseas. This may be the result of what is called a conflagration. As paradoxical as it sounds, when people confront a critical situation like a war, a flood, or an earthquake, they're less likely to end their own lives. What happens to their thinking when they're fighting on the battlefield? I don't know, but I imagine that they do not kill themselves because the potential lethal risk of war is felt to be an appropriate "task" or challenge for very depressed young men. I've developed this theory on the basis of accounts from two or three of my patients who were depressed and contemplating suicide and enlisted in the army as an alternative. So it's possible that the rise in suicide rates in the postwar period would be a statistical reversion to the previous "normal rate" that would have been seen in the absence of war. However, studies found no decline in the rates of suicide among young American men during the Vietnam War, but then that conflict did not fall into the category of a "general conflagration" since it didn't engage all, or even a sizable portion, of able-bodied young men.

# The Stigma of Suicide

The phenomenon of suicide presents an unusual challenge to doctors, social workers, and other caregivers, not to mention the friends and relatives of the deceased, because of the stigma attached to suicide. Social and religious taboos make many people reluctant to acknowledge a suicide in their family. While official statistics show that 30,000 Americans take their lives each year, the truth is that number could be considerably higher. Suicide often goes unreported even by coroners, who, perhaps because of pressure from or sympathy for the family, will ascribe the cause of death to an accident rather than the consequence of an intentional act. I've seen this influence as a factor in my own practice. I had a patient who was clearly depressed and was on suicide watch at home because his family was unable to afford the cost of hospitalization. The family didn't realize that the acetaminophen he took for headaches could be lethal. One day he took over 200 of these tablets when he was alone for fifteen minutes in his home office. He died of liver failure at the hospital. His family felt terrible, and worse yet they blamed themselves for failing him. I met with them together several times and repeatedly assured them that they were blameless. They didn't know enough to ask whether acetaminophen posed a danger and we didn't think to tell them about specific medicines, assuming that they understood what we meant when we said "all medicines" should be managed by the family and not the patient. After these sessions with them, I felt that I had helped them. They seemed to realize that they were not at fault and were able to air their feelings more openly. Then about three or four months later I heard that they were very upset to have read in the paper that their father's death was a suicide. They had somehow rationalized that his death wasn't a suicide at all.

In an even more bizarre case, I had a patient who shot himself in the head with a pistol. Miraculously, he sustained only a minor wound. Yet, against all evidence, both he and his parents insisted that it was an accident. He agreed that he was feeling despondent and had just had a fight with his parents. And it was true that he had gone upstairs and taken the gun out of the drawer and had pointed it at his head. All the same, the family assured me, the gun had gone off accidentally. Such episodes are not as uncommon as you might think. When any suicide occurs, families and friends are left to cope with an unforeseen catastrophe that leaves them disoriented and guilt-ridden. In some ways it might be easier to deny that the event took place at all. The families and loved ones who are so devastated need substantial support, education, and sometimes psychotherapy to help them deal with the loss. In my experience helping people confront their own impending death or the death of a loved one, whatever its cause, the deaths that I find the most difficult to handle involve suicide.

Then it should stand to reason that we should try to make suicide more understandable. Yet attempts to destigmatize suicide, however well intentioned, have generally proven unhelpful. An eighteen-month follow-up study on a school-based suicide education program, for instance, failed to provide evidence of the positive effects of holding group sessions in which the students talked about why someone might commit suicide. David Schaffer, a professor of child psychiatry at Columbia University, monitored the program and observed that those students who participated in it were significantly *less likely* to seek help for serious personal or emotional problems. They were also significantly less likely to encourage a depressed or troubled friend to seek professional help. Worse, those students who entered the program believing that suicide was not a reasonable response to stress were more likely to change their minds after they'd taken the program and considered suicide an understandable, possibly reasonable response to stress. This was the opposite result that the program's directors had hoped for!

The reason that the school programs failed, and even produced worse results than would have been achieved had the directors done nothing at all, was the misplaced emphasis. The focus had been on the act of suicide when it should have been the underlying cause: the depressive illness. Destigmatizing suicide makes it more reasonable to consider actually doing it. It would have been far better for students to learn about the diagnosis and the treatment of depression. That's the focus of our support group at Hopkins, called DRADA. Currently a group of dedicated and energetic doctors and staff is working with schools in Baltimore and Washington, D.C., to emphasize the importance of dealing with the illness rather than the act of suicide itself.

## Preventing Suicide

Many community-oriented attempts to prevent suicide have been tried, with varying degrees of success. Suicide prevention hotlines, for example, have proven not to work because callers are not the ones who are at greatest risk. Most hotline callers and crisis-service users are females, who are more likely than men to discuss their feelings, which is some protection in itself. The people who called, however troubled, were not those with severe major depression. Second, because suicide is often an impulsive act in a severely depressed person, many suicide victims will not take the time to consider alternatives or express their feelings to a stranger.

Many surveys reported in the newspaper or on TV suggest that 10–15 percent of high school students have thought about suicide. In a recent study of residents in New Haven, Connecticut, 10 percent said they didn't think life worth living; one in twenty had seriously considered suicide sometime in the previous year, while one in a hundred reported that they had made an attempt. (Such surveys have to be judged in context: people will not always answer candidly, or at all, when questioned about such sensitive issues as suicide.)

What can be done by the medical profession to prevent suicide? Historically, doctors have not always acknowledged that they had an obligation to prevent suicide because they shared the idea that most suicides were a result of a moral crises rather than the consequence of a disease (depression). Fortunately, this attitude has undergone a marked change. Yet in spite of striking advances in the medical treatment of mood disorders in the past half-century, we still have little evidence to show that we've succeeded in reducing long-term rates of suicidal acts in general, let alone in people with major affective illnesses. A few exceptional studies show a lower suicidal risk for people with manic depression who are on long-term lithium treatment and a few show that length of time in treatment in a hospital clinic for depression lowers risk. But the diagnosis and timely therapeutic interventions reach only a minority of psychiatrically ill persons at risk for suicide. Predicting suicide is also difficult in depressed people. Suicidal intent is not constant in an individual; people who harbor thoughts of suicide may never take any action to kill themselves and almost half of the people who do kill themselves give little or no warning about it beforehand.

Although there are numerous lists of "warning signs" that are of some use as a guide, the fact is that the signs are often ambiguous. There's also the reality that even the most suicidal people are ambivalent. It's surprising how sometimes a little thing—a missed phone call, an imagined slight—can snatch a life away. But it's also worth keeping in mind that sometimes it takes only a little thing to save these people, too, at least for the moment. The best-selling novelist Pat Conroy once recounted going into a gun shop to buy a gun in order to kill himself. While he was waiting for the clerk to serve him he was surprised to run into a former high school student of his. The student asked him what he needed a gun for and he replied that he needed it to shoot himself. The student laughed and said something about what a great sense of humor he had. Conroy says now that that heartfelt laugh caught him short and saved his life.

Any person contemplating suicide or parasuicidal acts may give voice to their intentions. A large number of people will say, "Yes, I've had suicidal ideas," or "I don't think life is worth living." It's surprising how frequently people have suicidal ideas and tell people what they are planning to do.

When a loved one or a friend tells you that he or she is thinking of suicide, what are you supposed to do? How do you respond? If you're like most people, you'd say, "Okay, let's go get some help." Yet what seems like the obvious thing to do may not meet with a receptive ear. Very often the person who has the suicidal ideas will rebuff any offer of help on the grounds that it won't be useful or else will insist that he or she wasn't serious. We need to emphasize that anybody who claims to be having suicidal thoughts certainly is in need of a psychiatric examination regardless of whether his or her actual intent is suicide.

So how should you respond if someone close to you talks about suicide? First, you should take what your friend or family member says very seriously. But at the same time you should remain calm and not overreact. Listen closely. Maintain eye contact. Ask direct questions. You should find out whether the person has a plan to commit suicide and try to learn the intended method. Acknowledge the person's feelings; empathy is called for, not a judgmental attitude. However, you don't want to relieve the person of responsibility for his or her own actions. Be reassuring; emphasize that suicide is a permanent catastrophe for everyone he or she cares about, and that their problems are temporary. Offer hope. Remind the person that help is available and that even though things may look bleak at the moment, they will eventually get better. Don't promise confidentiality—you will need to discuss the situation with a doctor later on. Remember that this is the kind of situation that you can't handle alone. And you don't want to put your own safety at risk, either. Always seek help. Contact a psychiatrist, therapist, or any health professional trained to intervene in a crisis. If it's an emergency dial 911 and get help immediately. Express your concern to the health professionals and clearly state why you believe your friend or family member may be in danger of suicide. If possible, don't leave the person alone until help arrives and he or she is in the hands of competent professionals.

I think we are on the threshold of major progress in preventing suicides. The evidence is starting to accrue that long-term effective treatments for depression help, especially lithium in bipolar patients. Less legal tolerance for drinking while driving and for adolescent drug use, combined with educational programs should help get more people diagnosed and treated, which would in turn help prevent suicide. We're certainly getting better at identifying and treating people who are among the suicide-prone. Because we are more alert about what to look for and more aggressive in prescribing drugs and other therapies, we are in a better position to break the grip depression has on our patients and pull them back from the brink. Where a great deal of work still needs to be done is in getting people who need help in for treatment before they put themselves in harm's way. And through education and destigmatization efforts of many groups ranging from the National Depression and Manic Depressive Association and National Alliance for Mental Illness (NAMI) to DRADA, we are probably starting to do just that. (To find out more about this organization and others involved in suicide prevention, see the resource appendix on helpful organizations.)

# PART FOUR

∞

# Treatments for Depression

In the following chapters I will tell you about a variety of treatment options. But before that, I'd like to give you a sense of what treatment means. Treatment can be pursued on two levels, tactical and strategic. On a tactical level I'm talking about the basics of care. As doctors we can list the treatments that are available for depressive illnesses and we can describe to you the advantages and limitations of each. And there's no doubt that a certain degree of skill is required to know which one to use on which patient and when. Without knowledge of the risks and benefits of various medications or without some skills in psychotherapy, it isn't possible to treat severely ill patients—inside or outside of the hospital. And if you are thinking about getting treatment, or are now in treatment, you should know what role your doctor will play in helping you. Beating depression is a collaborative effort between the doctor, the patient, and the patient's family and friends. If one partner in the collaboration is not doing his or her part, treatment will almost invariably be hampered. At the same time I also want to acknowledge that there are no risk-free diagnoses or treatments, nor are they written in stone.

So those are the basics, what I think of as the tactical level of care. The second level of care is strategic. By strategic I mean that the treatment of a patient requires an overall game plan that balances what the doctor judges to be medically necessary and what the patient and his or her family feel that they can contribute. However, the devil, as they say, is in the details. On the strategic level, doctors need to be more attuned to the individuality of each patient if we are to reach a successful outcome. After all, a variety of patients might have the same diagnosis or nearly identical symptoms when they enter treatment. That doesn't mean that they all should be treated the same way.

The most important treatment skill in my judgment is the ability to make a comprehensive assessment of the patient's symptoms, course of illness, temperament or personality traits, and history of behaviors (does the individual drink to excess or gamble too much?). I also want to hear from my patients about their lives from their own perspective. How do they see their current condition in view of their whole life? Just because a patient has a disorder doesn't mean that the disorder defines who the person is.

These are among the many factors that need to be taken into account in order to derive a comprehensive strategic treatment plan. Doctor, patient, and family all have to determine what hazards the patient will face if the treatment plan succeeds or if it fails. What goals are practical? Monitoring the progress toward these goals (or deviation from them) is the touchstone of good care. That means that we need to watch how our medications and other treatments are working, how the patient is responding to them, and adjust dosages or medications when necessary. If I have done a good assessment of all of these issues, I'll need only average technical treatment skills to succeed. On the other hand, if I misjudge the needs of the patient because I miss the diagnosis or misjudge the patient's or family's goals, then even great technical skill will not save the day.

For example, consider the needs of two patients with recurrent depressive illness (unipolar disorder). One is a twenty-one-year-old straight-A single college student when she is well but who has been ill 60 percent of the time in the previous five years. She is naturally introverted and when she becomes ill she tends to isolate herself, drink alcohol, and take too much medication so that she sleeps up to twenty hours a day. The second patient is a twenty-eight-year-old woman who is a married mother of two small children. A lawyer, she's fastidious in her habits and never touches alcohol; she always shows up to work on time and is immaculately groomed even when she is severely depressed. Because of her illness she has a hard time concentrating on her reading and on writing trial briefs, but she gets them done nonetheless. The effort to maintain appearances, however, isn't cost-free. As soon as she gets home from work she is so fatigued that she often climbs right into bed, so that she scarcely has more than a few minutes for her children. Her husband, a high school teacher, takes up the slack, assuming responsibility for caring for the children and making sure that the house is kept in good order. The couple is fortunate to have a good relationship with the patient's mother, who, now that she is retired, is able to help out when she's needed.

So what can we say about these two women when it comes to treating them? I would say that both patients would be well served by antidepressant trials as they begin treatment. It is virtually impossible to know in advance which antidepressant will be the best one for any given patient, although the odds are fairly good that the first drug I start each woman with will work okay if she takes it at sufficient doses for enough time (eight weeks to be sure that it has worked or failed). But how will each patient fare on medication? With the college student, I would have to take into account her disposition to use the antidepressant dangerously and not as it was prescribed. This means that I would be strongly inclined to give a medication that is very safe, even if it was taken in an overdose. So I would tend to prescribe a safer SSRI such as Prozac or Zoloft, even if she had a history that suggested to me that she'd respond better to a group of medicines, such as tricyclic antidepressants, which are riskier if taken in an overdose. Both patients could benefit from psychotherapy, but the lawyer will probably need more encouragement and supportive treatment if she isn't to fall into the trap of blaming herself for her condition. The college student, on the other hand, will need a more structured therapeutic relationship where she can receive the necessary support and supervision so that she doesn't abuse alcohol or overdose on her medications. She will be much more likely to need hospitalization as part of her treatment. With the round-the-clock nursing care she will get in the hospital, this patient will probably do very well. Moreover, her medication can be better managed. So the outcome in her case might be identical to the outcome for the second patient, only it will have been achieved at much greater financial cost due to her need for hospitalization. Her studies are also likely to be disrupted. Nonetheless, keep in mind that this patient is very smart and ambitious (remember, she gets straight A's when she's not depressed). If she responds well to the medication and becomes convinced that she can do well by stopping her drinking and is able to maintain healthy habits, the course of her illness could easily turn dramatically in a positive direction.

So where does the monitoring come in? Monitoring is vital. In most cases monitoring is more important than technical issues involving the selection of a medication. For the college student, the monitoring focuses on safety. Is any responsible adult readily available (perhaps her mother) to help with her illness, for example? Monitoring also means engaging the patient in frank discussions about how her behavior influences our ability to treat her. But these discussions have to take place when she is ready for them. We must make sure that she is not too depressed to handle the stress that talking about such sensitive subjects is certain to cause. That's why we always monitor mood. And if we see that she is tolerating the therapy sessions well, without sinking further into depression, then we will want to monitor her attitude, too, both in terms of her response to her illness and her commitment as a patient to do everything she can to get well and stay well. In fact, I have often seen how patients benefit from such commitment. Many patients tell me that it was some emotional experience that was unplanned strong enough to persuade them that life could be good and worthwhile and that they should live. She has to look at her illness in a more realistic manner and see it not as her destiny but as a series of high hurdles that can be overcome.

CHAPTER 12

∞

# Getting Help for Depression

What do you do when you or someone in your family is depressed? Well, most of what there is to do comes under three headings: medical, communication, and planning.

1. First, what should you do medically? The answer is, get professional help. You didn't cause this. Neither did anyone else. No one should expect it to be fixed without professional help. It's hard to see that it's the depression (or mania) that is the enemy and not you, or the patient, or anybody's mother! Once you understand that, it's a lot easier to look for help or persuade your partner to accept it.

2. Second, talk to each other about what you or your relative wants done while ill. This is much easier to do when feeling well since thinking and articulating your needs can be accomplished more clearly.

3. Third, plan for success. Figure on getting better. Given the success rates we can expect, that's a realistic thing to do. At the same time plan for some tough times with creative but sensible ideas. It's a give-and-take process between you, your family, and your therapist or doctor. It sounds more logical to say, "Hey, I'm depressed again" (or for a clinician to say, "Your depression is back") than it is to try and cope with the slights and hurts of the withdrawal or irritability that comes with depression. Admittedly, it's very hard for healthy relatives to deal with such an admission, since you're trying to hold back and not let yourself feel irritated, much less demonstrate it.

If you were in a body cast, your spouse would naturally understand that there were certain things you couldn't do. But it's not so easy even for someone close to you to recognize that you're crippled when you feel like your brain is unplugged. You can't concentrate on a conversation. You can feel stupid if your partner feels obliged to repeat things you didn't get the first time. People you love can seem angry even when they're really not. If, on the other hand, you're the healthy person in the relationship you need to understand that your partner is simply not as articulate as he or she would ordinarily be, and thus is unable adequately to express wishes or needs. Such partners may feel that they're doing even worse than they actually are. That explains why depressed people aren't as available in a confiding way as they would want to be. That's to be expected temporarily. They may even seem more apathetic or uncaring than sad. As we've said, the depressed person doesn't feel things, either positively or negatively, as he or she normally would. But the real person you love will be back: hang on and help your partner hang on.

Suppose you assure your depressed partner against all evidence (as he or she sees it anyway) that he or she is going through a bad patch and will snap out of it soon. How do you think your partner would react? He or she probably wouldn't believe you and might dismiss any suggestion about getting better, perhaps even trying to persuade you that you're mistaken. All you can do is reiterate your confidence that your loved one will improve and that you're not just trying to make him or her feel better, and explain that you understand that he or she can't believe you. Two of my most amazing patients, one a fifty-two-year-old woman and the other a sixteen-year-old boy, didn't know that they had depression, but they had learned a coping strategy for when they felt low. They reminded themselves how much they meant to the people closest to them, and that would keep them from going over the edge. That the sixteen-year-old was able to keep in mind that others loved him was the only thing that kept him from committing suicide.

When a couple knows that depression is the obstacle that's come between them, they're at least one step ahead of the game. That doesn't mean that knowing that depression is involved will make it easier to maintain the relationship. But knowing that depression puts a cynical or negative spin on feelings and that this is treatable should be of some consolation. It's not just something you have to "work out." And don't feel any compunction about letting your doctor share the burden of coping with the illness. That's why we are in the business.

## Getting Help for Manic Depression

The kinds of behavior that we have been describing act as alarms—as cries for help. If your spouse goes on a binge or disappears for days you may think he or she is crazy, or you may realize that a disease is the cause. Either way, you're very likely going to respond by trying to get professional help, urgently.

For manic-depressives, lithium treatment combined with psychosocial intervention can have a real and positive impact on family relations. Effective use of lithium does stabilize mood swings that require hospitalization. Once the illness is controlled it allows a more healthy adaptation to take place within the family.

Because manic depression is a remitting and relapsing illness, it places an additional burden on families. But we know that relapse rates are variable and believe that psychologically stressful events as well as other events can precipitate a relapse. What about how the family reacts to the patient? Researchers have called responses that are intensely emotional and critical as having "high levels of expressed emotion," and have observed that patients who live with their families who have high levels of expressed emotion are more likely to relapse within nine months than patients with relatives who are not so demonstrative. I can't disagree with the observation, as it has been a consistent across several studies. But I confess that I always react with negative emotion when I hear this research presented at a scientific meeting or a family support gathering. Since I have personally interviewed several thousand patients and families in crisis, I find it hard to imagine reacting *without* easily detected expressed emotion to the situations I hear about, such as finding the house ransacked, an unexpected $20,000 credit card bill, or worse. And I would challenge the research conclusions by asking whether the behavior of an ill person which evokes more, rather than less, expressed emotion is the cause of what we call relapses (i.e., needing to be in the hospital or to have their medication changed) instead of how family members react to the behavior. Having said that, we would probably agree that regularly experiencing the highly expressed emotion whether it is you expressing it as a family member or whether it being expressed by someone else is stressful. I think this is something to talk about with others, but perhaps best with someone who has also been there as a caring involved loved one, not just as a social scientist. Educating yourself as a family member about the illness helps to some degree, since it gives you an idea of what you can reasonably expect as you go through the ordeal with a loved one. But, for most of these people, there's nothing as helpful as education plus participating in family support groups. These groups are made up of parents, spouses, partners, and loved ones of patients. They are in the same boat as you are. I've found that they are loving people who, because they are coping with the same problems, can offer realistic and helpful advice (listen to it all without assuming the first thing you hear is the best), and perhaps more important, they are there to throw you an emotional lifeline in the event of a crisis. As the mother of a manic patient put it, "I owe my life to these people. I came here each week for four years until I felt I knew how to cope with his bipolar disorder. I found out why I had to take care of myself and still love my son."

## What to Look for in a Doctor?

I once had the privilege of attending a lecture by the late Canadian author Robertson Davies, best known for his novel *The Fifth Business.* During his talk he raised the very issue that I was grappling with myself. Patients, he said, weren't given adequate time to discuss problems with their physician and were compelled to rely too much on expensive technical assistance for care. In contrast, Davies recalled his own experience with a surprisingly understanding physician in England that made a great impression on him. At the time, Davies, a student at Oxford, was suffering from a bad case of the flu. Not only did the doctor spend considerable time with him but rather than limiting his questions to his symptoms, asked Davies about his background, how he was getting on at Oxford, and what he hoped to do in the future, issues that on the face of it had nothing to do with his illness. This doctor's approach reminded Davies of the techniques practiced by the doctors he'd known as a child. These old-time doctors, with their great black bags, would concoct preparations for him when he was sick, some were blue liquids and some were green. Did they do anything medically? Probably not. But the young Davies placed such confidence in his doctor's ability to make him well that he believed that they would help him, and they did. The doctor at Oxford acted much the way that those doctors had. Only instead of giving him a colorful compound of his own devising, the English doctor dispensed valuable advice. He urged Davies to make sure to take some time off from his studies now and again so that he wouldn't miss out on opportunities that life had to offer. The doctor recognized that the flu wasn't only a physical ailment. Something else was ailing Davies, only he hadn't realized it. By becoming too focused on achieving his academic goals, Davies was losing sight of what he should be doing. He was fortunate to find a doctor who was willing to look at him as a person and not just as a set of symptoms.

What both Davies's doctor at Oxford and the doctors of his childhood had in common was a willingness to give time to their patients and an intuitive grasp of what kind of treatment would be most effective, even if it wasn't, strictly speaking, a "medical" one. Davies hastened to add that he wasn't suggesting that he was against modern medicine. On the contrary, he was very grateful for the miraculous cures that modern medicine offered. What he deplored, though, was medicine's reliance on prescription drugs at the expense of personal care. To him, it made doctors seem like middlemen for large pharmaceutical firms, in marked contrast to the doctors of his childhood who seemed to possess the ability to produce magical potions on the spot. And because modern doctors have so little time to spend with their patients (which also gives patients the sense that they aren't very interested, either), Davies said, doctors are hardly in a position to evaluate the patient well enough to give advice that might have far more benefits in the long term than any prescription. After all, as Davies noted, the advice he received had no effect on the flu other than to reassure him that it wasn't fatal.

Davies's remarks helped me understand what my own patients were going through as they searched for treatment. I know I want the same kind of attention and consideration when I go to see a doctor. So just how should patients and families go about getting this kind of treatment? It makes sense to look for a doctor who is interested in you as an individual, but you also want one who is highly competent. You don't want a physician who will give you the benefit of his or her time but lacks the skills to diagnose or treat you. I know as a patient that I want a well-informed doctor who is a critical thinker as much as one who is wise and reassuring. One of the reasons that patients acknowledge for seeing alternative practitioners today is that their doctors don't spend as much time talking and listening to them. It is hard, Davies said, to believe that the doctor is in any position for critical thinking if he or she hasn't listened and probed the details of your illness; this very act of listening and asking good questions is experience and wisdom in action.

## Getting a Second Opinion

The best patient care requires three components: a well-trained, dependable clinician who knows what to do and is accessible to the patient; a well-informed patient who actively participates in his or her care plan and follows it; and a trusting alliance between doctor, patient, and family. If you don't understand or agree with a doctor's diagnosis, you should ask for an explanation of how he or she came to the conclusion. What factors weigh in favor of the diagnosis? What factors argue in favor of an alternative diagnosis? What possible diagnoses did the doctor consider before making this determination? What level of confidence does he or she assign to the conclusion? Optimally, you'd like to be 95 percent certain. It's your obligation to educate yourself so you can better evaluate the doctor's recommendations. You should also ask your doctor to tell you how he or she decided on the treatment plan. You can also do outside reading and/or talk to other patients who have had experience with the same treatments.

If you don't feel comfortable after this effort to clarify how good or risky the plan is, you should consider a second opinion. Whether you are a new patient or a returning patient, an inpatient or an out-patient, getting a second opinion shouldn't be considered an insult to your doctor. Many patients and their families worry that they'll hurt a physician's feelings or injure their relationship with their psychiatrist by requesting a second opinion. A second opinion can help you understand why your doctor has recommended your treatment and a second opinion may also help reassure you that the treatments are the safest and most effective. On the other hand, a second doctor might have ideas that will help your doctor get you the treatment you need faster. So no matter what decision you ultimately make about the treatment, the opportunity to have another psychiatrist, especially an expert in the field, evaluate your condition and offer diagnoses and suggestions for treatment will help you and your psychiatrist feel more comfortable with your decisions. In this sense, it can even reduce tensions for both you and your doctor, especially if you feel uneasy going ahead with a treatment. After all, there is no X ray or blood test yet to confirm the diagnosis of depression or bipolar disorder.

When do you decide to get a second opinion? The answer is simply whenever you, your family, or your doctor or therapist thinks it's a good idea. But, it is particularly helpful and reassuring to do so when the treatment isn't going very well or when a clinical decision, such as whether to go into a hospital for treatment, is a realistic possibility.

If you don't know of a consultant psychiatrist who specializes in conditions like yours, there are several sources you can turn to for a recommendation. You can ask your current doctor to recommend one, you can call a university or teaching hospital in your area; you can call the National Alliance for the Mentally Ill (NAMI) or the National Depressive and Manic-Depressive Association (NDMDA); or you can consult reference books that you can find in most libraries (including medical libraries), among them *The Best Doctors in America* and *Who's Who in Engineering and Science*. A search on the internet can also prove useful. Sometimes the best source of information proves to be a member of your family or a friend who has gone through treatment for depression. They may know doctors whom they would be happy to suggest.

When you do manage to see a consultant psychiatrist, make certain to request that your doctor sends your evaluation and treatment records to the consultant. Putting all this information together can take some doing, especially if you have had numerous physicians or therapists or even several inpatient stays. All the same, it's important to make the effort to get most of the records.

Some patients who have come to me for a consultation have expressed a concern that my judgment will be biased by the reports from their prior psychiatrist. I assure them that I or anyone offering a second opinion will want to come to their own conclusions independently. A consulting psychiatrist will regard previous diagnostic and treatment records in the same way a physician would look at previous X-rays or blood tests. The records can establish that certain symptoms or signs were present at some earlier date, but they wouldn't be used just to find out the doctor's opinion of your condition at the time. They can also document which medications were prescribed, in what doses, and for how long. If a medication was changed, the records could provide an explanation. The records alone are not sufficient to make a comprehensive evaluation, though. The consultant will always need to hear your own account. It is also extremely helpful for at least one family member to be present when you're being seen so that they can provide the consultant psychiatrist with their views about your condition just as they would be if you were being admitted to the hospital. If you feel they are your trusted confidants, it's very helpful for them to be brought in on the doctor's assessment with you or after you have spoken to the consultant alone. A patient often remembers only a fraction of what is said during these discussions, so it's helpful to have another set of ears present. And if the opinion given by the psychiatrist is upsetting, then the discussion is even harder to recall in detail because it's difficult to stay focused on what someone is saying when you are frightened or under a lot of stress.

What happens after the consulting psychiatrist has made an evaluation? He or she will typically call your treating psychiatrist and report the findings and recommendations. Usually a note indicating his or her conclusions will also be sent to your doctor. Keep in mind the bottom line: the goal of consultations is to help both the treating psychiatrist and you improve your options for treatment and to make your discussions more open and trusting.

# CHAPTER 13

∽

# Making the Diagnosis Is the First Treatment

What are my expectations as a doctor when a patient comes into my office seeking help for a possible depression or manic depression? And what can the patient reasonably expect from a visit? Keep in mind that not all doctors think alike and not all of them have the same expectations. I can speak for many of us, but my views may conflict with others.

Before I describe how I go about my examination I should make clear that on one important level it doesn't matter what a doctor's specialty is. Doctors and all health professionals strive to be good at examining patients and to be sympathetic, sensible counselors for patients and families. Although psychiatrists have more training in the diagnosis of "mood disorders," general practitioners, psychologists, social workers, nurses, and other professionals are all capable of diagnosing depression or manic depression. (You'll find an explanation of different types of professionals competent to diagnose and treat depression in the appendix.) Any of us will also miss the diagnosis sometimes, at least for a while.

Whatever the specialty of the professional you trust to approach, the critical skills in making a diagnosis of an illness are the same. The caregiver has to be discerning enough to know what to look for and have the ability to help you "tell the story" of depression (or whatever the disease). Of course, you're going to relate the story of the "problem" from your own vantage point. Drawing you out in order to make an accurate diagnosis isn't so much a skill as it is an exercise in patience and perseverance. The professional will be trying to establish a good relationship with you and acquire as much information as possible from as many different sources as available.

I want my patients and their families to understand what we as psychiatrists know and how we know it. Some of our knowledge comes from our training in medical school, of course, but much of our ability to diagnose and treat patients comes from our experience and intuition as well. The first thing that you need to be aware of is how we make our diagnoses of depression and manic depression and how we can tell when it is neither one nor the other but a different condition entirely.

## Understanding the Patient's Problem

The doctor has three basic tasks: to reach a diagnosis, to make a prognosis, and to craft a treatment plan with you that pulls in all the useful information and takes advantage of all potential resources. Another way of laying this out is to say that from the assessment I come to a formulation or understanding of your problem. In making this formulation I am not only trying to determine a particular diagnosis (sometimes that becomes clear in ten minutes), but I am also trying to understand you in terms of your own life story. In this sense my formulation is more than the sum of its parts. What I want to know is who is this person and how has he or she arrived at this point in life. What are the circumstances that have brought you to seek help now? Besides the direct physical and mental status examination of you and your current condition, I must take a history about your family background, your personal life, and your medical history, and learn whatever I can about past as well as current psychiatric problems. The family history should reveal who else might be affected with symptoms similar to the ones you have and the nature of your relationships past and present. This often bears on the outcome of treatment. For some patients the family can provide a vital resource that will help get the person through the illness. Other families, though, are dependent on the patient for their livelihood and sense of security.

While the personal history usually offers us clues about the nature of a patient's present condition, it also helps me get a sense of who the person is. A patient's personal and medical history covers a wide range of topics. When did he start to walk? When did he begin to date? Was he socially active at school? Was there a big change in his behavior at some point along the way? Has he been able to hold down a steady job or does he go for long periods without employment? What are his relationships like with his colleagues at work? Of course, I'm very interested in learning about the patient's personal relationships. Is he married? If so, is the marriage stable and mutually satisfying? Does he have children? How many and how are they doing? Has the patient had any scrapes with the law? Does he drink too much or use illegal drugs or have a dependence on prescription medicine? As you might expect, a doctor isn't going to get this kind of intimate and sensitive information from talking to the patient alone. In order to make the best evaluation possible, a doctor needs to talk to the patient's family and friends as well. I've found that talking with the patient's mother is usually the ideal way to learn about problems that may have arisen in early development. From longtime friends and relatives I can find out about the patient's normal patterns of behavior and how they may have changed over the years.

Sometimes, of course, few friends or family members are available to provide this information. This is especially true for a patient who is older or who has no family members left. In cases like that, I need to obtain information relating to the patient's medical history in its rawest form—from doctor or hospital records, for instance—which I can then use to help make our determination of the condition. I also need to know what medications a patient is taking and allergies to any drugs. (Many patients think that any bad reaction to a drug must be an allergic one, which is not always the case; sometimes it's just an unpleasant side effect.)

When I "take a history" of a psychiatric (or any medical) disorder from a patient, I'm looking for identifiable patterns. A pattern of depressive episodes may not be recognized by the patient at the start of the evaluation process but can emerge out of the flow of the questions and exchange between us. Sometimes a pattern of symptoms recurs in a way that suggests a broken record. I will want to know, for instance, when the more physical symptoms such as poor sleeping, loss of energy, and loss of concentration began. Which came first, the insomnia or the inability to concentrate? I will try to figure out together with the patient why these depressive symptoms have been continuous or episodic. "Was this always the pattern or was it different when you had your first brush with depression?" I'll ask. "Do symptoms change with the time of year? Do they occur whenever a challenging task or a deadline looms or only after the task is completed?"

In other words, in compiling a psychiatric history I want to know the story of a patient's problem. This may sound surprising, but the way in which most people experience and respond to specific diseases follows certain predictable patterns that change over time. Once I have heard the patient's story and have asked clarifying questions, I can compare it with classic story lines of several conditions. For instance, depression, anorexia nervosa, mania, schizophrenia, panic disorder, congestive heart failure, and asthma all have characteristic stories. Distinguishing one story from another is a key to reaching an accurate diagnosis. Let me give you an example of how confusion can arise. A medical colleague of mine, a cardiologist, sent a friend to see me whom he suspected had depression. The patient was the maître d' at the best steak house in town. I could see why my colleague was concerned; the patient's story did include three features of possible depression. He still hadn't gotten over his mother's death six months earlier; he was losing weight and not sleeping as well. But upon investigation his sadness turned out to be typical of bereavement: It came and went, which is normal, and, even though he would sometimes burst into tears he was also cheered by his mother's memory, not usually the case in depression, where cheer is notably absent. The eating and sleeping problems didn't seem typical of depression, either. When he ate an especially big meal, he told me that he'd suddenly become exhausted and leave half of his food untouched. His sleeping, too, showed a curiously erratic pattern. He'd suddenly wake up, short of breath, and need to sit up for twenty minutes or so before he felt able to go back to sleep. In an attempt to remedy the problem he began to sleep propped up in a chair or in bed. I realized that this was not a man suffering from depression. Rather his eating and sleeping disorders were indications of congestive heart failure. After examining the patient, my colleague agreed that he did not have depression but in fact had a heart problem that required treatment. That's what I mean about your doctor needing to be discerning enough to understand the symptoms he or she is seeing.

## The Mental Status Examination

In the course of this initial evaluation process I complete the mental status examination. If you have heard this term before, chances are you think it's a test of memory and orientation, meaning your ability to situate yourself accurately in terms of time and place. That's true in so far as it goes, but a mental status exam is much more. It's also an assessment of mental state that includes:

- Appearance and general behavior
- Speech and thought process
- Mood, vitality, and self-attitude
- Thought content, abnormal experiences, and beliefs
- Accessibility and cognitive state
- Insight and judgment

From the outset I pay careful attention to my patient's appearance, grooming, posture, and the speed and agility with which he or she moves and speaks. The coherence of ideas and choice of words provide several types of information. Most manic and a few anxious patients, for instance, will talk so quickly that it's difficult to get a word in edgewise. This is what's known as "pressured" (i.e., difficult to interrupt) speech. In addition, I assess the patient's emotional range, current mood, and vitality. I will ask the patient to describe how he or she feels now and then to compare this to when he or she felt well.

## Why Doctors Miss Important Signs of Depression

One of the things that make depressive disorders especially tricky to recognize when examining a patient is that only about half of the patients will describe their mood as sad or "depressed." While these patients are feeling miserable they don't associate what they are feeling in terms of the common use of the word *depression*. Many feel they're suffering from anxiety that's gotten out of control. Others feel unmotivated, apathetic, or simply "numb"—unable to experience any emotions at all. Each year I have a few patients who will tell me that they are unable to feel sad and can't cry even in situations that would otherwise move them to tears.

Another problem doctors run into when they're trying to make a diagnosis is that the milder or atypical forms of depression merge imperceptibly with normal moods and can be chronic rather than episodic. So asking patients to compare how they're feeling now to when they felt well can be problematic. If you're feeling low and discouraged your perception and your memory are naturally going to be affected. You may exaggerate your previous sense of well-being, or conversely, exaggerate how poorly you feel now. But just because you're feeling low and discouraged for a week or two doesn't necessarily mean that you are experiencing a depressive episode. But if it's severe enough and lasts long enough, I do want to make sure that I'm not missing this very treatable condition.

We can also miss making a correct diagnosis if we rely too much on a textbook description of mania or even the most typical type of depression. This is where the art of the interview (learned at the bedside) comes in. I remember a patient who told me that she had "toxic sleep" and that the doctors she'd seen were missing the boat by diagnosing her as having a personality disorder. It wasn't that she didn't think she had a problem, it was just that she and her doctors disagreed about its nature. She observed that her energy was so low that she couldn't get out of bed before noon. She felt that she was always at her worst when she woke up each morning. She also observed that she felt at her best late in the evening just before she went to sleep (when she could read, relax, and talk with friends), and so she reasoned that she needed the whole day to recover from the dire effects of sleep. Well, while parts of her story were unusual, it isn't so uncommon for people to feel their worst early in the morning and their best in the evening. To find out what was really the matter, I just had to listen to her until I understood her story. Then I had to persuade her that: (1) I had appreciated and understood what she observed; (2) that I had seen this pattern many times before; and (3) rather than get into an argument about what the diagnosis was I would simply let her know that whatever we called her condition, I thought we could successfully treat it. Actually I agreed that her problem was not primarily a personality disorder but clinical depression, which as I've explained is a medical condition. In that sense it was just as she suspected, even if she wasn't aware of its exact nature.

As this case illustrates, an examination of this kind, while definitely an inquiry, isn't just a matter of asking lots of questions. There is a negotiation going on between doctor and patient that requires the building of confidence for both parties. And sometimes it involves translating the story from one language (the patient's) to another (the doctor's).

Naturally you may wonder whether good doctors can make the wrong diagnoses. The answer, of course, is yes. So how might this occur? How would a doctor deal with such a possibility and how should you as a patient or a family member deal with it?

To answer that question we first need to look at the two different levels of diagnoses in medicine: the clinical level, and the level of cause (of symptoms) or, as it's known in the medical profession, the level of etiology. When I diagnose disease on a clinical level, I'm interested in a patient's symptoms and signs, which for the most part I can discover from taking a history and conducting an examination. If you can't recall the sequence of events leading up to your illness, however, or your doctor fails to ask the right questions, there are bound to be holes in the story of your illness. And without knowing the whole story of your illness, a doctor may make an incomplete or mistaken diagnosis. For example, if a patient comes in for a consultation, he may be asked how he has been feeling over the last year. If he says that he's been in a depressed mood, but has experienced no problems maintaining his normal level of concentration or energy and that he's been sleeping well and felt good self-confidence, then a doctor could not conclude confidently that the patient had no symptoms of depression, a depressive syndrome or disorder. Now a doctor might give a definitive answer and say, "No, you didn't have a major depression in the last year." By this he or she might mean, the symptoms alone don't meet all the *DSM* criteria for that diagnosis. But I would likely say, "Based on what you've told me, I can't say that you had a depression in the last year." An astute doctor might then go on to ask, "Who else has been close to you in the last several months?" The patient might have been in frequent touch with his mother, say, or have a girlfriend who saw him a few days every week. Then the doctor might say, "Since it's really important to us to get an accurate picture of how you felt, maybe I should talk to her about what she observed." Or, if the patient was seeing a therapist or doctor, then his medical records could help set the record straight. We don't have to just take the patient's word for it if some doubt or ambiguity prevents us from getting a complete story.

Depending on the patient's situation and urgency, I give them more information than diagnosis, treatment, and prognosis. I try to be honest about just how confident or uncertain I am about the diagnosis. I can be a bit more informative about the diagnosis. I can say what the other conditions that might be considered to explain the symptoms.

Now let's turn to the second level of diagnosis, the level of cause or etiology. Here things can get tricky in the sense that the doctor can be perfectly correct and say that the patient did have a clinical depression, and that because most clinical depressions are thought to be genetic, his must be genetic, too. But occasionally a patient can have another condition—a stroke, for example, or a brain tumor—that shows no clinical signs except for a depression. So, although this is a relatively rare occurrence, the doctor might miss the stroke or brain tumor and diagnose only the depression, which is real enough, but which in these cases is the manifestation of the brain tumor or the stroke.

In a situation like this, the doctor would have to have good reason to be suspicious that something else was going on (a tough call in many instances) in order to justify a neurological exam, such as a head MRI (Magnetic Resonance Imaging study), which can be very expensive, to detect whether another condition was partly or entirely responsible for the depression.

For both types of missed diagnoses—those that happen because a doctor failed to get the whole story, and those that happen because a doctor misses an unsuspected cause—the critical issue is *follow-up*.

By that I mean that, whether you are the doctor, the patient, or a family member, you should follow up on any concerns you have about diagnosis. Keep your mind open and remember that diagnosis is a weighing of probabilities, not an absolute certainty, at least not at the level of clinical assessments. When I complete a consult, I often raise the issue of other diagnostic possibilities and explain to patients and their families what might happen if my favored diagnosis is found to be wrong.

## What to Expect from Treatment

Most psychiatrists, and most other doctors, too, try to practice in such a way so that even the very act of making our exam and taking a history gives some confidence to the ill person. By carefully explaining our diagnosis and discussing why we have determined a certain prognosis and treatment plan, we are able to provide enormous relief and hope to our patients. Depressed patients generally believe that they cannot be diagnosed or treated and are often convinced that they will never recover from whatever is wrong with them. So you can imagine how gratified they feel when I'm able to tell them that their condition is, in fact, diagnosable and explain why I feel confident that I am correct. (If I'm not confident about my diagnosis I'll want to tell them that, too, and assure them that with time and additional tests, I will be in a better position to make the diagnosis.) I tell them that the diagnosis means that their suffering is caused by an as yet undefined brain disorder. I discuss the possible causes of their particular condition and how I propose to treat it. Given the current state of scientific knowledge, however, there is no test to identify the cause of a particular person's depression. Sometimes the family history points to a genetic predisposition. If, on the other hand, the patient has had the depression following a stroke or suffers from Parkinson's disease, I know that the brain injury in either of these two cases was a likely cause of the depression.

At the same visit, I try to make clear what patients should expect from treatment. When I put patients on antidepressants, I will caution them that for the first two weeks they are likely to experience mostly side effects. This is a critical time when families, the treating psychiatrist, and friends need to be especially supportive as the patient may often feel worse before their mood begins to lift. However, over the next couple of months they will begin to feel more energy and have a better ability to concentrate. Their appetite will return and they will be able to sleep well at nights—changes that usually occur before patients feel any difference in mood.

Typically, you look better before you feel better. It takes some time before you feel your self-confidence and self-esteem improve. That's why I discourage patients from making any major life decisions during this two-month period, except for the decision to seek and accept treatment. I have seen too many depressed patients change spouses, jobs, and locations in desperate attempts to fix their problem. Believe me, these radical fixes not only don't cure depression, they also bring grief both to the patients and to the people closest to them.

It's important for me to emphasize that psychiatrists should do more than diagnose and treat patients. I need to explain to a patient what is wrong, what I know about the illness, and what is not known. I should dispel the common myths surrounding the illness. If I can relieve some of the doubts and guilt about the disorder in my patients and their families, I can make it easier for all of them to be supportive of one another while we wait for the treatment plan to work.

# CHAPTER 14

# Medical Treatment

## Treating Depression with Medication

From an historical perspective, the current prospects for successfully treating depression are clearly much better than they were thirty years ago when I started out in medicine. More doctors and other health professionals are diagnosing depression and manic depression (bipolar disorder), without which no treatment would be possible. Although making a clinical diagnosis doesn't guarantee that it will be an accurate one, it is a necessary first step. In the 1970s, for instance, most nonpsychiatrists would have told you that they never diagnosed either depression or manic depression. This rise in the diagnosis of depression as well as bipolar disorder is related to the wide acceptance of the *DSM III* (and now *DSM IV*) manual,* which provides specific criteria for each diagnosis. The system has its critics—I count myself among them—but it deserves credit for raising the profile of depressive illnesses among professionals.

The outlook has similarly improved in terms of treatment. We have many more medical options available than in the past. Even Prozac, a selective serotonin reuptake inhibitor, or SSRI, first marketed in 1988, is now an old drug. Its patent period has recently ended and there are four other SSRI antidepressants on the market. In addition, completely new groups of antidepressant medications are soon to be introduced. The American pharmaceutical industry recognizes that the market for medications for clinical depression and bipolar disorder is huge, which was not the case twenty-five or thirty years ago.

---

*DSM* stands for *Diagnostic and Statistical Manual,* which is used as a guide for diagnosis of psychiatric illness; it's published by the American Psychiatric Association.

Almost all patients seen today in medical practices like mine with major unipolar depression need antidepressants and all manic patients need medication as an important part of their treatment.

We certainly know more about the most severe forms of depression. We know how to recognize them and we know how to treat the vast majority of them. Would we recommend antidepressants to the many millions who are now untreated? The answer, as you might expect, is that we don't know. Depression, like diabetes, asthma, and hypertension, varies in severity. Many patients with a milder form of diabetes do well on a careful diet and regular exercise and do not have to take pills or insulin shots. For depression, too, a nutritious diet and exercise may offer some benefit and I believe that their effects on the illness should be explored and studied. After all, diet and exercise proved their therapeutic value centuries before medications were developed.

However, for depressed patients who come to me for treatment there's no question that medication is usually very helpful. A fairly comprehensive survey of doctors (including many who were not involved in the mental health field) revealed that 90 percent of them would prescribe antidepressants for severely depressed people. For the vast majority of patients who have single or multiple episodes of depression (but not manias or hypormanias), antidepressants are recommended.

Not all doctors, however, believe in the effectiveness of antidepressants; some actually seem to have a philosophical bias against them. Pat Conroy, best-selling author of *The Great Santini* and *Prince of Tides,* volunteered to appear as a guest speaker at an annual DRADA gathering to talk about his own experiences with depression. He told the audience that he realized that he probably had depression only after two failed marriages. It was his third wife who recognized the same symptoms in him that she had experienced and told him how antidepressants were helping her. He knew something was the matter with him but wasn't sure what exactly. "I'm sorry. I'm crazy, baby," he told her. "So am I, honey," she replied, "but Zoloft really helped me. Maybe you ought to try it."

The idea that he might have a diagnosable and treatable illness was new to Conroy. Encouraged by his wife, he went to see his doctor. (He refers to him as his "Boy Doctor" because he was young and had recently taken over a much older doctor's practice, inheriting Conroy's care in the process.) He explained his situation, but Boy Doctor was dubious. "I don't believe in that," he said, adding that he didn't treat patients with antidepressants. Instead, he gave Pat St. John's Wort (an herb that is thought to have some value for depression). Conroy took it briefly but as soon as he began to do some research on it, he decided it wouldn't be of much help. Because St. John's Wort has never been subjected to rigorous scientific tests, there is little substantiated evidence that it is truly effective for depression, especially in severe cases. Having rejected Boy Doctor's treatment, Conroy wasn't inclined to consult another doctor and explore the possibility of taking antidepressants, either. He's hardly an exception. It doesn't take much to dissuade a depressed patient from seeking help! However, his attitude seemed to change after he attended our annual one-day symposium on depression at Johns Hopkins. He said that once he saw the data and heard other patients describe the benefits antidepressants could offer, he told the audience that he was now persuaded that his wife had been right all along. He shouldn't have shunned medication that had the potential to alleviate his illness.

## Treating Manic Depression with Medication

Twenty-five years ago, when I'd look at annual reports from large psychiatric hospitals listing the number of patients admitted each year together with their diagnoses, I was surprised to find that bipolar disorder was given as the diagnosis for only one or two out of every thousand patients. Compare that to today, when 25 to 35 percent of the patients admitted to these hospitals are diagnosed with bipolar disorder! As in the case of the increased diagnosis of depression, bipolar disorder has received more recognition because of the influence of the most recent *DSM* manuals. And just as many new antidepressants have been introduced in the last several years, the number of drugs we can use to treat manic depression has increased. For instance, several new psychotropic medications that have been introduced—which are effective in the manic state. They include atypical neuroleptics and anticonvulsants, which have a variety of chemical structures. They are not addictive or habit-forming, even though some of them can cause gastrointestinal side effects if someone abruptly stops the medication. This is why we recommend lowering of the dose over some period of time before stopping it altogether. This "weaning" should not be confused with stopping addiction or drug or alcohol abuse. Weaning, in this sense does not indicate that these drugs cause dependence or craving like alcohol or cocaine can.

These newer drugs have become basic to the management of acute mania and have substantially lower risk of long-term side effects such as tardive dyskinesia, a condition marked by abnormal movements of tongue, mouth, and body. This represents a decided advance over the neuroleptic medications we have used in mania for the past thirty years or more. While several medications have been shown to help with bipolar disorder, lithium, which was approved in 1970 by the Food and Drug Administration, is still unsurpassed and possibly unmatched for long-term efficacy.

First identified in 1817, lithium is a metallic element, that while it has some antidepressant properties, is mainly used for the treatment of manic depression. More than any other scientist, a Danish researcher named Mogens Schou helped lithium gain such widespread acceptance. When he proved that the drug was safe on animals he tried it on humans, beginning with his brother, who was suffering from manic depression. Now lithium is considered the most effective long-term treatment for 50 to 70 percent of patients with Bipolar I, the classic form of manic depression.

However, just because lithium shows remarkably good results doesn't mean that it is without its drawbacks. As is the case with antidepressants, about 30 percent of the patients with manic depression don't get much better on lithium and side effects occur for many patients though not all. Some patients will experience increased thirst and the need to urinate frequently. Some kidney problems may also develop. Most side effects, though, are not debilitating and are either transient or easily remedied. The use of lithium calls for close monitoring of the blood level to insure that the level of the drug in the blood is within the range of safety. If, however, the level gets too close to the toxic level and the patient still shows no signs of improvement, regardless of how he or she is doing otherwise, we'd have to consider an alternative treatment.

In addition to its known toxicity, lithium also takes time to work, generally 1–3 weeks before it has any discernible effect. In order to administer lithium successfully, a doctor requires a cooperative patient who will be able to take it correctly and be willing to give blood for testing—two conditions that a manic patient may not be able to meet. If someone is suicidal or experiencing delusions we need to do something immediately. We can't expect the patient to hold on for a week or two before he or she feels better. In such cases physicians will use neuroleptic medications, which, while not designed for the treatment of mania, do have a calming effect that alleviates the symptoms of psychotic behavior. Once the patient is well enough to understand the options, it's easier to persuade the person to take lithium while he or she is being weaned off the neuroleptics.

# What Exactly Are Antidepressants?

For all their differences, the many types of medications we call anti-depressants are consistently better than placebo tablets in reducing symptoms in depressed patients. These medications do not, however, have the capacity to change anyone's personality, but rather act to restore the normal chemistry in the brain. Antidepressants go by many names based on their chemical structure or activity, such as the tricyclic structure or the serotonin reuptake inhibitor activity; that's not to suggest that every drug with a tricyclic structure and every drug that affects serotonin reuptake is necessarily an antidepressant. While demonstrating antidepressant activity, almost all these medications have other useful properties, particularly in anxiety disorders or in the regulation of blood pressure. That's why the word *antidepressant* can be confusing. I prefer to describe these medications in terms of their structure or function; for example, this drug affects serotonin or norepinephrine in this or that way.

The drugs we call antidepressants fall into four basic categories: tricyclics, selective serotonin reuptake inhibitors (SSRIs), monanimine oxidase inhibitors (MAOIs), and a number of newer drugs we can lump together under the necessarily vague designation of "others."

Serendipity has played an interesting role in the development of drugs that are currently being used to treat depressive illness. Swiss researchers were trying to make a better antihistamine when they created a compound containing a property that proved very helpful in treating psychotics and schizophrenics. The drug they created turned out to be Thorazine. Then, when researchers sought to make a better Thorazine they produced not an antipsychotic (a drug used to treat severe mental illness), but a tricyclic drug called imipramine. While imipramine didn't help people suffering from manias or schizophrenia, it did help people with depression. Once the tricyclics began to enjoy wide acceptance, pharmacists went back into the labs to attempt to make a better imipramine; they instead came up with Tegretol (also called carbamazepine), the first anticonvulsant mood stabilizer not derived from lithium. But happy accidents, as we all know, rarely happen in a vacuum. The discoverers of these compounds were astute enough to know how to see things they weren't looking for directly and that's hard to do. (I've listed the various categories of antidepressants, neuroleptics, and anticonvulsants, including their recommended dosages and side effects, in chapter 15.)

While there are differences between types of antidepressants they are outweighed by their similarities. In fact, some experts have argued that, when you come right down to it, all antidepressants are basically the same, not only because the response rates are so similar, but because the chemical structure of these various drugs is much the same and overlaps in terms of activity. Generally speaking, these drugs act by blocking the reuptake of neurotransmitters such as serotonin and norepinephrine in varying degrees.

These drugs leave more of the signal-carrying neurotransmitter "out there" in the brain rather than allowing so much of it to be sucked back into the neurons and produce mental or emotional problems. Keep in mind that altering chemical balances in the brain is what these drugs *do,* and while they often evoke a favorable response in that the patient feels much better over time, what makes these drugs work, what their exact mechanism is in the brain that has an effect on depression, remains a mystery.

In the United States, we call medications antidepressants if they have been approved by the Food and Drug Administration (FDA) for treating patients with one or more forms of depression. Once a drug is approved by the FDA for one purpose, doctors can use it for other purposes that were not anticipated when the original approval was granted. The FDA requires substantial evidence that a medication is both safe and effective for its advertised use before it is willing to give its approval. Studies known as double-blind, placebo-controlled, and randomized clinical trials are conducted with hundreds of patients to test the drug's safety and usefulness. They are called double-blind because neither the patient nor the doctor/researcher who diagnoses the patient knows whether the subject is receiving a drug or a placebo. Only the pharmacist knows who's getting the drug and who's getting the placebo, and he or she is sworn to secrecy until the end of the study, which lasts from four to eight weeks. At the end of the trial the pharmacist reveals which patients were on placebo. This way the drug's efficacy (or lack of it) can be evaluated without the bias of the patient or the doctor affecting the outcome.

After hundreds of these studies on antidepressants we know that there are far more similarities than there are differences among these medications. In four to six week studies comparing about one hundred patients on antidepressants and another one hundred taking placebo, about 70 percent of outpatients with major depression will greatly improve on antidepressants, in contrast, about 20 percent of depressive patients do so on placebos.

# Treating Patients with Antidepressants

Once I have decided to treat a patient with depression with medication, how do I go about it? One of the most difficult and time-consuming parts of working out a treatment plan isn't making the choice whether to treat a depressed patients with medications. That's relatively easy to do once I've made my diagnosis. The hard part is in finding the one medication (or combination of them) that is going to be most effective. The different antidepressants do produce different side effects in patients, so for practical purposes we choose them on the basis of how each individual patient will tolerate a drug's side effects.

We take different approaches in treating patients with medication depending on the antidepressant we're using. For some drugs, particularly the tricylcic medications, I regulate dosage by using blood levels as a guide. I start the patient on a small dose and build it up to what I think is a reasonable dose. Then I take the blood test and reevaluate the patient with the blood level in hand and make an assessment as to whether the dose should be increased (or decreased). The level of the drug in the blood, while important, never takes precedence over the clinical condition of the patient. But since there is good statistical evidence that certain blood levels are more likely to produce beneficial effects than lower levels, I use them to guide decisions, especially early on in the first six to eight weeks of treatment. (We have also learned at which levels we ought to be concerned because of the potential for toxic side effects.)

In some antidepressants (tricyclics) there does appear to be a relationship between the level of medication patients have in their blood and the degree of improvement in their condition. For other types of antidepressants the blood level doesn't seem to have a value in predicting response. This is the case with the serotonin specific reuptake inhibitors (SSRIs), such as Prozac, Zoloft, Paxil, and Celexa. With these drugs we don't need to measure their level in the blood. We start the patient at a pretty standard dose since most patients tend to respond to these drugs at the same dose. We want the patient to stay on the standard dose for six to eight weeks before increasing it, since in the great majority of patients the standard dose will work as well as higher doses.

We also have a few antidepressant drugs in which the higher the dose, the greater the potential for toxic side effects. Patients taking medications such as Venlafaxine (Effexor SR) and buproprion

(Wellbutrin SR) face the risk of high blood pressure or seizures at high enough dosages.

As you might expect, one of our top priorities in working with these drugs is to insure that the dosages we administer are safe for the patient. Each drug has what is called a margin of safety, which is defined as the difference between the therapeutic dosage or blood level and the toxic dosage or blood level. The tricyclics have a fairly large margin but the SSRIs have a larger margin still. This doesn't mean that any one of these drugs is "better" or "worse" because of the differing margins of safety. It means that some drugs, such as Prozac, can be given without as much concern about life-threatening toxicity even at very high dosages or levels compared with other medications.

## How Do Doctors Decide Who Gets Which Antidepressant?

Since we've said that all the drugs we have are of more or less equal efficacy how do we decide that one patient gets nortriptyline, while another gets Prozac or Wellbutrin? Generally we choose a medication for a patient on the basis of two considerations: potential adverse effects and ease of use. "Ease of use" refers primarily to the number of times we have to adjust doses and how much we will need to monitor the patient for side effects. Side effects also discourage a patient from continuing the course of medication. A number of studies show that over the long haul approximately the same proportion of patients—15 to 30 percent—will stop taking their medication because of its side effects, regardless of which drug they're on. For the physician the challenge is to try to determine what side effects a drug will have and weigh that against what side effects a patient is willing or able to tolerate. Before we make our decision as to what drug to prescribe, we first have to evaluate the patient's condition, physically as well as mentally. If a patient has chronic insomnia it is important to ask whether a sedating or nonsedating antidepressant will be better. Even if the patient's depression isn't getting any better we can't focus exclusively on the illness if at the same time he or she can't get to sleep. Optimally, we'd like to see the person get better *and* get a good night's sleep. So for that reason we might choose a medication that has a sedative side effect.

Ease of use also refers to the ease with which a patient can use the medication. If a patient needs to take a medication only once or at most twice a day he or she has a much better chance of sticking to the regimen. More than that and the patient is liable to forget to take the medication regularly or else give it up altogether because it's too much trouble.

In addition, we have to take into account the subjective response to side effects. Some patients will shrug off side effects that might disturb a doctor while other patients will complain vehemently about side effects that the doctor would be inclined to dismiss as relatively trivial. But fortunately we're in a position where we aren't limited in our choice of antidepressants; if one medication doesn't work or is too unpleasant for the patient, we have many others available to try in its place. In fact, we have twenty-five to thirty medications in our arsenal now, with more being added all the time.

How long does it take these medications to work? The answer is: It depends. If, however, the medication is proving effective, typically it's not the patient who notices but his or her family! They'll begin to observe some improvement in about two weeks. While the patient may still be grousing that the drug isn't working, the family is already celebrating his or her return to the land of the living. That's because the patient's self-image is still partially trapped in its depressive mode while the body races forward, more animated and energetic by the day. The self-image still has a lot of catching up to do, so it usually takes about three weeks or even longer for the patient to feel that he or she is really doing better. I try to prepare patients for a two-month trial period so they won't feel the drug has failed before we've given it a fair shot. About 65 to 70 percent of the patients we treat with anyone of the effective medications will have a good response over a two-month period.

However, there is still a significant proportion of our patients for whom the task of finding an effective medication can take years. So does that mean we have to give up on these people? Not at all. As you'll discover shortly, our arsenal of therapies is hardly limited to drugs alone.

# CHAPTER 15

# The Different Kinds of Drugs

## Selective Serotonin Reuptake Inhibitor (SSRI)

The SSRI drugs are popular antidepressants that are so named because they selectively block the reuptake of serotonin into the nerve cells. Evidence suggests that serotonin is an important neurotransmitter (a chemical messenger in the brain) in depression, but whether this is the primary mechanism that makes these medications work remains unproven. An SSRI called Citalpram was developed in the early 1970s but was not marketed until recently in the United States under the commercial name Celexa. Prozac was the first SSRI introduced in the United States and has become a huge market success story despite organized misinformation claims and popular misconceptions. Fluvoxamine and paroxetine (already in use in Europe somewhat earlier) and fluoxetine, and later sertraline, were introduced in the United States in the mid- to late 1980s. In particular, Prozac, because it could be taken in the form of a simple dose, reduced the need for medical testing, and a favorable side-effect profile, made the SSRIs attractive first-line therapies for most patients.

The most common side effects related to SSRIs are nausea and other gastrointestinal difficulties. Fortunately, these side effects tend to pass quickly. A long-term problem for some 20–30 percent of individuals is delayed or absent orgasm and decreased sexual interest. (These side effects appear to be relatively independent of one another.) Other noted side effects include headache, sweating, transient anxiety, tremors, drowsiness, or insomnia. Patients should allow adequate time to pass before switching medications—especially to MAO inhibitors—to allow the body to clear itself of the earlier drug and metabolites (especially for fluoxetine).

| Generic Name | Trade Name | Use | Side Effect (Insomnia) | Side Effect (Jitteriness) | Side Effect (Sedation) | Other Effects (Inhibits Cytochrome p450 enzyme 2D6) |
|---|---|---|---|---|---|---|
| Citalopram | Celexa | Depression, Anxiety | +/− | +1 | +/− | +0 to +1 |
| Fluoxetine | Prozac | Depression, Anxiety | +1 | +2 | +1 | +2 |
| Fluvoxamine | Luvox | Depression, Anxiety | +1 | +1 | +2 | +1 |
| Paroxetine | Paxil | Depression, Anxiety | +/− | +0 | +2 | +3 |
| Sertraline | Zoloft | Depression, Anxiety | +1 | +2 | +1 | +1 to +2 |
| Zimelidine (no longer on market) | — | No longer available | — | — | — | Severe flu-like syndrome with rash |

# Tricyclic Antidepressants (TCAs)

Tricyclic antidepressants (TCAs) were the first antidepressant medications developed. They are all derivatives of the first neuroleptic, Thorazine (as is carbamazepine). These three-ringed compounds inhibit the reuptake of norepinephrine and serotonin by nerve cells. The reuptake of these neurotransmitters by the same neurons that release them is the primary mechanism for turning off the inhibitory effect of norepinephrine and serotonin. By blocking the inactivation of these neurotransmitters, TCAs allow them to remain active in the space around the target neuron and to prolong or intensify their effects. Although it was assumed that leaving more serotonin and norepinephrine around the target neuron must be related to how they achieve their antidepressant effects, this theory is in doubt today.

From the early 1960s until the early 1990s, TCAs were the treatment of choice for major depression. Approximately 70 percent of the treated patients experienced substantial recovery from their symptoms over eight to twelve weeks in "efficacy studies." Admittedly these studies involve somewhat idealized study conditions and the "response" rates of 70 percent are not all responses to medication alone since about 20 percent of placebo-treated patients also show substantial recovery. However, to date, no set of medications do any better than TCAs. They are now prescribed as second-line medications, but are still considered very important antidepressants.

Fortunately, many of the side effects of the TCAs are largely temporary and most of them are tolerable. The most common side effects involve dry mouth, blurred vision, constipation, urinary retention, sedation, a fall in blood pressure when standing, and hypotension (low blood pressure). Nortriptyline in particular has been widely studied in medically ill and older patients. A very close relationship exists between blood levels and therapeutic response to the medication. It causes less orthostatic hypotension (the drop in blood pressure when rising from a sitting or prone position, which can cause dizziness) and has relatively fewer anticholinergic side effects. (These effects, related to action on the peripheral and sympathetic nervous system, include blurred vision, dry mouth, constipation, and confusion.) Electrocardiograms are necessary at least prior to prescribing TCAs because of increased slowing of conduction when conduction defects are present prior to prescription. (Conduction refers to nerve impulses transmitted to the "natural" pacemaker in the heart. This pacemaker is composed of a bundle of tissue in the heart muscles. A

| Generic Name | Trade Name | Use | Side Effect (Anticho-linergic) | Side Effect (Weight Gain) | Side Effect (Sedation) | Side Effect (Lower Blood Pressure) |
|---|---|---|---|---|---|---|
| Amitriptyline | Elavil | Depression | +3 | +2 | +3 | +3 |
| Amoxapine | Ascendin | Depression | +1 | +2 | +2 | +2 |
| Clomipramine | Anafranil | Depression, OCD | +3 | +2 | +2 | +3 |
| Desipramine | Norpramin | Depression | +1 | +1 | +1 | +2 |
| Doxepin | Sinequan | Depression | +2 | +2 | +3 | +3 |
| Imipramine | Tofranil | Depression | +3 | +2 | +2 | +3 |
| Maprotiline | Ludiomil | Depression | +2 | +1 | +1 | +2 |
| Nortriptyline | Pamelor | Depression | +1 | +1 | +1 | +1 |
| Protriptyline | Vivactil | Depression | +1 | +0 | +1 | +2 |
| Trimipramine | Surmontil | No longer available | | | | |

disturbance of this function can cause the heart to have irregular beats or stop it from beating altogether.) On the other hand, at therapeutic doses, the TCAs actually reduce common cardiac ventricular arrhythmias (pvs), although at toxic levels they may exacerbate them. For this reason TCAs are more dangerous compared to SSRIs and serotonin antagonist reuptake inhibitors (SARIs) if patients take an overdose. When patients have failed one or two full trials of other antidepressants they should receive a trial of a TCA such as nortriptyline.

## Monoamine Oxidase Inhibitors (MAOIs)

Monoamine oxidase inhibitors were developed in the early 1950s as a treatment for tuberculosis. Doctors prescribing this medication found a few of their patients to be unusually euphoric after taking the drug, more so than might be expected from recovering from their disease. Researchers looking into this phenomenon discovered that MAOIs inactivated the enzyme monoamine oxidase, which is responsible for breaking down norepinephrine, serotonin, and other monoamine neurotransmitters. By using MAOIs, the body did not break down the neurotransmitters, allowing them to accumulate.

Like all others, MAOIs have several side effects, some of which can be severe. The most common side effects include nervousness, insomnia, perspiration, dizziness, weight gain, and sexual dysfunction. Less common but more severe side effects associated with MAOIs are nausea, sweating, chills, migraines, or vascular headaches.

The most worried about side effect is hypertensive crisis. This rarely occurs, but it's usually associated with the ingestion of certain foods and medications (see list on page 186); very rarely they can occur spontaneously. This is due to the monoamine oxidase enzyme being present in the lining of the intestine and the liver. The enzymes are responsible for breaking down the amino acid tyramine naturally found in many foods. With the presence of an MAOI, the amino acid tyramine cannot be broken down. Tyramine can raise blood pressure, and so the accumulation of this amino acid can lead to hypertensive crisis.

Patients should be aware of the signs of a dangerous rise in blood pressure, including headache, stiff neck, or pounding heart. Less frequently, nausea, vomiting, and dilated pupils will occur. Should a patient experience such symptoms, he or she should immediately go to an emergency medical facility.

## Foods That Should Be Avoided:

Aged cheese, broad bean pods, beer, red wine (especially Chianti), and active yeast products (Breads are safe, as are most forms of yogurt.)

## Foods That Should Be Taken in Moderation (Unlikely to cause reaction):

Alcoholic beverages (besides beer and red wine), pasteurized cheese products, fava beans.

## Serotonin Antagonist Reuptake Inhibitors (SARIs)

Two drugs, nefazodone and trazodone, combine the ability to prevent the reuptake of serotonin and the ability to block serotonin-2 (5HT2) receptors on the neurons. By doing this, the SARIs enhance serotonin transmission via the serotonin receptors other than 5HT2 receptors. Nefazadone is also capable of weakly inhibiting the reuptake of norepinephrine.

The side effects associated with SARIs appear to be more pronounced with trazodone as compared to nefazodone. Trazadone causes frequent and more severe sedation and orthostatic hypotension (which is dose dependent), probably related to its antihistamine properties. Side effects from nefazodone include mild somnolence, and less frequently nausea, dizziness, constipation, and blurred vision compared to trazadone. Nefazadone is reported to have a lower incidence of agitation and sexual side effects as compared to tricyclics and SSRIs. Trazadone is most frequently prescribed at low doses (below doses that would have antidepressant properties) to promote sleep in depressed patients. It is not as efficient as short-acting benzodiazepines, but creates no dependency in those who use it.

## Norepinephrine Reuptake Blockers (NRI): Buproprion (Wellbutrin)

Since the 1980s several antidepressants have become available that selectively block the reuptake of norepinephrine. Buproprion is an

| Generic Name | Trade Name | Use | Side Effect (Anticholinergic) | Side Effect (Weight Gain) | Side Effect (Sedation) | Interactions |
|---|---|---|---|---|---|---|
| Phenelzine | Nardil | Depression | 2+ | 2+ | 1+ | Same as above |
| Tranylcypromine | Parnate | Depression | 1+ | 1+ | 0 | Same as above |
| Isocarboxazid | Marplan | Depression (No longer available in the U.S.) | — | — | — | Stimulants, decongestants, antihypertensives, narcotics, sedatives |
| Meclobamide | | Depression (Not available in the U.S.) | — | — | — | — |

| Generic Name | Trade Name | Use | Side Effect (Anticholinergic) | Side Effect (Weight Gain) | Side Effect (Sedation) | Other Effects |
|---|---|---|---|---|---|---|
| Nefazadone | Serzone | Antidepressant | +1 | +1 | +2 | Inhibits cytochrome P450 enzyme 3A4 |
| Trazodone | Desyrel | Antidepressant; sedative at low doses | +1 | +1 | +3 | Inhibits cytochrome P450 enzyme 3A4 |

aminoketone compound that inhibits the reuptake of norepinephrine and, to a lesser extent, dopamine. The adverse reactions associated with bupropion include gastrointestinal distress, headache, mild constipation, dry mouth, and insomnia. Three of the tricyclic antidepressants (protriptyline, desipramine, and nortriptyline) share the relatively specific noradrenergic reuptake activities of buproprion and reboxetine. Reboxetine is not yet marketed in the United States. Its side effect profile is similar to buproprion except that reboxetine is associated with mild tachycardia in about 7 percent of patients.

| Generic Name | Trade Name | Use | Side Effect (Anticho-linergic) | Side Effect (Weight Gain) | Side Effect (Sedation) | Other Side Effects |
|---|---|---|---|---|---|---|
| Buproprion | Wellbutrin | Depression, ADHD | +1 | 0 | 0 | Dyspepsia, nervousness, insomnia, headaches |
| Nomifensine | Merital | No longer available | +1 | 0 | 0 | Blood dyscrasias |
| Reboxetine | | Not available in U.S. | | | | |

# Miscellaneous Antidepressants

**Venlafaxine (Effexor):** This drug is similar to SSRIs and to the tri-cyclic antidepressants. Like the SSRIs it blocks reuptake of serotonin somewhat selectively at low doses and has a side effect profile that for the most part is like the SSRIs. Like the TCAs, it blocks reuptake of both serotonin and norepinephrine (particularly at doses above 150 mg./day). Although the side effects have the same profile as SSRIs, the exception is the risk of a sustained elevation of blood pressure at higher doses of the medication. This could be a significant risk for someone who already has high blood pressure. Venlafaxine is avail-able as a sustained release preparation which can be taken once daily. The usual plan with this medication is to increase the dose of the drug gradually until therapeutic benefit is achieved. Unlike TCAs, blood levels do not appear helpful. But unlike SSRIs, the dosage likely to produce the best result is not so predictable (i.e. fluoxetine 20 mg. per day with little benefit from increasing the dose). On the other hand it appears that the response rate is greater for each dosage increase, in the pattern of steps. The usual dosage is between 150 mg. and 375 mg. per day. Side effects include nausea, gastroin-testinal upsets, and headaches in addition to high blood pressure.

**Pindolol:** This drug is a mixed beta-blocker and agonist that has revealed some antidepressant properties in combination with other antidepressants. French studies several years ago suggested that beta agonists (including some asthma medications) might help depres-sion. Adding Pindolol to SSRI appears to be a useful either to speed the response to SSRIs or to augment them when they provide less than ideal results when used alone. Its major side effect, seen at high doses (about 40 mg per day) is moderate lowering of blood pressure or slowing of the heart rate. The usual dosage is 2.5 mg. three times a day but I have patients who have responded best at 40 mg. per day.

# Medications for Mania or Maintenance of Bipolar Disorder

Several medications exist that have antimanic effects. However, only two medications have been shown to decrease the frequency and severity of episodes of mania and depression in long-term maintenance in people with bipolar disorder (carbamazepine and lithium). While most drugs that have antidepressant effects can precipitate mania reactions (at least in bipolar patients), some do so to a lesser extent or not at all (e.g., lithium). All of these medications have anticonvulsant properties, except for lithium. Although no

| Generic Name | Trade Name | Use | Side Effect (Anticholinergic) | Side Effect (Weight Gain) | Side Effect (Sedation) | Other Effects |
|---|---|---|---|---|---|---|
| Carbamazepine (CBZ) | Tegretol | (1) Antimanic; (2) maintenance; (3) possibly antidepressive | +1 | +2 | +2 | Decreased WBC; auto-induction |
| Lithium carbonate | Lithium, Eskalith, Lithobid | (1) Antimanic; (2) antididepressive; (3) maintenance proven and FDA approved | +1 | +2 | 0 | HCTZ, NSAIDS, and low-salt diets raise levels |
| Valproic acid (VPA) | Depakote | (1) Antimanic; (2) possibly maintenance | +1 | +3 | +2 | See LTG |
| Lamictal (LTG) | Lamotrigine | Demonstrbly an antidepressant; not clear if it has anti-manic or preven-tive properties | +1 | +1 | +1 | Rash, and liver changes, especially with rapid dose escalation or with VPA |
| Neurontin (GBP) | Gabapentin | Not clear | 0 | +2 | +2 | — |
| Tobamax (TBMAx) | Topirimate | Possibly antimanic | — | weight loss | +2 | May cause depression |
| Ozcarbazepine (OCBZ) | Trileptal | Antimanic; more studies needed | +1 | +1 | +1 | Autoinduction at high doses |

one knows how these drugs work, it is believed that several diffferent anticonvulsant mechanisms found in these drugs are worthy of study.

The administration of lithium and anticonvulsant medications can be more challenging than some of the others categories of medication. The dosage is influenced by the individual's sex, age, weight (especially muscle mass), salt intake, and kidney capacity. Several of these drugs interact strongly with other medications. Frequent serum monitoring is necessary for many of these drugs in order to assess the dose–blood level relationship.

While side effects can be numerous, most of them are manageable. The most common side effects for the CBZ, VPA, and other anticonvulsants include sedation, nausea, ataxia, and weight gain. These side effects usually subside with continued treatment or with a temporary reduction in dosage. Other adverse reactions may include hand tremors, hematological effects, and impaired renal function.

## Typical Neuroleptics (Antipsychotics)

In 1952, the first conventional neuroleptic, chlorpromazine, was found to be therapeutic for schizophrenic patients. Since that time a multitude of neuroleptics have been introduced and have been found to help in several conditions other than schizophrenia. The main effect of these drugs is to block the postsynaptic dopamine receptors within the brain, which produces an almost immediate calming effect.

Many of the typical neuroleptics are sedating. Sometimes this effect can be advantageous for treatment of mania, especially to promote sleep. At other times the sedation is a serious drawback since manic patients dislike being slowed down. In addition, their families often see this effect as resulting from overmedication or else worry that the patient is being turned into a zombie. In very severe mania, however, it is difficult to get control of the manic symptoms without some degree of this sedation. Other short-term side effects observed with these neuroleptics include low blood pressure upon rising from sitting or lying position, dry mouth, constipation, blurred vision, weight gain, and sexual dysfunction. The more severe problems involve muscle tone and movement. These are called extrapyramidal side effects. Occasionally patients will exhibit Parkinsonian-like symptoms, spasms within the head and neck region, and experience an intensely uncomfortable need to walk to relieve restless sensations in their legs. These side effects are quite treatable and

| Generic Name | Trade Name | Side Effects (EPS) | Side Effect (Anticho-linergic) | Side Effect (Weight Gain) | Side Effect (Sedation) | Other Effects |
|---|---|---|---|---|---|---|
| Chlorpromazine | Thorazine | +3 | +2 | +2 | +3 | +3 hypotension |
| Fluphenazine | Prolixin | +3 | +2 | +1 | +1 | +1 hypotension |
| Haloperidol | Haldol | +4 | +1 | +1 | +1 | +1 hypotension |
| Droperidol | Inapsine | +3 | +1 | NA | +1 | For I.M. use only, +2 hypotension |
| Loxapine | Loxitane | +2 | +1 | +2 | +2 | +2 hypotension |
| Mesoridazine | Serentil | +2 | +2 | +2 | +2 | **QTc prolong,** +2 hypotension |
| Molindone | Moban | +2 | +1 | +2 | +1 | |
| Perphenazine | Trilafon | +2 | +1 | +2 | +1 | |
| Pimozide | Orap | +3 | | +1 | +1 or less | **QTc prolong** |
| Thioridazine | Mellaril | +2 | +3 | +2 | +2 | **QTc prolong,** +2 hypotension |
| Thiothixene | Navane | +2 | +1 | +1 | +1 | |
| Trifluoperazine | Stalazine | +3 | +1 | +2 | +1 | +1 hypotension |

usually short-term. The most worrisome side effect is the development of tardive dyskinesia. This sometimes debilitating disorder consists of repetitive involuntary movements of the mouth and tongue and sometimes other body parts. This unusual movement disorder was rarely reported in unmedicated schizophrenics, but now occurs with greater frequency in bipolar or depressed patients (and female and older patients) who have been on long-term neuroleptics. The syndrome initially gets worse when neuroleptics are stopped but after four to eight weeks it usually improves. It is often no longer noticeable after twelve weeks or more off the neuroleptic. For a minority of patients, the syndrome may be episodic or continuous thereafter even with the cessation of typical neuroleptics. Higher-potency D2 receptor blockers (haloperidol and fluphenazine) are more likely to produce the effect than are lower potency typical neuroleptics (and atypical neuroleptics least of all).

QTc is defined as that part of the electrical record of the electrocardiogram that reflects the depolarizing of the electrical or pacing fibers of the heart. This measurement is important because, when this effect is very prolonged, patients are more vulnerable to irregular heartbeats.

# Atypical Neuroleptics

Atypical neuroleptics have a similar efficacy and different side effects as compared to typical neuroleptics in the treatment of mania. These medications are occasionally used as part of a regimen for depressed patients, especially if they are agitated, have "psychotic" symptoms such as delusional ideas, or if they are bipolar and shift rapidly into mixed or manic states. Compared to the traditional neuroleptics, they cause EPS or "extrapyramidal" syndromes (characterized by Parkinsonian-like side effects) less frequently. They are similar to the traditional neuroleptics, in that they block dopamine receptors in the brain. The atypical neuroleptics also have a high affinity for some serotonin receptors.

The term *atypical neuroleptic* came into usage, at least in part, to describe neuroleptics that had good effects on decreasing so-called negative symptoms of schizophrenia as well as decreasing hallucinations and delusions (so-called positive symptoms) in these patients. As a group, these medications also tended to cause fewer extrapyramidal syndromes. They tend to block certain serotonin as well as dopamine neurotransmitter receptors. It turns out that none of these distinctions provide a simple way to divide these compounds into two groups (typical and atypical). Generally speaking, though, the so-called atypical neuroleptics cause less EPS.

These drugs have some side effects that are not so frequently seen with typical neuroleptics that should be taken into consideration; these include weight gain, hypotension, hypersalivation, nausea, and gastrointestinal disturbances. In addition to weight gain, which is due

| Generic Name | Trade Name | EPS | Side Effect | Side Effect (Weight Gain) | Side Effect (Sedation) | Other |
|---|---|---|---|---|---|---|
| Clozapine | Clozaril | + | Diabetes risk; occasional seizure; fainting | +3 | +4 | — |
| Olanzapine | Zyprexa | + | Diabetes risk | +3 | +3 | — |
| Quetiapine | Seroquel | + | Fainting; diabetes risk | +3 | +4 | — |
| Risperidone | Risperdal | +2 | | +1 | +2 | — |
| Ziprasidone | Geodon | + | — | 0 to +1 | 1 to +2 | Appears to have lowest rate of diabetes mellitus and weight gain |

to change in appetite levels, several of these medications are associated with a risk of type 2 diabetes mellitus (the type in which insulin levels are normal or high, but the body tissues are relatively insensitive to insulin).

## Benzodiazepines

Benzodiazepines were introduced in the 1970s as powerful and rapid-acting antianxiety or hypnotic drugs. Since that time they have been prescribed as anxiolytics, anticonvulsants, muscle relaxants, and as sedative hypnotic agents. These drugs have long been used as effective treatments for anxiety, insomnia, and more recently as additional treatments in manic states.

In patients who are acutely manic, short-acting benzodiazepines have been found to be effective tranquilizers, especially in combina-

| Generic Name | Trade Name | Use | Side Effect (Withdrawal) | Side Effect (Daytime Sedation) | Interactions | Other |
|---|---|---|---|---|---|---|
| Alprazalom | Xanax | Anxiety | +4 | +3 | Alcohol | |
| Chlordiazepoxide | Librium | Anxiety | +1 | +2 | Alcohol | |
| Clonazepam | Klonopin | Anxiety, Agitation | +2 | +3 | Alcohol | Long duration of action |
| Clorazepate | Tranxene | Anxiety | +1 | +1 | Alcohol | |
| Diazepam | Valium | Anxiety | +1 | +3 | Alcohol | |
| Estazolam | ProSom | Sleep | +2 | +2 | Alcohol | Short duration of actoin |
| *Flurazaepam* | *Dalmane* | *Sleep* | +1 | +2 | Alcohol | |
| Halazepam | Paxipam | Sleep | +1 | +1 | Alcohol | Short duration of action |
| Lorazepam | Ativan | Anxiety, Agitation | +2 | +1 | Alcohol | |
| Oxazepam | Serax | Anxiety | +2 | +1 | Alcohol | |
| Temazepam | Restoril | Sleep | +1 | +1 | Alcohol | |
| Zolpidem | Ambien | Sleep | +1 | +1 | Alcohol | Short duration of action |
| Zaleplon | Sonata | Sleep | +2 | +1 | Alcohol | Short duration of action |

tion with neuroleptics. Benzodiazepines can occasionally be used to break an incipient hypomania or mania. However, they are very effective as a sedative to calm a patient down until other medications become effective. In patients who are depressed, benzodiazepines can be used for anxiety and insomnia. Lessening these symptoms can be particularly helpful for the first two weeks of a manic episode.

The major side effects associated with benzodiazepines occur within the central nervous system. These symptoms include drowsiness, muscle weakness, ataxia, and impaired reaction time, motor coordination, short-term memory, and intellectual functions generally. These adverse effects are dramatically enhanced by the use of alcohol.

It is important to note that benzodiazepines can be abused and it is possible to become physically and psychologically dependent on them. Moreover, their effectiveness as tranquilizers and as sedatives decreases over time; therefore they are best if used in short-term regimens.

# Three Principles of Medication Use

## I. All Drugs Are Toxic

The first rule of the Hippocratic Oath is "First do no harm," and when it comes to proper use of medicines, doctors are taught that all drugs are toxic so they should be prescribed carefully and monitored in the same way. Medications act by interacting in some way with human biochemical processes. Even insulin that's prescribed for those who lack it (juvenile diabetes), because it is administered by injection, is not acting in precisely the same way that insulin made by the living human (pancreatic beta-islet cells) acts. Prescribed insulin can be given in too large an amount and can cause a fatal hypoglycemic attack. It can cause a fatal allergic reaction (since it usually comes from and is manufactured with small amounts of nonhuman products). All the same, it also is a life saver when used properly and under doctor's supervision.

## II. Profitable Drug Companies Are Good Things to Have

The above sentence sounds almost anti-American if we are to judge from public opinion polls. Drug companies come in for special condemnation these days for making "obscene" profits off people who can't afford their products. Dr. James Watson, the Nobel laureate who started the U.S. Human Genome Project, said that he learned a few surprising things as he went around the country in the early 1990s to marshal support for the $3 billion effort to sequence the entire genome. What he discovered was that "you couldn't use the term 'bad genes'" without arousing a great deal of consternation, and that Americans didn't like the idea that scientific discoveries would be turned into "profit-making products for large drug companies." His point, of course, was that the companies didn't invent the system and that the U.S. Government almost never invested enough in research to bring a drug safely "to market," in other words, to make it available for widespread use.

For better *and* for worse, the pharmaceutical companies are the only institutions that can do the work necessary to develop medications and distribute them to the people who need them. If they didn't expect to reap a big profit at the end of a successful venture, they would never venture in the first place. Although some question the exact number, the pharmaceutical manager's association estimates that it costs $500 million to get a new drug to the market.

## III. The DSM/Managed Care/ Pharmaceutical Complex

In his farewell address President Eisenhower told the country that the size and scope of our military forces mission could cause unforeseen problems. He called it the "Military-Industrial Complex." In psychiatry we see a similar thing developing in our strange managed-care system for psychiatry. I call it the *DSM*/Managed Care/Pharmaceutical Complex. Overzealous classifying and splitting of psychiatric symptoms especially in the anxiety and depression arena has the effect of creating more "indications" for the pharmaceutical firms to target in order to get new drugs into the market. These successful hits create the rationales for managed care companies to limit the access of anxious and depressed patients to any treatments other than pills. This creates greater interest in expansion of the *DSM* whenever the committee reviews possible additional categories.

# CHAPTER 16

Psychotherapy:
Treating the Person

Medical professionals are increasingly accepting of the idea that depression is a real disease and are using practical methods of treatment that are specifically designed for patients with serious psychiatric conditions. Almost no mental health professional follows Freudian theory in that they view depressive states as diseases not as a product of unconscious drives. As a result, there are more therapists who offer valuable support to the medical management of patients with depression, manic depression, and practical therapies for patients in different stages of illness and recovery. In addition, these newer "name-brand" psychotherapies—such as interpersonal and cognitive—require less training and are not as expensive or time-consuming for the patient compared to the psychotherapy of thirty years ago.

Throughout this book I've made the statement that classical depression isn't the same thing as being discouraged. But its social impact is large enough to discourage the patient and all of their loved ones. It affects not only the individual who is suffering from the illness but families and friends as well. Treating depression—like treating cancer or hemophilia—is more of a partnership of doctors, patients, and loved ones than it is a matter of just writing prescriptions It's one thing to recover in terms of mood and vitality; it's quite another to regain functioning and adapt to everyday life at home and on the job. In a five-year study, one of the longest controlled studies done maintaining a recovery, patients who had first been treated for acute depression and then recovered were put on one of five regimens. One received antidepressants in doses equivalent to what they took when they were ill; a second group received antidepressants, also at the same dosage levels, but in addition received psychotherapy once a month. The three other groups either received psychotherapy alone or received placebo pills and brief medical checkups. The patients who were given both antidepressants and psychotherapy did best. They experienced the fewest relapses and remained well for longer periods. The patients on medication alone also did quite well though they had more relapses in the first year. Among those groups who were treated without medication but did participate in psychotherapy sessions, relapses had occurred at a much higher rate. The patients on placebo pills and who received no therapy did worst of all.

My interpretation of the message from this study is that we must treat the disease and the patient with empathy. Psychotherapy and counseling encompass a wide range of psychological strategies that can promote recovery. I am not convinced that there is only one best method to achieve this goal. One of my teachers, Dr. Jerome Frank, noted in his book, *Persuasion and Healing,* that very small, symbolic things can help a patient—like a doctor wearing a white coat, perhaps because it is so identified as the sign of a healing person in much the way a uniform distinguishes a police officer or a solider. Dr. Frank found in his studies that if the patient regarded the doctor as competent, genuinely concerned, and as someone who could be confided in, then the patient would derive greater therapeutic benefit. It is largely the doctor-patient relationship that makes psychotherapy work. First of all, you have to expect that you're going to get the help you need. You then become more ready to become emotionally engaged in the therapy. And you retain more and get more out of the sessions since you are emotionally stimulated. These elements predict success at least in achieving the realistic goals of therapy, regardless of the particular psychiatric theory espoused by the therapist.

## Setting Goals for Psychotherapy

What is the role of a doctor in a therapeutic setting? Or to put it another way: What is the implicit contract—the treatment contract, if you will—between the doctor and the patient? The first order of business of the doctor is to examine and diagnose you, then make a formulation including a diagnosis, prognosis, and treatment plan in a helpful and constructive way without misleading you about your chances for recovery. In broader terms, the treatment contract commits the doctor to connect with a patient's experience or "walk in your shoes" in order to understand what you are going through.

What are realistic goals in psychotherapy for severely depressed patients? I believe it is crucial to help patients understand and accept the diagnosis of what they have (the clinical diagnosis). If you're the patient you need to understand and accept that the disease responds best to a combination of medication and psychotherapy. You also need to accept the doctor's traditional, pastoral caring role, at least partially, and view us as modern competent practitioners in treating a diseased body or body part. As you might expect, balancing the humanistic and more mechanical or scientific part of a doctor's job is not always easy. None of us do it as well as we'd like every day. The ancient symbol of medicine, the caduceus, which shows two snakes twisted around each other on a staff, exemplifies the dual role of the doctor. One snake represents the god of knowledge and science (the words are derived from the same Latin root) and the other the god of humanity or conscience.

In a well-intentioned effort to give patients more responsibility for their own treatment we may be saddling them with a burden that is too much for them. To take just one example, in a study of informed consent—in this case it was agreeing to electroconvulsive shock therapy, or ECT—a panel of judges and lawyers was asked to give opinions about the value of a number of doctor-patient sessions recorded on film. When asked whether the patients had understood enough of what the doctor had told them to give their informed consent to the procedure, the panel was unanimous in its verdict. The jurists and lawyers said no. It wasn't that the doctors weren't getting information across (these conferences went on for two or three hours) but patients confronted almost insurmountable difficulties in understanding it. For one thing, there was a disparity between the amount of knowledge the doctors had (a great deal) and the amount the patient had (not very much).

It is not possible for a doctor or anyone else to compress twenty years of medical training and experience into a half-hour or even a half-day. Even if we could, the patient has so much riding on the outcome of the treatment that his or her mind is clouded by emotion. Informed consent relies on contract law (the signing of a contract) but this can leave the patient feeling on his own. The doctor-patient relationship has shrunk too far.

In treating the depressed patient, the psychotherapist's starting point is probably as important as the method of therapy. If the therapist believes that your problem is a normal reaction to an abnormal situation and does not consider the possibility of depression, then the therapy might do no good at all. Actually, the therapy could actually be counterproductive if the therapist held the view that taking medication was somehow a sign of weakness based either on his or her failure to diagnose your condition or on his or her perception that depression is not a real disease.

For example, I once had a suicidal patient who had been abused when she was eleven. She didn't repress the memory or let it fester, not at all. She brought it up with her mother and talked it through shortly after the abuse happened. The mother was very supportive and they dealt with the perpetrator through appropriate channels. My patient never felt any guilt over the encounter. She did acknowledge, however, that the incident affected her sexual life with her husband, though it hadn't ruined it altogether. She'd remained otherwise healthy until she was in her forties, when she had her first episode of severe major depression. The therapist she first went to, however, was convinced that the depression had to be caused by the abuse. He felt that she was having this problem three decades later because she hadn't confronted it well enough when it had happened. While the therapist was well intentioned, he was blinded to the reality of her depressive illness, which was very clear-cut. He said that the psychotherapy wasn't helping (despite meeting twice a week for one and a half years) because, in his opinion, "She's gotten into this hopeless thing." Once, he went on, she was over this "hopeless thing," the psychotherapy would allow her to deal with the "real" problem. What he didn't understand, of course, was that the "hopeless thing" *was* the problem. Treatment wasn't working in this case because the therapist hadn't recognized the illness and the patient was too ill to engage in psychotherapy. It was all she could do to hold onto life and call for help.

Experienced clinicians (no matter their degree or guiding theory) are more apt to recognize the depression and to adapt their treatment plan to the patient and his or her illness. So assessment and diagnostic skill are critical for the success of psychotherapy.

## Which Psychotherapies Work Best

Let's turn to the methods of psychotherapy. In the most severe forms of depression and mania, interpersonal and cognitive psychotherapy (the two most-studied psychotherapies for depression) require that a patient be able to concentrate and have a modicum of hopefulness in order to work with the therapist. So if you are severely depressed and despondent, and perhaps unable to get out of bed, well, you just won't benefit from much psychological help. The most we can do is to keep reminding patients of the simple truth: that eventually they will get better and that we will keep treating them until they do.

When it comes to recommending psychotherapy, only two types of therapy—interpersonal and cognitive—have been shown to have positive effects when used alone in moderate depression. A number of studies suggest that patients in either type of therapy for a year can benefit. But my guess is that, as in the case of antidepressants, several different types of therapy will work equally well if we know when and where to apply them.

I said at the outset that depression can be especially insidious in terms of its impact on relationships. Interpersonal therapy, which was formulated in the 1970s, can be thought of as a form of common-sense psychoanalysis; its objective is to resolve difficulties in relationships. There's no doubt that helping patients cope better with their relationships has a carryover effect during and after the illness, especially if the illness is acknowledged as a force unto itself and not the consequence of a problem in any relationship. For one thing, if you can be assured that your family is supportive your anxieties about the treatment and recovery are likely to diminish. For another, having an opportunity to work out problems in your relationships in therapy may have a more beneficial effect if you suffer a relapse in the future. You and your family will be better prepared to contend with the stress, which might help mitigate its impact. But don't let me overdo it here. This illness, like asthma, can come on when you have done everything possible to prevent it. If you do have a relapse (and you didn't stop your medication and weren't abusing drugs or alcohol), then you can hardly hold yourself to blame.

By contrast, what cognitive therapy does especially well is to help patients address what seems to be a catastrophic event or an undeservedly injurious event. Let's take one example from an astute researcher named Ellen Frank, who has worked with rape victims. What Dr. Frank found in her studies was that the classic reaction of a rape victim is a feeling that her life has been ruined. In such cases the cognitive therapist tries to be supportive while gently challenging the belief that the patient's life is destroyed forever. The therapist's goal is to make the patient understand that what happened was surely terrible but that it was not her fault. The therapist asks the patient if she can think of any positive aspects to her life. Usually she can. *Your husband has been very supportive you say, so what's that about?* Or think of it another way: "*My life is ruined*" *is one story, but it isn't the only story. I've been hurt, but I have love and support and the resilience to put my life back together—that's another story.* On the other hand, if someone is too severely depressed, she might not buy into any other version of her story than the one she is fixated on: *My life is over.* When she gets somewhat better she'll be able to recognize and appreciate the fact that her husband isn't going to leave her and still loves her.

In the past some cognitive therapists drew a cause-and-effect association between what they characterized as "negative thinking" and depression. That is no longer the belief of Dr. Aaron Beck, who developed cognitive therapy. He says that he doesn't believe that "bad" thinking habits cause depression. I agree with him. So it's important for people who are depressed to realize that they may not be able to stop negative thinking until we do something to relieve the depressive illness.

Many other aspects of depression are amenable to forms of psychological therapy. Several types of behaviors—anorexia nervosa and alcoholism are two strong examples—may worsen the depression and can make prospects for recovery much more difficult. In many cases, where alcoholism and substance abuse is a problem, you may first have to deal with the destructive behavior before you can effectively treat the depression. Most of the time if the patient is not too addicted or enslaved by the behavior, the patient and doctor will be able to work on both the behavior and the illness at the same time. This kind of psychotherapy is behaviorally oriented.

How does a behaviorist work with these patients? At Johns Hopkins program for people with severe eating disorders the plan is to reinforce good eating habits by having a nurse sit with the patient to ensure that the patient not only eats, but normalizes their eating patterns. We'll tell the person when he or she is falling back in "eating disorder behavior" since that is how their behavior will again go out of control. Behaviorists would say that we're gaining "stimulus control" by putting these patients at a table, giving them silverware, and making sure that they exercise "normal" eating manners. Our objective is to encourage the patient to practice normal (nutritional and social) eating behavior to readapt the behavior to normal purposes rather than allow them to focus solely on losing weight. Weight gain or loss follows the behavior. Patients with eating disorders usually regard this type of therapy as intrusive at first. But they have lost control over their eating. So the staff needs to take control temporarily in order to help the patient regain control later. Behaviors are in many ways tougher to deal with than diseases and sometimes patients refuse our attempts to help them. By and large, though, we can succeed with these patients by being as persistent as possible, encouraging their healthy instincts and discouraging their unhealthy urges.

## The Future of Psychotherapy

With the breathtaking pace of research on depressive illness, it's certain that psychotherapy is going to change dramatically over the next few decades. One change I hope to see is a greater focus on particular illnesses and patients and less focus on the specific theory of psychological dynamics. That is to say, psychotherapy ought to be addressing such questions as, what do depressed patients have in common and what do they best respond to? Similarly, what are the psychological needs of their families and what helps them feel less guilty and more realistically optimistic and supportive? Just as I believe we will need general practitioners to diagnose and treat depression, so I also believe that all health care professionals will be able to help patients and their families recognize that it's the disease that is the cause of the psychological mayhem and not the reverse.

## The Different Kinds of Healers

Just as I was about to begin my clinical rotations as a Johns Hopkins Medical School student, I attended an introductory lecture called "Who Is a Clinician and What Does He Do?" Although the topic didn't mean much to me when I saw it listed, it was to have a lasting influence on all my work since then. This lecture, by professor of medicine Dr. Philip Tumulty, was given to all members of the Johns Hopkins Medical School class of 1972. Dr. Tumulty explained that clinical training would teach us the methods for taking histories and conducting physical examinations, ordering laboratory tests and interpreting test results. Learning these skills was important, he said, insofar as they served our primary function, which was to manage all aspects of an illness and its impact on the patient. He went on to say, "We need to understand that some diseases might be terminal, but none are hopeless." He emphasized that even terminally ill patients respond positively to treatments that alleviate their physical and psychological pain and sense of isolation. These patients are most responsive when a positive doctor-patient relationship develops. The doctor's task, he argued, is far more psychological than it might at first appear.

Many people think of psychiatrists in terms of their skills in the use of medications and psychotherapies. I believe the central role of a psychiatrist—and of any physician—is to evaluate and formulate the patient's problem so that an accurate diagnosis can be made and a prudent and helpful treatment plan emerges. Just as central to the clinician's mission is educating and supporting the patient through his or her illness. This objective remains true when the diagnosis is clear and when it is not, when treatments work well and when they don't, as long as the patient and the family need us. As I said, Dr. Tumulty's talk carried a powerful and unexpected message.

Given the importance of the doctor-patient relationship, you might ask what type of doctor is in the best position to help you. That brings us to the question of what exactly psychotherapy is and who psychiatrists are.

The answer to this question is a contentious one. That's because the field of psychiatry (like medicine at the turn of the twentieth century, with its competing osteopaths, homeopaths, herbalists, and the like) is still bedeviled by battles between different "therapeutic camps." We have, for instance, psychoanalytic, psychodynamic, behavioral, cognitive behavioral, psychopharmacological, and biological camps. As confusing as the situation is today, it's not as bad as it was a few decades ago. The trouble is that we have yet to realize the ideal of a common understanding of the condition we treat and an appreciation of the training and talents that different health professions bring to their patients. Put plainly, all professional counselors, physicians, and health professionals, regardless of which camp they come from, are psychotherapists.

So what does a psychotherapist do? Simply stated, the psychotherapist uses psychological means to help patients. A psychotherapist is a physician, a psychologist, a social worker, a nurse, or any other type of health professional who understands a patient's condition and participates in treatment. Psychotherapy constitutes an important part of the work of all these professionals. For example, psychiatrists, because of the specialization of their training, will be better able to treat patients in some situations, while a social worker will be more critical in others.

Some psychiatrists refer to themselves as psychopharmacologists, a term meant to describe their expertise in the use of psychotropic medications. In the United States, psychopharmacology has never been recognized as a professional specialty; no school offers a degree in psychopharmacology nor does any state license a psychopharmacologist to practice. (Psychopharmacology is, however, officially recognized in Italy and possibly other European countries.) I should note that recently an organization called the American College of Psychopharmacologists was formed, which offers membership and gives exams to psychiatrists.

Given the number of camps that exist, and the emphasis on "therapeutic orientation," I can understand why people often ask me what my orientation is or whether I believe in drugs or in psychotherapy. Some psychiatrists, for instance, refer to themselves as psychodynamic, while others call themselves biological or psychopharmacological. Still others, like myself and the majority of psychiatrists, believe that labels are less important. Our critical job is to evaluate patients' problems and to apply medical and psychological treatments based on the different needs of our patients. This objective should be the same for all clinicians, regardless of specialty or orientation.

So, you might ask, what *is* the best type of treatment for depression: drugs or therapy? The answer is that it's usually a combination of both. The trick is knowing which types of medicines and therapy to use and when, and that comes from training and experience. We don't pick doctors to treat diabetes based on whether they prefer insulin therapy to diets; we expect them to know when and how to use any treatments that are available to them. By the same token, it doesn't matter whether someone is a child psychiatrist, a geriatric psychiatrist, or a forensic psychiatrist; the basic skills and responsibilities are the same: helping the patient and the family through the illness from start to finish.

## Different Kinds of Mental Health Professionals

When you decide to go for help for any emotional problem or behavior problem, whom do you go to? Many medical professionals are available who can and will help. Who you should see naturally depends on what is wrong with you and what is needed to fix it. It would be a great deal simpler if you could consult one group of professionals who would be able to tell you what is wrong and then arrange your treatment with the ideal health professional, if one is needed. In many countries this is actually how it works because their health care systems are centralized. But in the United States however, where the system is a hodgepodge of private doctors, health care networks, and government programs such as Medicare, you have to educate yourself if you're going to make it work for you.

As it turns out, several types of health and mental health professionals can help you even though their approaches to diagnosis and treatment may differ because of their training and background. However, it should be noted that the critical first step of making the evaluation and diagnosis can be done, to some extent, by all the professionals described below.

**Psychiatrist**: The psychiatrist is a college graduate who has completed four years of medical school, a year of internship, and three or more years of residency training, evaluating and treating patients under the direct supervision of senior psychiatrists. All psychiatrists are physicians who have had four additional years of specialized training in psychiatry. They are trained to assess and treat patients who have problems in mental life, regardless of the cause. In order to practice they must pass a licensing exam (national or state) and obtain a medical license from the state in which they work. Fulfilling these conditions makes them "board eligible" to take the examinations (written and oral) for certification by the American Board of Psychiatry and Neurology. While being board certified isn't necessary to practice, it is a professionally recognized sign of qualification. Some psychiatrists have special qualifications in child, geriatric, or forensic (legal) psychiatry in addition to board certification as a general adult psychiatrist.

**Psychologist**: Psychologists, with a doctoral (Ph.D.) degree, are trained to see patients for evaluation and treatment. Psychologists are not trained in pharmacology or physiology. However, they have extensively studied cognitive or intellectual functioning as it relates to normal and abnormal brain structures. Clinical psychologists usually must have obtained a Ph.D. or Psy.D. (Doctor of Psychology), served a one-year internship in a hospital or a clinic, and have completed a research thesis. A doctoral degree requires three or more years of graduate study. Psychologists with a Ph.D. qualify for a wide range of teaching, research, clinical, and counseling positions in universities, medical schools, hospitals, school systems, private industry, and government. Psychologists with a Doctor of Psychology degree usually work in clinical positions and use the title "doctor" before their name.

**Clinical Social Worker:** *Social Workers* provide much of the psychotherapy in the United States. They work in a variety of settings, such as, hospitals, public and private agencies, and health clinics to name a few. The setting, qualification and expertise of the social worker will determine his or her role in the treatment of patients/clients. Social workers have an MSW (Masters in Social Work), which includes 2 years of closely supervised field placements or "internships." An LCSW (Licensed Certified Social Worker) has passed an exam for certification from the Board of Social Work Examiners and has been licensed to practice in his or her state. An LCSW-C (Licensed Certified Social Worker-Clinical) or clinical social worker must have 2 years of post graduate clinical training and also pass an exam for certification and licensing from the Board. Some clinical social workers have a national license which is a BCD (Board Certified Diplomat). Continuing education is mandatory for all. In order to practice psychotherapy independently one must have their LCSW-C.

**Nurse:** Many levels of nursing qualification are relevant to mental health treatment. However, registered nurses are more likely to be involved in mental health intervention than are licensed nurses (LPNs). Because licensed nurses have less extensive training, they usually do not practice psychotherapy outside of a supervised setting. To earn a degree as an RN, nurses have two options: they can either obtain an undergraduate degree and then go on to nursing school for two years, or else they can go directly from high school into a university nursing school and earn both an RN and an BS or BSN. Nurses are required to take basic science courses in anatomy, physiology, and pharmacology; in addition, they also spend time practicing under supervision in clinical settings such as hospitals and clinics. Their training also gives them the expertise to function as counselors. In that capacity they are in a position to educate patients and families about their treatments (dosages, names of medications, side effects, and so on) and offer the patient crucial support through difficult illnesses in collaboration with other medical professionals. Nurse practitioners have a master's degree and further years of clinical training and in certain states they can prescribe medications.

**Occupational Therapist**: Occupational therapy (OT) is a health and rehabilitation profession that helps people regain, develop, and build skills that are important for independent functioning, health, and well-being. Occupational therapy practitioners work with people of all ages who, because of illness, injury, or developmental or psychological impairment, need specialized assistance. OT practitioners can be credentialed at the professional (occupational therapist) level after completing a four-year baccalaureate, five year masters, or at the technical (occupational therapy assistant) level with a two-year associate degree program. More than three hundred accredited baccalaureate or associate degree programs in OT are offered at colleges and universities throughout the United States. OT practitioners must also complete a supervised fieldwork program and pass a national certification exam. Until recently occupational therapists seldom assumed the role of psychotherapist for patients with depression or manic depression, but this situation may be changing, for two reasons. First, occupational therapists have expertise in making functional assessments: how well does a person carry out his or her daily routines at home and on the job. Second, successful treatment doesn't end when the patient no longer requires a doctor's care; it also means making sure the patient is able to transition back to previous roles once the illness is over. This trend suggests that the role of occupational therapists as active participants in psychotherapeutic treatment process will grow in coming years.

**Physicians**: All physicians (general practitioners, family practitioners, internists, and specialists in other fields) attend medical school, intern at a hospital, and must pass state or national board tests to qualify to practice in the state where they live. With the exception of the general practitioner, all physicians must complete residency training ranging from two to seven years before they are able to practice in their field of specialty. How good are doctors without psychiatric training in diagnosing and treating depression and manic depression? The answer, which is applicable to every other health profession we've cited, is that it depends on the professional's training and experience. As far as experience is concerned, the more the better, so long as it includes treating patients for depression.

## Why Can't Psychiatrists Go It Alone?

There are too many patients in the U.S. with depression and manic depression for psychiatrists to help everyone who needs us. Even if the load is shared with the large number of available professional psychotherapists, there simply aren't enough psychiatrists to provide the initial evaluation and medication management for all depressed patients. If we're to meet the needs of everyone with depression and manic depression we have to call upon the services and skills of all health professionals (and not just those I've described here). Because most patients consult their family physician first when they have depression, these physicians have a special role to play in diagnosing and treating patients with the illness in collaboration with other professionals—especially psychiatrists—when it comes to more complicated cases.

# CHAPTER 17

∽

# ECT, Light, and Other Medical Treatments

All along, I've been underscoring the fact that medications can alleviate about 65–70 percent of major depression within a two-month or two-year period. What about those who have gotten little or no help from these drugs? Several other treatments, some old and others new, are available and some have proven effective. I'll start by discussing one of the oldest treatments, which, while still regarded as controversial in the press, is actually used more today than twenty years ago.

Many years ago I was practicing at a large city hospital when I became aware of a pronounced thumping that reverberated throughout my office. It went on for days, but I didn't think anything of it because of the noise from a construction site nearby. I assumed the thumping was coming from pile drivers. Then one of the psychiatric residents popped into my office and said, "Ray, we've got a problem. That noise you hear is coming from a manic patient we've got in the seclusion room on the inpatient unit. She's so agitated that if we let her out she'd be injuring people. She's determined to get out—she's beating her arm against the wall and the wall is starting to come down." What's more, the resident went on, it seemed that she'd bitten off a piece of her plastic bedpan and swallowed it. The resident was desperate; he didn't know what to do. Already she was on a huge dose of the most powerful neuroleptic we had, receiving over 200 mg when the usual dose was 3 to 30 mg a day. "We've got to consider this a medical emergency," he concluded. When I later took a look at the seclusion room for myself I discovered that the resident hadn't been exaggerating: the wall had been reduced to chicken wire and slats, and would have to be rebuilt.

The solution that suggested itself to me observing this wreckage was a treatment that has a long history but to this day carries an undeserved stigma reserved for leeches and dunking chairs: electro-convulsive therapy (ECT), otherwise known as shock treatment. Com-pared to medication and other treatments available to us, ECT is the most immediate and strikingly effective treatment for severe depres-sion and mania. After giving her consent, the patient needed only two ECT treatments to get to a point where she could participate in group therapy. And she needed just another two and a half weeks to make a full recovery from the episode. The transformation, achieved by ECT, in this patient and others like her was little short of miraculous.

## How ECT Was Invented

As a treatment, ECT predates all antidepressants and lithium by ten to fifteen years. It owes its origins to a Hungarian psychiatrist named Lazlo Meduna, who theorized that epilepsy and psychosis were incompatible; that is to say that people who had epilepsy had some natural protection because of their illness against the delusions and psychotic episodes that are a central part of schizophrenia. So, Meduna reasoned, if you, in effect, "gave" epilepsy to people with schizophrenia or other mental disorders by inducing seizures in them, you might relieve their psychotic symptoms. His theory was mistaken on a number of counts. First of all, epilepsy does not pro-vide protection against schizophrenia, nor did convulsive therapy prove very effective in schizophrenia, either. However, as is done with most new treatments in medicine, a variety of patients were tested on it. Two groups of patients showed marked beneficial responses—those with severe depression and those with mania.

At first Meduna employed inhaled camphor, a naturally derived compound, to trigger seizures. But these seizures were difficult to control once they started. Injections of another drug that was also capable of inducing seizures presented the same problem. Then two Italian researchers—Dr. Lucio Bini, a psychiatrist, and Dr. Ugo Cer-letti, a neurophysiologist—began to use electricity to produce seizures, first in pigs and then in humans. Electrically induced seizures, they discovered, were both effective and safe and could be easily controlled.

Up until their discovery of the value of ECT, the two scientists had been trying to determine whether epilepsy caused the brain damage during the seizures or whether the occasional obstruction of the air-ways during a seizure was responsible. The results of the Italians' research showed that while the shocks themselves caused no brain damage they did have a calming effect on both the animals and the humans they tested. To stop the flow of the current all they had to do was remove the electrodes placed on the forehead. Like Meduna, they found that patients with the most severe forms of depression and mania experienced a relatively quick recovery once they underwent treatment. The early forms of ECT, however, carried some risks that have been reduced by modern methods of anesthesia and advances in electronics.

Before anesthesia was used, a few of the patients sustained fractures of their limbs or vertebrae during ECT treatment. With anesthesia, however, fractures are almost unheard of and compression fractures of vertebrae have disappeared except among aged patients who might have osteoporosis ("brittle bones"). And perhaps just as reassuringly, patients now receive anesthesia during ECT and so they don't feel a thing under ECT.

## How Much Memory Is Lost After ECT?

Memory loss is another concern about ECT. One form of memory loss comes about in the immediate aftermath of the treatment when the patient is confused and disoriented but usually recovers in one to two hours. A more persistent type of short-term memory retrieval comes on slowly but also resolves more slowly, between one to six months. In any case, the first type of memory loss is largely due to the anesthesia rather than the procedure itself. Patients coming out of any surgery will experience the same thing. Actually, patients who have undergone ECT recover more quickly since they've been given less anesthesia to begin with. The second form of memory loss involves an inability to recall events that occurred just before and just after the treatment. This does not appear ordinarily until a patient has had four to six ECTs. The memory loss may extend a few months back; the loss is spotty and it's more intense the closer you get to the ECT time period. However, the memories might not be truly lost. "Misfiled" might be a more accurate term since they can be retrieved in large chunks by patients after ECT stops. Some patients may lose a degree of spatial orientation ability and find themselves confused if they get behind the wheel. This type of "loss," too, is usually transient.

There is yet a third form of memory loss: a temporary reduction in the patient's ability to learn new things. While the loss is often not noticeable either to the patient or the family, it can be detected by memory tests after three to six ECTs. At nine months after ECT, however, there are no detectable differences between the learning abilities of those who have undergone the procedure and those who have not.

Recent advances in administering ECT have also helped reduce memory loss. Whereas in the past the electrodes were placed on both sides of the patient's head, equally good results have been attained when the electrodes are deployed only on the right, or nondominant side. Most patients benefit as much with this type of unilateral (one-sided) ECT as opposed to bilateral ECT. At the same time, researchers have succeeded in cutting down the amount of electricity per treatment and delivering it in a more concentrated way. By administering electric pulses, lasting no more than a fraction of a second, instead of in one large wave, the patient gets less current while still receiving the full benefit of the treatment.

A vivid account of what transient memory loss after ECT is like comes to us from an English psychiatrist who received ECT while he was battling his own depression: "When an event, entirely forgotten, is brought to one's notice, it sounds completely strange, foreign and unknown. One has the feeling that a confabulation is being presented: the details of the account seem unnecessarily elaborate. . . . Then a fragment of the story rings true; a name is recognized, for example, and a series of events or facts come suddenly to mind, in a linear sequence. One is suddenly aware of a curious faculty to feel one's way along the sequence, as one element leads to the next. The revelation has a marked quality of unreality. . . . Although it is a strange experience, it is in some ways quite delightful. It is as if one is seeing at least some aspects of life through new eyes."

He then proceeds to describe what it's like to experience a temporary loss of one's "map." "With the second course of ECT . . . my topographical schemata have become totally disorganized. I must look at a map to visualize the route from A to B, and I have forgotten completely the patterns that previously have been almost second nature to me."

And yet for this patient the ephemeral memory problems were well worth it given the outcome. "Whereas before treatment I became tearful with very little provocation and felt intensely sad out of all proportion to the stimulus, after one single treatment I was no longer crushed by my chance sadness. The troublesome symptoms of irritability also subsided early in the course of treatment."

There are also some physical side effects that can result from ECT about which patients should be, aware. Frequently, it can cause headaches and muscle aches, especially in the jaw, that are probably attributable to the local dispersion of the current in the muscles of the face. And as with any surgical procedure, general anesthesia (the effect of which lasts only three to five minutes) poses some risk, with only a very slight chance of death. Twenty years ago the risk was about 3 in 100,000 treatments but that risk is probably less now due to recent significant improvements in anesthesia techniques and monitoring.

## How Effective Is ECT?

About 80 percent of the patients who undergo the ECT procedure will do better after two to four weeks. They show a higher response rate and a quicker antidepressant response than they would on medication. So why don't we use it for more patients? The reason is that ECT has demonstrated effectiveness in the short-term. The rate of relapses, in the absence of medication, is fairly high. We're talking about a matter of months. As a result, almost all patients who have recurrent depressions will need medications after ECT.

Whom do we consider the ideal patients for ECT in light of the pattern of benefits and risks? We recommend ECT for the most severely ill patients because they are less likely to respond to medications. A depressed or manic patient who needs to be in the hospital because of delusions or intense suicidal thoughts would be a prime candidate for the procedure. Patients who refuse to eat and as a result may be at risk of dying of malnutrition or else whose depression or mania has aggravated an existing medical condition would also benefit from ECT. The basic criteria for using ECT are:

- Intensity of suffering
- The risks inherent in the patient's condition
- The likelihood of immediate success

ECT is also useful for severe mania as well as for depression, although we have more rapid-acting medicines for mania. In addition, it can be difficult for a doctor to gain the manic patient's trust and persuade them that he or she needs ECT.

How frequently is ECT used? At Johns Hopkins, for example, we may have as many as fifty severely depressed patients on our wards at any one time; about 10 percent of them will receive ECT. It remains a powerful treatment with major benefits whose risks are both minor and relatively short-lived.

Why does electroshock therapy work? We don't know. The mechanism of therapeutic action is not understood. But there's some evidence, from studies on animals, that ECT and antidepressants cause similar responses in their effects on neurotransmitter receptors and the activity of genes in specific brain regions.

## Why Did ECT Get Such a Bad Reputation?

If we know ECT works for so many patients, even though we do not know how it works, why has it gotten such a bad reputation? Certainly the way in which it has been portrayed in many movies, particularly the Oscar-winning *One Flew Over the Cuckoo's Nest,* has instilled a fear of the procedure in people's minds. When I was a first-year medical student I also had the impression that ECT was outmoded and harmful, until one of my professors introduced me to a patient who was getting ECT. I witnessed firsthand the transformation of the patient from hopeless back to a relaxed caring person. That was all it took to shake off my bias, but I regarded it like all treatments for depression and mania—as a blessing even if it did have certain drawbacks, such as being effective for only limited periods. Still, many patients recommended for ECT, especially for the first time, tend to believe the worst about it. It's very difficult to imagine yourself going through it. But when you're talking about medical procedures you have to keep in mind that other surgical procedures—a spinal tap, let's say—often aren't pleasant to watch in spite of the fact that both ECT and a spinal tap are very safe and pose little risk to the patients. ECT also acquired a tarnished image because of its overuse soon after it was introduced in the United States. It worked rapidly and so effectively in many patients—and with few serious side effects even when it didn't work—that a few psychiatrists were impelled to apply it for almost all of their psychiatric inpatients. But as happens in so many instances, the pendulum swung too far in the other direction and ECT almost disappeared from hospitals altogether. Since the 1980s, however, ECT has made a comeback and is regularly used for the most severely depressed patients and the occasional manic patient who doesn't respond to other treatments.

The apprehension with which patients look upon ECT is borne out in a recent survey conducted in England, showing that about 40 percent of patients approach the therapy with some degree of anxiety. But their attitude undergoes a sharp reversal once they've actually had ECT. In retrospect, 82 percent of the patients interviewed considered it no more anxiety-provoking than a dental appointment. More important, 78 percent said they were helped by the procedure and 80 percent stated that they wouldn't mind having it again if they needed to.

What happens, though, if ECT doesn't work? Does that mean that there's nothing more we can do for these patients? Quite the contrary. We have patients who fail ECT and yet who will respond favorably to the next medication we pull out of a box. There is a misconception that ECT is a last resort-treatment for depression.

## Lifting Mood with Magnets

Someday it's possible, perhaps even likely, that electricity, too, will no longer be needed to induce therapeutic seizures. That brings us to another, still experimental, treatment called repeated transcranial magnetic stimulation (rTMS). Like so many other treatments we've talked about, magnetic stimulation came about as a result of chance. In an effort to develop lighter and cheaper imaging machines to study the brain, researchers at the National Institutes of Health found that the small magnetic resonance imaging instrument created a sudden lift in a patient's mood when it was held on the right side of the head. (When they experimented on the left side they found that the magnetic stimulation made patients feel depressed.) The use of magnetic stimulus to produce a localized magnetic field seems to produce at least temporary changes in mood. Since certain regions of the brain seem more implicated in depression and others in manias, these devices may one day make it possible to treat patients with a less potent but more precisely localized stimulation. Transcranial magnetic stimulation is also being studied as a way to perform convulsive treatment since a strong magnetic field can induce a seizure with many fewer side effects compared to electrical current.

## Lifting Mood with Lights

Of all the therapeutic tools we have at our disposal, none could possibly be more economical, more low tech, or more easily accessible or convenient than bright lights. The use of bright lights to treat what has become known in the popular press as Seasonal Affect Disorder (SAD) came about because of the experience of a single patient. An astute observer of his own condition, he kept meticulous notes, recording the dates each year when he would be hit with a depressive episode. He proceeded to share his observations with his doctor, who agreed that there was a definite pattern to his episodes: they invariably began in the fall with diminishing sunlight and went away in spring. Though he was the first to bring the disorder to the attention of the medical community, he wasn't alone in his suffering from it. In the northern hemisphere SAD starts around mid-October; it is characterized by low mood, overeating, oversleeping, and a strong sense of lethargy. Although SAD moderates throughout the winter compared with other forms of depression, many SAD patients also have temporary and very mild hypomania when they emerge from their depression in spring.

Light alone can make a substantial difference for many patients. However, many if not most of them find that a modest dose of an antidepressant (usually an SSRI like Prozac or Zoloft) is also very helpful at the same time. The standard daily treatment is 10,000 lux (the common measurement of brightness intensity denoted in terms of light candles) for thirty to sixty minutes per day during the darkest months. All you need to do is sit in front of the lights, so your eyes are within sixteen inches of them, to benefit from the treatment. (There's no need to look directly into the lights.) There are few side effects, if any, associated with the use of bright lights apart from occasional headaches or a bit of agitation, which abates if the time spent in front of the lights is reduced somewhat. (Occasionally bright lights can also induce a mild hypomania.) If, however, you find yourself basking in the sun on Aruba in the middle of the winter you can probably do without bright light therapy for the duration of your sojourn.

## Sleep Deprivation and Other Rare Therapies

The bright light story suggests that interfering with some natural cycles can have positive effects on mood. Another instance in which we can see something similar is when we deliberately deprive depressed or bipolar people of sleep.

The idea that there might be some therapeutic benefit in altering sleep patterns came from a German research group studying circadian rhythms. Circadian rhythms (the twenty-four-hour clock system wired into our brains) govern fluctuations in body temperature and the secretion of several hormones. In about two-thirds of patients with severe depressive illness, researchers noticed a temporary improvement in mood if they were deprived of sleep during the night. The effect didn't persist, though, if they were allowed to take a brief nap in the morning. Subsequent studies show that optimal results can be achieved if the patient is kept awake for the second part of the night, from two to six in the morning. But even if the patients remain awake throughout the next day the effect disappears when they sleep through the next night. Of course, there's a big trade-off here. By rousing themselves from sleep, my patients often temporarily alleviate their low mood but they're still going to feel groggy and irritable, as anyone would be when deprived of sleep. So obviously sleep deprivation as we currently do it is not going to be an answer to our prayers. We've also learned that sleep deprivation, like bright lights, often induces mania in bipolar patients. In fact, if they're already starting into a manic phase, they'll deprive themselves of sleep on their own. This may be one of the reasons mania seems to get worse so fast and lead to manic attacks. We could call this a feed-forward mechanism, as opposed to a feedback mechanism, in mania. You feel you don't need sleep, you don't sleep, and that in turn brings on an even more severe mania.

The findings about circadian rhythms and sleep deprivation, while not yet offering us an effective treatment, have given us a focus for research, allowing researchers to investigate specific aspects of brain function for their impact on mood. At this point we know more about how to study sleep than we do about how to study mood. We have now succeeded in "cloning" about seven genes that regulate biological functions in animals and in humans, making it more likely that we'll one day be able to control our body's clock for the treatment of depressive illness.

# Rare Treatment Options:
## Vagal Nerve Stimulation and Brain Surgery

Two additional therapeutic techniques, though seldom used, should be mentioned here. One is vagal-nerve stimulation and the other is brain surgery.

The vagal nerve occupies a crucial role in regulating gastrointestinal function. The nerve runs down part of the length of the spinal canal, culminating in the abdominal end of the stomach. In epileptic patients it has been found that stimulating this nerve—no one really knows why—has the effect of reducing the seizures in many patients. The procedure is not very different from inserting a pacemaker. A small loop of the vagal nerve is brought to the surface of the skin, and a stimulator is attached to it and covered over with a flap of skin. Some researchers feel that if vagal-nerve stimulation could help epileptics, it might also be able to help some people out of depression. Even as scientists look into the potential of the technique, most doctors would be reluctant to try it on their patients (unless a person has already had it done to treat epilepsy) because, however safe, it remains an invasive procedure. Active research using the vagal nerve stimulator is underway so that we will shortly learn if it offers effective treatment for major depression.

We have long wondered about why brain surgery in certain intractable cases of depression could result in a cure. By far the most common—and controversial—of these surgeries was prefrontal lobotomy, which involved removing much of the frontal lobe or else severing its connections to the rest of the brain. Introduced in the late 1930s, it was successfully employed as a means of controlling aggressive or violent behavior and relieved some depressions. The procedure began to be used for many other causes of mental disorders—too much so. Unfortunately, because so much brain tissue was removed, a large number of patients suffered from a blunting of their personality. Like electroshock therapy, it proved to have enough lasting positive effects for so many patients that physicians began to overuse it. So it's understandable why lobotomies fell into such disrepute.

While prefrontal lobotomies had established that some surgical procedures did produce benefits, it wasn't until very recently that brain surgery has undergone reconsideration. It is now being used again, albeit with great caution and for only the smallest minority of patients. Recent improvements in mapping the brain have made it possible for surgeons to achieve their objectives while destroying only an extremely small fraction of brain tissue. Surgeons use radio- and X-ray guided probes to target precise regions of the brain and burn away a tiny bit of tissue. Since so little of the brain is involved in the surgery, there are few if any complications even if no benefit is achieved. The procedure, as carried out now, carries no danger of blunting personality.

Brain surgery remains extremely rare. I myself have seen only one such case out of eight thousand in my career, but it was no less memorable for being rare. The patient, a young man, was totally disabled by his depression. He was hospitalized as many as twenty times a year. When all other treatments had failed, he underwent brain surgery at the recommendation of several doctors. For the first six weeks he did perfectly well; then he seemed to relapse, reverting to a state little better than he had been before the surgery. Naturally the patient and his family were devastated. But then he began to make steady progress again and now he's working as a full-time writer. He has been well for four years and has not needed to be hospitalized in all that time. It does appear as if the surgery resulted in a near complete cure.

The problem with a case like this, no matter how spectacular, is that you can't use it as a precedent. Because these cases are so rare there aren't enough of them to do a controlled study to determine how often surgery works and to what extent. Nor would I yet want to recommend surgery for many patients. While medications are improving and are much to be preferred over other current treatment options, advances in the use of techniques like ECT and brain surgery give me a good deal of confidence that we will have many new and perhaps unexpected ways of helping people with depression and mania in the near future.

# CHAPTER 18

∞

# Alternative Treatments

Many doctors now advocate for patients to take responsibility for their own health but the rest of the medical profession has been slow to take up this common-sense idea. We doctors generally tended to act in an overly paternalistic way, prescribing drugs and procedures while consigning patients to a more or less passive role in their own treatment. Many patients, look for alternatives. In other cases they are so desperate that they turn to any source that offers a solution even if it proves to be bogus. In its most limited sense, self-treatment can be as simple as a regimen of eating well and getting regular exercise. But self-treatment goes beyond nutrition and exercise. Today's so-called alternative or "natural" treatments include everything from herbs and nutritional supplements to chiropractics, acupuncture, and aromatherapy. Like many other "allopathic" doctors, I tend to react to each new alternative treatment I learn about with skepticism, at least initially. (Allopathy is defined as a system of medicine that relies on proven remedies for treatment.) To be sure, I am skeptical of *all* new medical treatments until they are shown to work. Alternative treatments, though, pose special difficulties and sometimes make for some contentious exchanges with patients or their families. By expressing any doubts about a treatment that they believe will work for them, all I am doing is reinforcing the belief in their minds that I am being close-minded. They lump me in with all those in the medical profession who either dismiss or condemn alternative treatments out of hand. In some sense that's how we came to call these alternative treatments in the first place. They are not the treatments that your doctor will prescribe. After giving the matter a great deal of consideration, though, I began to think that it might be possible to find some middle ground rather than viewing the situation starkly in terms of black or white.

# Why Patients Seek Out Alternative Treatments

Before I did anything else, I needed to understand why so many patients seek these treatments, often in apparent disregard of their doctors' reservations, even though in the past their doctors may have enjoyed their unquestioning trust. Second, I had to understand why doctors are so skeptical to begin with. This represented a departure from my usual approach. I like to remind people that the first tenet of the Hippocratic Oath is "First do no harm." Doctors are paid to be skeptical of all treatments, no matter what we call them. Whether a treatment is standard, alternative, allopathic, or experimental, each one must be carefully studied in terms of its risks and benefits before it can be approved for widespread use. But those are the concerns of doctors, researchers, and regulators. People who are suffering with serious illnesses have different motives and different needs and I understand these as well. One of the first things—and one of the most surprising, too—I learned when I started reading the literature on this subject was that most people who seek alternative treatments are not patients who shun conventional treatments. In fact, just the opposite is true.

Basically, 10 percent of the U.S. adult population made at least one visit to an alternative practitioner—including acupuncturists, chiropractors, and massage therapists—in 1994, the last year for which reliable statistics are available. It is now estimated that 42 million Americans seek out some form of alternative treatment. Surprisingly, the people who saw an alternative clinician also made *twice as many* visits to physicians as did individuals who did not see alternative practitioners. These patients nonetheless reported that they had very high needs for medical care that weren't being met by any practitioner. It would seem then that these are people who are very concerned about their health. However, it would be a mistake to assume that they are consumed by hypochondria or excessive worrying.

In one study of patients who were receiving care in a melanoma clinic in Austria, 14 percent (or 30 out of 215) sought alternative treatments compared to another 54 percent who, while reporting interest in alternative treatments, never sought them out. Melanoma is a serious, potentially fatal form of skin cancer. Those who sought alternative treatments had more advanced melanomas than those who did not. The study also showed that those who expressed interest in alternative treatments but never sought them were, as a group, younger and had more active coping styles compared to those who had no interest in alternative treatments. What's more, this group of the "interested" also displayed a marked propensity to search for personal or religious meaning in their disease. Nonetheless, all three groups—those who received alternative treatments, those who were interested in them but never acted, and those who wanted nothing to do with them—did not differ in either their faith in their doctors or in their compliance with conventional treatments. But the patients who did express interest in alternative treatments were virtually unanimous in their feeling that they weren't getting the attention they'd hoped for from their physicians. Many of them were especially concerned that their treatments weren't working, an understandable worry in patients with advanced melanoma. One thing that this study demonstrated was that it wasn't so much the type of *treatment* per se that made alternatives attractive, but the attention and the sense of shared hope that the patients felt they were receiving from the alternative treatment providers. On the average, alternative providers spent longer with each patient, administered more treatments themselves (rather than relying on nurses or technicians), and by and large prescribed fewer medications than the average medical practitioner did. In contrast to the cost-control focus of medical corporations, which encourages psychiatrists as well as other physicians to see patients for very short visits, alternative treatments represent a much more patient-friendly picture.

## What Exactly Is Natural?

If you walk into a store specializing in nutritional supplements and herbs, you will find an astonishingly large number of them on the shelves. Some, of course, are better known than others and as a result of their popularity have stirred some interest in the psychiatric profession. These include St. John's Wort, SAMe, DHEA, omega-3 fatty acid (fish oil), and L-tryptophan. Since I get so many calls from friends and professional colleagues about these treatments, I'm always looking for studies comparing them to standard treatments or to placebo. I'm also looking for studies that ask, "Well, if this works for something like depression, then how does it do it?" What strikes me about the advertised benefits for these herbs and supplements is that they are supposed to alleviate anywhere from eight to twenty different conditions each. St. John's Wort, which was believed to have some antidepressant effects, is also said to promote wound healing, and cure skin diseases, various cancers, AIDS, and lung and kidney disease. That doesn't sound like a sensible set of claims to me. Pharmaceutical companies couldn't make so many claims for their products because the Food and Drug Administration (FDA), which has control over the claims they can make, wouldn't allow them to without substantial proof to back them up. However, since 1994 these supplements have not been under FDA control because they are considered neither drugs nor foods. I know that many herbs have been in use for centuries and, though argumentable, that most of them are generally quite safe.

But there's another argument about safety, which hinges on the definition of the term *natural*. Neither the FDA nor any other regulatory or medical body has an acceptable definition of natural that any company marketing an alternative substance would have to adhere to. I would point out that arsenic and cyanide are natural, too. And poisonous mushrooms are very natural. The most conventional treatment for bipolar disorder is natural: lithium is a salt derived from the earth.

There is another argument that advocates of alternative treatments advance, which goes like this. The FDA will approve only drugs that have been rigorously tested in both animals and human beings and are found to be safe and effective. But drug companies, which spend billions of dollars to do research and produce these drugs, have no interest in testing nutritional supplements or herbs because they are "natural" and so can't be patented, depriving them of any future profits.

As it turns out, this perception is quite mistaken. First, these are very profitable products. They command a very high retail price and are much in demand. In addition, pharmaceutical companies are very interested in these products. They have bought many of these nutritional supplement companies. So while the label on the bottle of ginseng or gingko might look like it was printed in the back room, you might end up buying a product that is marked by Pfizer or Roche Lab. There may be a silver lining to this buying binge. Once makers of these supplements and nutrients come under the control of big pharmaceutical companies, they will probably have to institute more uniform quality control to avoid lawsuits.

## When Supplements and Herbs Can Be Dangerous

One of the big problems we face is trying to discover what actually goes into the contents of a particular substance. You may read that a bottle contains gingko, a Chinese herb said to improve memory, but there's no guarantee that that's what's inside, or whether there might not be other ingredients in addition to gingko. In one study, it was found that something on the order of one-third of the bottles being sold in nutritional supplement stores were adulterated with substances not listed on the label. In some cases, substitutions were made or there was less of what you probably thought you were getting. Many of these substances are diluted and the study found little standardization of concentration. Sometimes ingredients that are added to these herbs or nutritional supplements have dangerous side effects. When researchers examined some bottles of gingko for their study, for instance, they discovered significant amounts of drugs that could raise blood pressure.

Luckily, most herbal remedies are relatively inert: they don't interact much with the body and so they are almost perfectly safe even though they haven't been subjected to controlled human studies. However, when patients take them in addition to antidepressants or other prescription medicines, they may put themselves at risk for dangerous drug reactions. That's why I always encourage my patients to be honest with me and let me know whether they're using supplements or herbs. As we know, though, many patients are embarrassed to admit that they're doing anything of the kind. The result is that the doctor misses out on important information.

Let us take a closer look at some of the most popular supplements and herbs on the market that are reputed to have therapeutic value for depression and manic depression. A word of caution: what is called an alternative treatment has a way of changing quickly. So I will confine my discussion to those substances that enjoy popularity as of this writing. But, as they say in the fine print of ads for airline tickets, everything is subject to change without notice.

## St. John's Wort

The best known herbal treatment for depression today is St. John's Wort. It is also the best studied of all the herbal treatments with antidepressant claims. Known to botanists by its Latin name, *Hypericum Perforatum,* it's an attractive yellow flower (weed might be more appropriate) that grows in warm to moderate climates including the southeastern United States. Taken alone, it is safe and has few side effects at recommended dosages. In fact, I have found more information about the toxicity of St. John's Wort in the agricultural literature than in medical literature. It seems that the occasional grazing cow cleared a field of the wild flower in the morning and got a very bad skin reaction when exposed to the sun. Recently there have been greater concerns about drug interactions in AIDS patients who take St. John's Wort and their anti-viral medications, but it is not clear how big this risk is. A recommended dose of 900 mg a day of St. John's Wort costs 30 cents to $1.50 per day (the cost of standard antidepressants runs 30 cents to $2 per day) and I have friends who have sent me cans of tomato soup and teas fortified with it. In 2000 Americans spent $195 million on the pill form of the herb. About twenty patients have seen me while they were taking it but I couldn't be confident whether it was helping them or not. Most of them said they were taking it because it might help, and that they sensed that since it is an over-the-counter "natural supplement" that they could do it on their own. Most of them had no idea that because of its recent popularity, large pharmaceutical firms manufacture and sell it.

The early studies of St. John's Wort (23 of them) were done in Germany in the early 1990s. These studies concluded that the herb was more effective than placebo and equally as effective as standard antidepressants in treatment of mild to moderate depression. Isn't that enough? Not really. Unfortunately, the studies do not include a standardized diagnostic evaluation so we could not compare the diagnostic groups and the severity of the group of patients compared to the patients in trials of other drugs as possible antidepressants. They provided some information on the condition of the patients before they entered the study. The patients had depressive symptoms and in addition we know their age, sex, and score on a depression scale. Did the patients have major depression? Some did but it is not clear how many. Other standardized random clinical trial procedures may have been rigorously followed, but in most of the early studies I couldn't answer these questions because they are not included in the papers. Another problem is that the doses of antidepressants administered in the study for the sake of comparison were dosages that were too small. The doses given, in fact, wouldn't have been expected to be any more effective than placebo treatments.

In May 2001 this changed, the *Journal of the American Medical Association* (JAMA), published the results of a large U.S. multicenter study of St. John's Wort. This study was by far the most rigorous one done to date. The findings weren't very promising for advocates of the herb. The study found that it was no more effective in treating depression than a placebo tablet. But another study of three hundred patients is still being analyzed at the time of this writing. Unless the result from that study is more hopeful, we'll have to conclude that St. John's Wort is not an antidepressant, at least not for major depression.

# DHEA

DHEA (short for dehydoepiandrosterone) is a naturally occurring substance in the human body. Present in small amounts, it is known as a prehormone or a precursor to testosterone. It is known to have potentially serious medical and psychiatric side effects based on its relationship to testosterone and other steroid hormones. It is banned by many sports authorities (swimming and biking), but the FDA doesn't regulate it and Major League Baseball used to permit its use. This was of more than a passing interest because Mark McGwire was taking the substance faithfully in the 1998 season when he hit a record 70 home runs. There is, however, no evidence that it does anything to improve strength, which was McGwire's motivation in taking it. Does it have any effect on depression? A number of years ago some researchers published a few very small but inconclusive indications that DHEA might help the performance of other antidepressants. While researchers found no proof that it doesn't have any effect, they found no proof that it did. What is perhaps more revealing of their views of DHEA is that they stopped using it for depressed patients in their research programs. DHEA is extremely expensive ranging from $17 to $42.50 per 400 mg pill. The most common side effect is menstrual irregularity. But some severe mixed or manic states have been suspected to be related to DHEA.

# SAM-e

Recently wide attention has been given to SAM-e. Several books have come out in recent years promoting SAM-e as a "natural" cure for depression. SAM-e (short for S-adenosylmethionine, which naturally occurs in humans and in other organisms), was first discovered in 1952 and has been commercially available in Europe since the 1970s. An amino acid that acts as a catalyst in a number of metabolic reactions, it is involved in the manufacture of joint cartilage and the maintenance of neural cell membrane function. It was thought that perhaps it might be a useful treatment for some psychiatric disorders based on the old theory that schizophrenia and possibly depression were related to levels of methionine in the blood. If you read the promotional literature for SAM-e you'd think the substance has been thoroughly tested. Here, for example, is a pitch from one distributor of SAM-e: "The reason behind much of the attention being paid to

SAM-e is the significant amount of scientific evidence supporting its use. There are over 75 clinical studies on SAM-e worldwide, involving thousands of people that appear in scientific publications. One respected medical journal published a very positive collection of studies on SAM-e totaling over 100 pages." To the uninitiated, all this might sound very impressive, but in fact, while some of these studies in the 1960s and 1970s suggested that SAM-e might be a useful anti-depressant, they failed to demonstrate any clear benefit. The studies were not vigorously done and the research stopped, and although some individuals in these studies clearly got better, we cannot say that they did any better on the SAM-e than off it. Again, there is no proof of in effectiveness, just an absence of proof that it has any effect at all.

## Omega-3 Oils

Dietary difference between Americans and Japanese—characterized by a fondness for fatty foods on the one hand and for fish on the other—have long been thought to be a possible explanation for the lower rates of heart disease and gastric cancer in Japan. As researchers began to study the therapeutic benefits of a diet rich in fish, they found some evidence that fish omega-3 oils might also be a possible treatment for depressive illness. It has been noted that people with depression have lower cholesterol levels than other people do.

While the Japanese eat a lot more fish on a regular basis than the average American does, it isn't clear that Americans have more depression than the Japanese. Some studies suggest a small difference in rates. Even if the small differences reflected real differences in disease rates, though, that doesn't mean that diet had to be the cause. Nonetheless, some studies are now going on to find out whether omega-3 oils may in fact hold some promise in treating depression and so far one has indicated that it might be helpful. We will keep listening but we will maintain the professional skepticism until the data is all in.

## The Business of Hope

In addition to these herbs and supplements, you can find all kinds of other alternative treatments supposedly useful for depression ranging from acupuncture and astrology to aromatherapy, yoga, and meditation. Now, just because there is no good evidence that any of these practices work, we shouldn't discount the potential power of placebo. If we can get more people with moderate depression to come forward for treatment because they're interested in trying alternative treatments, their experience may turn out to be very therapeutic, especially if the treatments are less toxic and less expensive than standard medication. Again, though, we have to emphasize that for people who have severe depression these alternatives are unlikely to do as much good as proven antidepressants, therefore I always recommend an initial evaluation to establish a correct diagnosis.

How do I react when a patient comes into my office and tells me that he or she has been taking St. John's Wort or seeing an acupuncturist? Well, to be honest, my reaction over the years has changed. On the one hand, the skeptic in me still comes out very quickly (though I'm discreet enough to bite my tongue). On the other hand, my reaction is now usually tempered by the notion that most of these treatments are fairly safe in terms of pharmacology. That, of course, is both their greatest strength and their greatest weakness. As I said, most of the herbs and supplements on the market are pretty inert in terms of their effects on physiological systems (though there are exceptions). What concerns me most about patients resorting to alternative treatments is whether conventional treatment is failing them. What exactly are they looking for? The illness may be so severe and recovery so slow or imperceptible that they may have lost faith that we have all the answers. That certainly is a legitimate concern. What we want to do is get patients to air their feelings honestly so that we can discuss treatment and consider what options are available.

All the same, I must speak up as the skeptical doctor who is concerned about maintaining the proper balance between patients' needs and their hopes. *Hope* is probably the operative word here. If you want to look at medicine as a business, then the currency of our business is hope. And I'm talking about realistic, credible hope, not false or magical hope. My practice and advice is to use what is proven first, but never quit, so that if all "proven" treatments have been given fair trials then unproven treatments should be given a fair shake as well.

# CHAPTER 19

∞

# Hospitalization: A Guide for Patients and Families

In a number of situations, hospitalization or an emergency evaluation is absolutely necessary. Sometimes hospitalization is desirable, but it's not an emergency. But in this section we'll talk about what happens in an emergency, whether the person involved is currently being treated for depressive illness or not.

The need for hospitalization arises if a person is endangered because he or she is suicidal, or so paranoid or so irritable that he or she is threatening or exhibiting violent behavior. Similarly urgent measures are called for if the ill person has developed hallucinations or delusions or is so confused as to be unable to care for basic personal needs. For example, if the depressed or manic person cannot get out of bed for days at a time, or is so mistrustful that he or she can't or won't take medications as prescribed, then admission is usually warranted. While there are exceptions, these symptoms or signs should be viewed with concern and most likely require an emergency evaluation if not admission. Inpatient admission will be needed in a number of other circumstances as well, especially when a treatment is required that presents a significant health risk for a patient. For example, if a person has another serious medical condition in addition to depression or manic depression, admission would be justified so that the patient's medical condition could be carefully monitored while he or she is treated for the depressive illness.

If possible, patients and their families should tackle the difficult but necessary task of dealing with the health plan reviewers before a crisis strikes. (For more on this topic, see the appendix on insurance.) By thoroughly familiarizing yourself with your health plan, you will know whether you have inpatient coverage, how much, and in which hospitals you can get inpatient care.

It's also very useful for patients and families to prepare a logistical emergency plan well in advance in the event that an emergency situation does arise. Too often, though, families have to go through a crisis once with no preparation in place before they actually do draw up a contingency plan. It's extremely helpful for the family members and friends of the patient to have assigned areas of responsibility defining what each person will do in an emergency. Who will take the agitated family member to an emergency room? If you think you will need three people to control the situation, bring four or five. Nothing helps calm a situation down more quickly than the presence of a familiar but irresistible force. Injuries occur most often (either to the patient or others) when there are not enough people to protect the individual or they're not organized well enough to control the situation.

In the event that a depression worsens or a mania develops, each member of the family should have a role to play. The question each person should pose to the doctor or other key person is: "What can I do to help in this situation?" It's very helpful for everyone, including the patient, to sit down with the doctor and discuss these issues when the patient is in outpatient care. That way everyone is on the same page, as it were: each member of the family knows what is expected of him or her and what is likely to occur if the patient becomes severely depressed or manic and requires emergency intervention. A small but thoughtful number of patients now sign legal "advance directives" about who should make medical and financial decisions on their behalf if they become "psychotic."

## Hospitalization Day

Even in instances where the patient isn't exhibiting extreme agitation, going through admission procedures at the hospital is a very stressful experience for both the patient and the family. It is so stressful, in fact, that we know that about one-third of patients who receive certain hormonal tests will show abnormal results if they are tested on their first day in the hospital due to stress alone.

When a patient is admitted to the hospital, family members or friends should accompany the person and be prepared to help him or her deal with the stress of admission. Just getting to see a doctor or nurse or getting assigned to a room can be a cause of stress because of delays that often last for hours. So the presence of a family member or friend can provide not only great moral support during the waiting periods but can also actually make a big difference in how the treatment at the hospital gets started.

When the psychiatrist examines the patient, the family should be able to provide any information they have about the patient's prior treatment, medications, whether other family members have also had psychiatric illnesses, and so on. They should also report any observations they have about the patient that might bear on his or her condition or treatment. I recommend that families write down their observations so they won't forget any important points, and be sure to bring them along to the hospital. They should also remember to bring any medical records in their possession. It's important to get as much pertinent information into a doctor's hands in as comprehensive and organized a fashion as you can manage given the constraints of time. How much opportunity the family will have to share this information with the doctor depends on the doctor's workload. The family might need to tell a nurse or social worker what they've observed about the patient if the doctor has only limited time for them during an emergency situation. Obviously this situation isn't ideal since the most accurate and detailed information available about a patient with delusional ideas or disordered thinking often comes from the family. Nonetheless, at nights and on weekends and especially in a very busy hospital, the doctor, who may be admitting three or four patients, may not have sufficient time to gather this information in a face-to-face meeting. That's why it's so important for families to bring a written copy of their observations about what the patient's symptoms were prior to admission.

Sometimes families can provide doctors with a more balanced impression of patients' condition than the patients themselves. While depressed patients can be too negative about their condition or else try to minimize the severity of their illness because they are afraid of going into the hospital, manic patients will often deny their symptoms altogether. I also encourage the family to speak up, to make their wishes clear, and to arrange a regular channel of communication with a contact person at the hospital regarding the patient's diagnosis and treatment plans, if not at the time of admission then soon thereafter.

## Family Participation During Hospital Stay

Different hospitals have different expectations and structures for the family's involvement in hospital care. Nonetheless, in almost all cases, families can play an extremely valuable role in aiding recovery by offering support, encouragement, and a willing ear. More than the relatives might realize, they can perform a useful service as reporters on the patients' progress. A family, after all, knows a patient much better than any hospital staff. Besides, we aren't only treating a disease, we're treating a person who happens to have a disease. The family member can fill in the gaps about the person's background. Their reports serve to remind the staff that the patient has a personality that the disease has temporarily hidden from view and that on recovery can be expected to return. While we doctors see patients in their most vulnerable moments, we need to learn about their strengths, hobbies, talents, hopes, and ambitions as well. Such information is important as we plan for what kinds of things the patient should try to do when recovery begins. For instance, the patient may be a passionate fly-fisherman or chess player. This kind of information might be just what a doctor or a nurse needs to get a shy and depressed patient to start talking about his or her life. You'd be surprised how talking about the fish you caught—and the fish that got away—can also make you feel comfortable enough to open up about more personal things. We want patients to think beyond their illness even when they might still feel trapped by it. At the very least, raising these subjects reinforces in the patient's mind the fact that we have the expectation that he or she will return to the life they knew before becoming so ill. Patients naturally worry about their problems when they are depressed. Sometimes we refocus the direction of their conversation (and thoughts) by reminding them of the things that brought pleasure and inspired dreams and ambitions. But in order to do this we need to know what to listen for.

The family should always report their impressions on how they see the patient's progress to hospital staff after they visit the patient. Providing these reports is especially important if the patient has been allowed out of the hospital ward in their company on a day pass. Did the patient participate in meals, or was he or she sociable during the few hours spent at home? Did the patient get along well with other family members? It can be embarrassing for the family to admit that the patient is irritable, but they shouldn't consider their comments as criticisms of the patient. Candid observations of the patient's mood and behavior can provide the staff with a better idea about whether the patient is making progress.

What happens after the consulting psychiatrist has made any evaluation? He or she will typically call your treating psychiatrist and report the findings and recommendations. Usually a note indicating his or her conclusions will also be sent to your doctor. Keep in mind the bottom line: the goal of consultations is to help both the treating psychiatrist and you improve your options for treatment and to make your discussions more open and trusting.

## Support Groups and Peer Support for Patients and Families

Patients and families have a need for support and education about depressive conditions, and this is especially true when hospital treatment has occurred since it is often followed by a period of great worry. I emphasize support and education in my writing and speaking because both are equally vital in terms of treatment. Studies of patients with cancer and diabetes show that patient and family education programs are more effective in promoting healthy behavior if emotional support is also part of the experience. The best way of achieving this emotional support is by pulling together other patients and/or families who have gone through similar experiences. I have worked with mutual help groups through a great organization, Depression and Related Affective Disorders Association (DRADA), which has spearheaded the training of volunteer support group leaders for the past fifteen years. As a result of DRADA's efforts, more than seventy-five support groups have been established and sustained for a decade or more in the Baltimore metropolitan area. They are now working to train leaders in a joint program with the National Depressive and Manic Depressive Association.

Such groups can be very helpful for patients and families. They are in some ways similar to support groups such as AA or ALANON in that they offer support and reduce the stigma of illness. But they also differ, since with alcoholism, an addictive behavior, the ultimate goal is to refrain from drinking alcohol; clinical depressive and bipolar disorder, on the other hand, are diseases; the ultimate goal is to be free of the symptoms. However, to achieve this requires patients to avoid damaging behaviors and to trust the wisdom of others in sustaining treatments and a group's support can help immeasurably, especially since the group is formed of people who have done it. The groups are also run somewhat differently in that patients and family members actively participate in a general discussion in support groups. This "cross-talk" does not ordinarily occur in AA, where the standard procedure is for one person at a time to tell his or her story and get a show of support from the group at the end of the talk.

In spite of the differences in the disorders and the rules governing their meetings, these support groups and groups like AA have a great deal in common. All of them encourage and sustain supportive relationships with other survivors of the disease or addiction. These groups also do much to reduce the strong sense of isolation that patients and families feel, while at the same time increasing a sense of hopefulness. In addition, these groups allow for an exchange of information and experiences among their members so that they have a way of getting hold of practical advice on how to cope with and solve problems, and just as important, how to avoid pitfalls of various types.

Most people feel almost as if they're aliens when they attend their first group meeting. Sometimes the experience makes them feel so uncomfortable that they don't want to return. Resist the impulse to not come back; it usually takes four meetings before it's clear whether a particular group is what you want. In most cities, if you find one wanting in some respect, there are others to choose from.

Of all the important lessons that these family support groups teach, two in particular stand out in my mind. The first lesson is the need for all of us (patients, families, and professionals) to recognize our limitations. As a family member, you should have a general sense of how much stress you can manage and what things you should and should not try to handle. If you're a family member responsible for caring for a patient, there's a related lesson to learn: You need to look after your own health and welfare. You're not going to be very efficient at taking care of an ill spouse or child who will likely need your help at various times over the next several years if you're exhausted or burned out. Your health and welfare are not only important for you, but are essential to the well-being of the patient and other members of your family. These two fundamental lessons are quite similar to the ALANON message as it distinguishes between what you can do for your family member (love him or her) and what you can't do (make him or her stop drinking). Actually, I think a careful inventory of our limits is ultimately an empowering exercise so long as we don't forget what we *can* do to help. This is also true for doctors and therapists. I want to be certain that I make myself accountable to my patients for what I can do (treat the illness), but I also have to admit my limits. I can't know ahead of time which medication is the best one for a patient. I can prescribe drugs prudently, I can assess how they are working, and I can give them in adequate doses for the right amount of time. I can make myself readily available to patients and provide them with supportive and even protective care if they can't get up or take their medications or keep themselves safe and ask for help. But I can't make the patient take the medicines correctly, or make the patient magically stop destructive behavior unless he or she is ready to work at it, too. I hope if I make clear what I see as reasonable expectations and limits for my role in a patient's treatment, I help make it that much easier for families to accept their own limits.

Other types of support groups exist that are accessible from your own home. In recent years, for instance, Internet support and education opportunities with a variety of structures have become available. I've included the names of internet support groups from helpful organizations in the resource appendix. Simply type the name into whatever search engine you're using, such as Yahoo or Google, or type the Internet address directly.

These groups can take several forms, including bulletin boards, chat rooms, and "listserve." The listserve groups are for members only and so are not open to anyone who happens to access their site. You have to write to the group to request a membership and agree to its rules. These rules apply to every member who posts a message responding to an issue related to the same general topic.

Internet bulletin boards, on the other hand, function more like a radio call-in show. You never know what responses you will read and from whom. You will see some original postings getting hundreds of responses and dozens of posted messages getting none. By contrast, a chat room allows users to communicate in real time, often without the intervention of any moderator. Both bulletin boards and chat rooms can be a source of good or very bad information, since there is no way to be sure who is communicating (and users frequently employ aliases), nor is there any way of controlling the flow of information or judging its reliability.

Of the three types of on-line mediums I've mentioned, listserve groups provide the closest thing to a live support group. For one thing, some of them have a professionally qualified moderator who accepts individuals for membership. All messages are routed first to his or her computer and from there out to all the "members." If there is some message that the moderator feels is not constructive, he or she can respond or even stop the conversation for a time by disconnecting one or more of the members from access to the group while the issue of concern is worked out. A situation like this might occur, for example, if one person makes a suicidal threat but claims not to want help to change his or her mind, or if a member makes a disparaging or mocking comment. Situations like these arise very infrequently, though, and are far less likely to occur in a listserve group than in a chat room.

# CHAPTER 20

Getting Back to Normal

Once you know for certain that you have depression the next thing you'd want to know is when it will end or will you ever get back to yourself. Treatments are usually very helpful but the severity of your condition and whether you have any other conditions besides depression or bipolar disorder also affect prognosis. The three basic tasks for a doctor are to make a diagnosis, develop a treatment plan and a prognosis. Most difficult in these three is prognosis. It comes from the complex life, your temperament, your habits, your knowledge (real and potential) of the illness, and your particular form of the disease. Then this feeds back into your long-term treatment or rehabilitation work. If it proceeds naturally you will come to understand the severity of illness as well as to determine how your temperament is either helping you or making it harder for you, what kind of support you need and what you can do to foster this. Doctors have to take all these things into account when they make a prognosis and you need to come to use this for recovery and even growth.

That said, we have several fairly reliable ways of assessing your prospects for getting better. When Dr. Emil Kraeplin distinguished "manic depressive insanity" from dementia precox (later called schizophrenia), he also sounded an optimistic note about prognosis for "MDI." As many as 80 percent of patients with either depression or manic depression, he wrote, could expect to recover from a manic or depressive episode. This was in marked contrast to people with schizophrenia, where only 20 percent recovered fully and 80 percent did not. Obviously the news wasn't entirely positive for people with depression. After all, about 20 percent of depressives didn't recover and even the 80 percent who did were likely to have relapses. What Kraeplin observed a century ago has important correlates today but even the 20 percent who didn't recover in Kraepelin's day can obtain substantial improvement with vigorous treatment today. These are the patients for whom I set an 80 percent improvement, 80 percent of the time goal—and usually we reach that.

As I've said many times, most people who have recurrent episodes of depression never seek treatment. What we know about diagnosing and treating depression comes mainly from people who are seriously ill and either are or have been in treatment. But what do all those other people with depression do when they become ill? In many cases, their depression or manias, while incapacitating to some degree, are not so serious that they would feel compelled to see a doctor. Often they will try to do something for themselves to alleviate the symptoms or else sit tight and wait out the storm. Even many patients who do seek treatment from doctors will also try other treatments on their own. Some of these self-treatments may be benign (getting regular exercise, for example) and some may be counterproductive or even dangerous. This brings me back to a subject I touched on in talking about alternative treatments.

## Education as a Treatment

To begin with, it's crucial for people with depression to know what they're dealing with. Education makes a huge difference. If you know what you've got, if you know what's causing your illness (at least in terms of the current state of our knowledge), and if in addition you are aware of the kind of treatments that will probably help, you are already several steps ahead of the game. The problem arises, of course, when you try to evaluate your own condition rather than get a professional judgment.

All the same, some common-sense approaches to good health apply to most people with depression, just as they do for anyone else. Getting a good night's sleep, for instance, is hardly a radical piece of advice. Everyone knows that getting regular exercise, maintaining a nutritious diet, and eating three meals a day, managing (not avoiding) stress, and keeping to an appropriate daily routine all contribute to good health. Doctors have been making these recommendations to their patients for centuries. So have millions of mothers. There's good reason that these prescriptions have stood the test of time: they work.

However, if you have severe clinical depression, you won't always be able to make use of the wisdom of generations of doctors and mothers. Even people with moderate depression may not be able to benefit from these traditional prescriptions for a healthy life. That's because depression disrupts your routine and throws your life out of balance, creating a pattern of disorganization. People with depression can't concentrate as well. What used to take ten minutes takes an hour and even then it doesn't come out right. So if you are depressed you may tend to put off some task awaiting your attention because you know you won't be able to do it efficiently. That's why one of the first things to go when you're depressed is a regular schedule.

Many people with depression will get into a rut where they stay up too late and they also have trouble getting going in the morning. Once they do get to work (late or not), they perform less efficiently, but may feel as if they can get by okay. If they're professionals with demanding jobs they may be able to keep functioning, but only at half-speed. Then they feel guilty because they're not accomplishing what they should. So instead of recognizing that they're ill, they keep pressing on, working late into the night at the expense of a good night's sleep. Yet in spite of their resolve, they won't get done anywhere near as much as they would have ordinarily. On the contrary, they will tire far more quickly and their efficiency will drop dramatically.

If you're in a situation like this, the problem is that you are judging yourself against an unrealistic standard, though it's one that you would have had no trouble meeting if you were well. If you were in bed with the flu, you wouldn't hesitate to stay home a couple of days to recuperate. But if you mistakenly believe that your depression is something like a trivial "cold" that you can beat by ignoring it, you can make things worse. Working twice as hard, staying up till all hours, and still getting less done, could make you even more discouraged. If, however, you can set reasonable goals and expectations and prioritize getting a good night's sleep instead—you will probably function better even though you might not feel better. But you will have taken a concrete step to improve the situation.

Often personal initiative is not enough. Someone with mild depression may still be able to get to a gym a few times a week. That's all to the good. But if the depression is very severe, exercise is probably out of the question. Someone who's flat on his or her back in bed isn't going to be able to get to the gym. Even if the person could, no matter how long on the Nautilus machine they won't beat a severe depression. So in addition to keeping a regular diet and getting regular exercise, my third rule is not to get down on yourself in the belief that if you had just done what you were supposed to do, you'd be okay now. That's not so. Remember the biggest trap of the depression is an unjustified feeling of worthlessness. This underscores the importance of seeing a doctor who can reiterate these points even when you can't.

## Diet and Depression?

What about diet and depression? There are two concerns here. The first is whether eating or avoiding certain types of food might have some therapeutic value for people with a mood disorder. The second is the tendency for many patients to experience weight problems as a result of depression or as side effects from antidepressants.

Until recently, clinicians specializing in depression paid little attention to their patients' diets. For one thing, no particular diet, as far as we know, has any beneficial effect on the illness. Some claims have been put forward for a diet rich in carbohydrates because they raise serotonin levels, but there is more theory than good science behind this.

However, where weight problems arise because of side effects from medication, clinicians are in the position to do something for their patients. Weight gain doesn't result only from side effects of medication; it also can occur because of the coping mechanisms patients develop to deal with their illness. People who are depressed—and who, in addition, tend to stay up late—have a tendency to overeat. Either they think: *Why not eat? I can't enjoy anything else.* Or else they will begin to graze between meals, indulging in candy and junk food. As anyone who has ever tried a diet will know, it's a lot harder to lose weight than to put it on. And as you gain weight it changes your self-image, which has already taken a big hit from the depression. Not long ago an internist who was an expert on weight addressed a gathering of psychiatrists and took us to task for ignoring the problem. "You say there's a trade-off between taking medication and gaining weight, but treatment has a lot to do with how people feel," he said. "You can do something for these people and you're not. You've got to monitor your patients' weight and once it climbs five pounds you've got to intervene. You can't wait to do something until after they've gained twenty pounds. This is part of the treatment."

What he said was correct. Some of the antidepressants and anti-manic medications have a powerfully stimulating effect on appetite. Used correctly and with doctor's advice the meals marketed by Weight Watchers or Ultra SlimFast can be helpful because they have appropriate nutrition and you will be able to keep your home junk-food-free. Can I count on patients always adhering even to this diet? Of course not. There's bound to be some slipping up. But I can support their efforts. Interesting research is now underway to find safe ways to offset the appetite stimulating effects of these medications. The ones that my patients have most difficulty with include: quetiapine, olanzapine, and clozapine. And from experience, I can tell you that many patients do in fact manage to restrict their eating and others improve in their mood and self-image even though they gain weight.

## Recovering from Depression

If you have a depression, how can I as a clinician determine your chances of getting better? Or to put it another way: which patients are at the greatest risk for staying ill or relapsing? Studies over the last twenty years suggest that those who are at greatest risk are patients who have chronic and mild forms of depression. They have to drag themselves through the day and feel miserable most of the time but still manage to keep going, that is until they're hit with a full major depressive episode that puts them out of commission entirely. As I've said before, this chronic form of depression is called dysthymia. For dysthymic patients recovery doesn't mean that they aren't still depressed. It usually just means that they're *less* depressed. They recover back to their dysthymia. Now most of these people didn't start off life depressed; they developed their dysthymia along the way. But they have certainly suffered from it for a long period of time. So that's one group of depressed patients about whom I'd have to say that the prognosis is not easy. I must also say that with persistent medical treatment, psychotherapy, and both mental and physical exercise, patients do get better than they were before the depression. But it generally takes quite a while.

What if you have manic depression? Who in this group is at the greatest risk for nonrecovery? Basically, I can say that it's those patients who have mixed states, which Kraeplin characterized as a "lingering form" of depressive illness. Remember I defined a mixed state as one in which both depression and manic depression are present, with different mixtures of blue and red. It's a disorder that sticks around long after the depressive episode has passed. The prognosis for individuals suffering from mixed states becomes even worse if they are abusing or dependent on alcohol or drugs.

Alcohol and drugs can play a particularly insidious role in the progression of *any form* of depressive illness, as I've said several times in this book. What we can say about drugs and alcohol in terms of prognosis, though, is that substance abuse makes it less likely that they'll recover. I draw a graph for my patients to demonstrate the approximate chance of staying well if they continue to use drugs and alcohol when measured against the chance for those who abstain. What my graph shows is that about 75 percent of those who abstain from substance abuse will go on to recover for a sustained period of time while 25 percent will relapse within two years. But if they don't abstain the situation is almost completely reversed. Approximately 80 percent of the nonabstainers will relapse in two years. I don't take the view that if you don't abstain that all is lost. After all, about 20 percent of my patients persist in abusing alcohol and drugs and do okay while other patients who do exactly what the doctor orders will still relapse. But if you were a gambler would you take the odds? Even after you do swear off alcohol or drugs, recovery doesn't magically happen overnight. Based on clinical experience, I think it takes a while after you've stopped to fully benefit from treatment. It appears to require eighteen months to two years free of alcohol and drugs before the brain is going to respond really well to medication like the brains of nonaddicted patients do.

Simply giving up drinking or drugs alone in the absence of any treatment can have a positive effect, although I'd be the last person to suggest that anyone forego needed treatment. I had one such patient who stopped drinking but refused all medication. Nonetheless, he went on to recover from his depression and stayed well, except for some minor periods of depression, for about twelve years. Then he started drinking again and all his symptoms came back. His long recovery can probably be attributed to his abstinence.

Given the risk that drinking and drug abuse pose to depressed persons, we have to ask ourselves: When is it worth attempting to treat depression or manic depression in substance-abusing patients and when is it not? The answer is that it depends. I have to make my decision on the severity of the abuse and our assessment as to how easy it would be for the person to stop for a couple of months. If I have someone who is willing to do that, I am in a better position to treat the person and am better able to predict the outcome.

## The Episodic Nature of the Illness

When we talk about prognosis for recovery we also have to consider another basic element of this disease: its tendency to remit and relapse. Almost all patients experience relapses at one point or another regardless of treatment. The critical questions for me are: how many episodes will you have over a given period of time, and how severe will they be? The frequency of episodes is just as important as the severity because the disruption of lives depends on both. If you recover for only a month you're in an entirely different place than someone who recovers for a decade. We don't know why some people have sustained recoveries while others suffer frequent relapses, but we do know that the duration of recoveries varies enormously. As I pointed out, substance abuse puts people at greater risk for relapses and jeopardizes their chances of a good recovery as well.

In preceding chapters I've spoken quite a bit about life events and how they can influence the onset of depression. It also appears that life events can tip the scale enough so that they may cause relapses as well. One of my patients with manic depression, for instance, fell ill just before an anticipated event in her daughter's life. Her first manic depressive episode occurred when her daughter became pregnant; she experienced a second episode when her daughter got married; and she had a third episode when her daughter had the baby. Note that each of these episodes was precipitated by an event in her daughter's life that had to do with sex. In fact, my patient developed a delusion about a sexual relationship involving her husband. The problem, of course, in judging the impact of life events in terms of the prognosis is that you can never be certain how much influence they have. It's like the famous Agatha Christie novel *Murder on the Orient Express,* where nearly every character is a suspect. When bad things happen, as you know, they usually happen all at once, so we don't know what's the chicken and what's the egg. When it comes to alcohol and drugs, however, I can say to the patient, "Stop doing these things and you'll have a much better chance to recover and stay well."

But what can you do about your life events? Obviously, it's very difficult to stop life events in your child's life, to take just one example. Relapses can also occur because of changes in the season. Though we may think that winter puts people at greater risk I've had patients who are prone to having depressive episodes mainly in the summers. I have one patient who in the last three years has had a relapse in the week before July 1. She believed that it had something to do with a change in her responsibilities at work, but she'd experienced the same shift in responsibilities every summer for the last twenty-five years without incident. And we can safely say that the cause wasn't primarily genetic; she had the same genes all along. So the most likely culprit was the seasonal change. But why has the depression only occurred for the last three summers and not the summers before? And how can we be absolutely certain that it wasn't some other factor? We don't know. It could have been something else that we aren't aware of.

How many episodes can a patient expect to have over his or her lifetime? Is there any average number? Well, some studies have looked into the question, but the results are far from satisfying. One reason is that most of the research has focused on hospitalized patients, so we don't know that much about the rate of relapses among the moderately depressed who are never seen for their condition by a doctor. The frequency of relapses will also depend on the age of the people we're studying at the time. Rates of depression may be rising in one population (teenagers, for example) and falling in another (the aged), so that trying to calculate the number of episodes someone is likely to incur becomes even more problematic. If, however, someone pressed me, I would say that the average patient will probably have three to six depressive episodes in a lifetime, but I would also point out that variation is the rule. And it doesn't tell us all that much to say how many episodes a person is likely to have if we don't also know the duration of each episode, which also varies. You would have to measure the duration of wellness against the duration of illness. Manic-depressive (or BPI) patients, for instance, tend to have clear-cut intervals between episodes of illnesses. Bipolar II patients usually have depressions as the primary form of illness interrupted by occasional hypomanias (mild manias). They have more depressive relapses and spend less time well than those who have a pattern of severe manias followed by depressions. Depression is more prominent in women; they're more likely to have depression and there is some evidence suggesting that they tend to respond less well than men do to certain antidepressants (i.e. tricyclics). Although women and men have equal rates of severe manic depression (Bipolar I), women have much higher rates of Bipolar II—that is, depression with mild highs. And among the severe BPI patients, women have more depressions than the BPI men do. Ironically, the more moderate the depression the more likely women are to have it and the more likely the depression is to be chronic and frequently recurrent. Why? We don't know. Having said all this, I always like to stress that new medications are coming on the market about every six months, so the future may be much more positive.

## The Stages of Recovery

Now that I've talked a bit about how depression affects daily functioning and the various factors that can influence or impede recovery, we need to look at how recovery proceeds. It certainly doesn't happen all at once just because your symptoms may have disappeared. Naturally, when you're ill you want to get back on your feet so that you can do the things you did before you got ill, with the same degree of vitality and interest. But you have to be prepared to get better just as you would if you were recovering from any other serious illness, a heart attack, say, or a catastrophic injury. Improvement occurs in stages. Your job functioning and functioning at home, especially if it involves a significant amount of homemaking and childcare, takes considerably longer to get back to normal than the resolution of symptoms. One study showed that it took about four months for people after their depressive symptoms disappeared to function normally at home. Function on the job took considerably longer. Years may have to pass before a patient completely recovers, and in some cases recovery may never occur. Some studies show that patients took a year to return to fully normal function. One study of patients who were free of symptoms for more than two years found that they still experience psychological problems. While these disadvantages may diminish with time, we still don't know how long it takes for full recovery to occur. And because of the likelihood of recurrence of symptoms, some degree of impairment may actually last for years. When researchers in Iowa reevaluated patients thirty to forty years after their first hospitalizations for unipolar or manic depression, 17 percent of unipolar and 24 percent of manic-depressive patients were rated as "occupationally incapacitated" due to mental illness.

So why does it take so long between the time the symptoms go away and the time you feel back to normal? (And, as I just said, in some cases, patients never completely get back to normal.) What usually happens first, after you've been in treatment for a month or two, is that you begin to look better. You are no longer "leaning into the wind"—your posture is better, you move with more agility, your skin tone and color are better, and you speak more animatedly. You begin to regain some of the vitality and energy that you'd lost when you were depressed. Yet if you were my patient and I told you that you were looking better you'd probably think I was out of my mind. In fact, this used to happen with some of my patients. When I was a young psychiatrist and didn't realize how differently they were seeing their situation, I would comment on how much better they looked. They insisted that I was mistaken and that I was just trying to encourage them because they knew that they certainly didn't *feel* any better. They were perfectly accurate about how they felt, of course, but so was I about my observation (albeit not perfectly.) That's because the physical improvement regularly occurs before the psychological improvement. I always tell patients, "You'll look better before you feel better." The inner symptoms of hopelessness and low self-esteem take more time to recover than vitality and physical condition. Now I'm more cautious about expressing my views. I just tell my patients that I've noticed that they seem to have more energy and point out that this is usually the harbinger of things to come, throwing it out as a casual observation to give them something positive to think about.

## Returning to Work

In the most severe depressions, the inability to function for a time, it reinforces the loss of self-esteem and self-confidence that patients already experience just from being depressed. When you recover from most of the symptoms of the illness, you feel you have to prove to yourself and to others that you can do your work with as much competence as you did before you became ill. And you're also likely to be sensitive and worried about what your coworkers or your boss may be thinking, and how they'll be judging you.

Some of your friends and fellow workers face a bit of a dilemma, too. They may be unsure what to say to you when you come back to work, especially if you were in a hospital and they knew about it. So there's an unnatural atmosphere. No one knows what to say. The net effect of this situation is that you may feel more isolated. Once you've returned to work you'll probably need some time to get up the nerve to talk to coworkers and vice versa. If the circumstances are appropriate, however, I recommend an open discussion at least with one or two trusted friends or coworkers. The objective is to help you regain your sense of belonging. Letting a friend or two in on the story will allow them the opportunity to tell you what they and others were thinking. Usually you'll find out that they were worried for you or that they have other friends who have gone through the same ordeal you have. On the other hand, you don't want to make your depression the story of your life. You can be honest without making a big deal of it. *I had depression, now I'm coming out of it, but it may take me a while.*

If you or your supervisor is worried about job stress levels, you may want to ask your supervisor if you could start off part time just to get adjusted rather than plunge right in. From my experience (I've been working with depressed patients since 1977), people are generally more understanding about depression now than you might imagine. My patients tell me that, for the most part, their employers and colleagues are more sympathetic than they'd expected them to be. There is now a greater public awareness about the disease. And by now, virtually everyone has heard about lithium or Prozac. Even more important, they may know someone who's depressed and on medication themselves.

This isn't to say, however, that there's no stigma attached to depression. Most of my patients worry that they will be stigmatized and not well regarded by their colleagues when they find out why they missed work, if they did. The sense of being stigmatized causes many people to shun seeking help from a psychiatrist. So they may not get help at all. Alternatively, they may feel less embarrassment about consulting another kind of doctor, like a general practitioner, who is not officially associated with psychiatry.

If you feel that in seeking help you are at risk of losing your job or alienating friends or family, you may be far less likely to get help. Although I don't think that stigmatization of depression is as bad as it was twenty years ago, I know that the situation is still not as good as it should be. People are growing more comfortable with the vocabulary of depression, though, and some of the new medications seem less stigmatized because they're so widespread (Prozac) and because they're widely advertised on TV and in popular magazines. Ads are constantly appearing in newspapers and magazines, advising people to be on the alert for several easily identifiable symptoms: low energy, lack of interest in life, persistence of symptoms over a long period, and the like. Unfortunately, these ads also suggest that being nervous while speaking in front of an audience is also a disease. A lot of people either get the idea that clinical depression is no tougher than overcoming anxiety about public speaking, or even conclude that the whole claim that depression is a disease is an exaggeration or worse. The key to destigmatizing the illness is for people to understand it as a medical condition, like heart disease or diabetes, and to know that treatment will help.

However, because there still is a stigma, some recovering patients will experience situations in which the reception at work or at home isn't likely to be as welcoming as they'd like. My advice is to use common sense in determining whom you want to tell about your illness, what you think is appropriate to disclose, and when. Getting extra support in a group or from your doctor or therapist can help you make these decisions.

How your boss reacts will probably depend on whether you've already proven your worth to the company. If your employer already sees you as valuable, he or she will be far more inclined to take you back and offer support. I have to say that it often turns out that the employer or someone in his or her family has had the illness, too. One patient's supervisor told her, "I've got it too and I've been under treatment for five years. So let me know if there's anything I can do for you." And all the time, my patient never had an inkling that the boss was fighting depression. If your boss has already had a good or bad experience with a depressed employee, he or she might prejudge your situation either optimistically or pessimistically. If you know what that experience was it can help you use or change the boss's expectations. In some situations you may ask your boss if they'd like to speak with your treating psychiatrist so they can ask questions that they might have.

What kind of a situation a recovering patient can expect to find when returning to work is often influenced by several external factors, among them the size of the company. If you work for a small firm, for example, your absence may have more of an impact than if you worked for, say, General Electric or IBM. Small businesses tend to have a greater financial burden when an employee gets sick for an extended period of time for any reason, because of the lost productivity and the insurance costs. So the owner will probably take into consideration how much disruption the illness caused the company. Has the boss lost confidence in the patient as a reliable employee? How many times has this employee been absent in the past? Will it happen again? And if so, how often? One of the things I point out to patients who want to leave the hospital before they're ready is that they're better off being away from work for five weeks at one stretch than getting out in four and relapsing a short time later because they weren't ready. Even if a subsequent hospital stay is only for two days, your boss is likely to wonder whether you can be counted on to get the job done.

The situation is significantly different in large companies; while they're often more impersonal, their attitudes toward employees who become seriously ill are usually consistent and neutral or positive. Many companies have human resource or personnel departments that offer confidential assistance to employees so that they can get help. It doesn't do a company any good if a worker isn't performing up to speed. And larger companies are better positioned to provide the support that's necessary to smooth the patient's reentry into the workplace. In this regard one of the best employers turns out to be the federal government because its policies have a very predictable set of rules and regulations for dealing with mental illness; there's a great deal of flexibility and tolerance built into the system. The situation is similar in many large companies. Our hope for the future is that all companies will recognize that depression is one of the leading causes for decreased work productivity and absenteeism, spurring them to take a more active role in identifying employees who are at risk and getting them into treatment.

## Can You Speed up Rehabilitation?

We can't really talk about recovery without talking about rehabilitation. What is the difference? Recovery implies that the illness has gone into remission—symptoms are resolved and presumably the brain disorder is at least inactive. Rehabilitation refers to regaining the ability to function at home, at work, and in social circumstances. What can we do to help patients regain function who have been disabled but who are recovered? Well, the field of vocational rehabilitation is not specialized in terms of disease and so many of the guidelines governing rehabilitation seem pretty generic. We're still not at a point where we can say what kind of rehabilitation is appropriate for a depressed patient.

What is the ideal way of helping patients who have missed two weeks of work as opposed to someone who's missed six weeks? That's hard to say. We work with the patient, social workers, employee assistance personnel, and others to put together a plan that seems suitable to the individual, but the plan is by no means precise. Certainly the patient is the most important person in the recovery process. Obviously, refusing to come for appointments or to take medications faithfully is harmful and disrupts your treatment plan. When these issues are raised we often hear the term *compliance* used to refer to how well or poorly patients are working with their doctors. I prefer the term *treatment adherence,* because it implies to me that the treatment plan is one that both the patient and doctor commit to. The doctor does his or her part, and the patient adhering to the treatment plan does his or hers. We are collaborators with the same objective in mind, but with different roles and insights. If the diagnosis is on target and the medication is appropriate then trust and personal commitment to the treatment plan is one of the most powerful predictors of positive outcomes.

## Treatment Adherence

Of the big three or four behaviors that reflect the outcome from depression and bipolar disorder, the most obvious one is whether the patient stays faithful to his or her treatment program. Almost no patient does this perfectly (anymore than we doctors always make the right diagnosis or start off with the best medication plan). However, over a one- to two-year period, it becomes obvious which patients have the right idea and carry out their side of the treatment plan.

I look for certain key factors that act as early indicators of whether a patient is committed to treatment. One of these indicators revolves around the issue of stigma. Does the patient accept the need for treatment? Some patients feel that using medications carries a stigma that will cause them to lose their job if they admit to taking them. Other patients shun only certain treatments, like lithium. The bad reputation that lithium is getting is relatively new. Twenty years ago lithium was more acceptable, but today I have patients who assure me "That's only for really crazy people." I have patients who will take anything *but* lithium. They tell me they consider lithium a drug you take only when you're seriously, psychiatrically ill—it's big-time stuff. When you say lithium many people think manic-depressive illness, which they tell me sounds less benign than calling it bipolar disorder. One of my patients—a very bright school teacher—insisted that she wouldn't take any substance as unnatural as lithium, but unfortunately she had no compunction about doing cocaine because, she said, it came from the cocoa leaf. I told her that if you want natural substances you couldn't do much better than lithium. Lithium, after all, is an element found in the ground. I'm afraid, though, that she didn't find my argument particularly persuasive. Another young woman regularly indulged in cocaine and took excessive amounts of Xanax and Valium as well, but told me that she wouldn't touch antidepressants because she felt she could work her emotional problems out on her own. These cases are by no means isolated ones. Even for patients who really do know about the illness and are widely read on the subject, it's still very hard to commit to taking medication that controls moods on a long-term basis. And when they do take medications, patients often have a different judgment about the effects than doctors do. Doctors may think a side effect—a dry mouth, for instance—is pretty trivial, but the patient may find the side effect especially aggravating and may think otherwise. (The situation can work in reverse, too: a patient will dismiss a side effect as inconsequential that the doctor will regard as quite significant.) But the point is that if you find the side effect too troublesome you may give up the medication altogether; and if in addition you don't receive the understanding or support you expected from your doctor, you're less likely to stay with a treatment. Some Bipolar patients have another explanation as to why they give up their medication. They miss their highs. Even the knowledge that we are sparing them from the worst of the lows may not be a sufficient inducement to maintain their medication.

Unfortunately, a fairly high number of patients don't follow their treatment plans as prescribed; 30 to 50 percent will stop their treatment even after only the first six months. Their reluctance to take their medication, may have several causes. Possibly the treatment wasn't well explained to them. Maybe they don't have confidence in the doctor. In that event, there is less likely to be an open and frank collaboration. The patient can't trust it when the doctor tells him or her what will work and what won't.

A few patients openly reject following doctors' orders. They can say to the doctor, "Look, I don't need you," and walk out of the office. Or else they may sit back and wait for their medication to kick in and figure that they don't have to do anything else to get well. In this case, I'd say they feel they have no role in their treatment. In both cases—whether you walk out or act passively—the situation is essentially the same: a refusal to cooperate.

But at this point I have to put in a caveat. When people are extremely depressed they're so ill that a doctor has to take care of them. That doesn't mean that they don't want to cooperate. It's just that they are incapable of cooperating at the time they are seriously ill. When these patients are no longer severely depressed and can return to work, their active commitment to treatment is critical. The purpose of getting patients to accept the illness is for them to be a more informed and active patient. You can say, "This medication isn't helping me, what else can we try?" How much improvement is reasonable to expect? Both of us have jobs to do in order to get the best results.

# CHAPTER 21

∞

# Going Forward

I hope that I have succeeded in conveying what we know about depression and what we don't know. As a community of professionals, patients, families, and friends concerned about depression, we know so much more now than we did twenty to thirty years ago. We have many more demonstrably effective treatments, both medical and psychological, and we have far more confidence that we will find the important genes that contribute to the predisposition to depressive disorders. In addition, we know more about the limits of knowledge in genetics, brain structure, and neurochemistry. We have made the great leap from simplistic ideas to good questions. It will take time and more bright careers dedicated to this work to get the answers. In my judgment, this is the great biomedical challenge of our age. The age of discovery of insulin, penicillin, and cancer treatment are past or just upon us now. Brain diseases like depression, manic-depressive illness, schizophrenia, Alzheimer's, and others are on the horizon. I know that knowledge of this research and the hype for better treatments, can serve to some extent as an antidote against the feelings of aloneness and hopelessness that depression creates.

I also hope that what I've elaborated about the impact of depressive illness conveys why I feel it's so urgent to accelerate our educational efforts to spread the word about depressive illness. At the same time I also hope that I've made clear how excited I am about the opportunities to define the physiological pathways to these diseases and the hope for rational treatments in the future. In other words, we are closing in on what happens in our brains to cause depressive and bipolar disorders. The sequencing of the human genome, achieved in 2000 and 2001, is certain to provide us with new approaches to finding the genes responsible for depression. These genes will lead to more accurate diagnosis and to more accurate predictions of which treatments will be most effective and which will be safest. Eventually this can be done individually for each patient. Throughout this book I've tried to emphasize the most important lessons that I've learned from eight thousand patients (and thousands of families) affected with depression and manic depression. Based on what I've seen and what we've learned from recent research, a strong case can be made that none of us—whether we have depression or not—can afford to remain indifferent to these often devastating but highly treatable conditions. As a leading cause of disability worldwide and one of the most burdensome diseases for millions of people throughout the world, in both economic and human terms, clinical depression affects all of us, directly or indirectly.

No one, as I've said many times, really understands what goes wrong in the brain during clinical depression. But what we do know too well is that it is the leading cause of suicide, that it increases the risk of developing heart disease and suffering fatal heart attacks, and that it contributes to increased fatality after strokes. Even though we cannot yet comprehend the mechanism of these diseases, all trained clinicians can diagnose them with a substantial degree of accuracy. Psychiatrists are as consistent in diagnosing clinical depression as other physicians are in diagnosing pneumonia, heart attacks, or enlarged prostate glands, once they've taken a direct history and examined the patient. Moreover, even in spite of gaps in our knowledge, we are able to provide effective treatments for most patients with depression and bipolar disorder. We can also make reasonable predictions about the outcome of our patients' cases; depending on how well they take care of themselves and how faithfully they work together with their caretakers to limit the impact of the illness.

## What We Will Learn

What I would like to do in this last chapter is give you some idea about what we might learn beyond the important practical matters when we are able to chart the basic elements of the genetic and brain pathway in depression and manic depression. In practical terms, our increased understanding will allow us to make the diagnosis earlier in the illness and we will make fewer diagnostic errors. I suspect that we will probably learn that there are six, twelve, or eighteen different genetic types and six nongenetic types of depressive illness.

When we do finally find the genes and environmental factors that cause depressive illness, we will obviously be in a far better position to determine how they promote these disorders. We will have a much clearer picture of how today's common treatments work and for which patients they will be most effective.

I expect that some of these discoveries will satisfy our intellectual curiosity, too, by providing us with insights about how moods influence all of our everyday activities. You may remember at the beginning of this book I talked about the confusion that often resulted when people mistook a clinical illness (depression) for a normal state (feeling distressed or down for a short period of time). What is illness and what is "moodiness" is not always an easy question to answer. You can't spend half your life trying to outwit an adversary like depression without gaining both respect and fascination for moods and our affective functions. Thanks to the dramatic experiences of my manic patients, I long ago became fascinated by the mysterious power of mood. Among the traits that our genes contribute to, in addition to intelligence, physical characteristics, and athletic or musical ability, are the affective temperaments.

Many of you may feel the way I do, that it is somehow counterintuitive to think of genes as holding any influence over our moods, whether those moods occur in periods of depression or are the kinds of moods that we experience normally in our daily lives. (Probably at least some of you are wondering, with all the attention I'm giving to genetic influence, whether I think there's anything genes don't do! Answer: make the coffee or find my car keys each morning.) As it turns out, though, genes do play an important role in moods. A lot of impressive research is shedding more light on the link. For example, some researchers studying the role of mood in cognition believe that moods make a key contribution to the tone and quality of an individual's thinking. Other researchers tend to believe the reverse, that "thinking" is how we set the tone and quality of our moods. If the former mood researchers are correct then we'd have to say that if it weren't for mood, we'd be indistinguishable from computers. (If moods were generated by intellect alone, then in theory, a computer could generate moods, too.)

Thus, moods seem to be real things in themselves, present in all of us, not just in people with depressive illness. And moods or affective responsiveness are part of what we call temperament, which by our best calculations is about 50 percent genetic. (Remember what Galen said about how personalities could be categorized by the four "humors"—phlegmatic, melancholic, sanguine, and choleric? He was actually talking about temperament.) Yet moods, it turns out, might play a role in distributing genes in a population. So what I'm suggesting is a kind of evolutionary (selection) dynamic: genes influence moods, moods influence our behavior and relationships that are part of the dynamics of sexual behavior, which is how our genes are distributed as they help define the next generation.

This idea may sound a bit wacky. Try to recall what you heard in high school biology about the theory of evolution: nature tends to preserve those genes that help us adapt, thrive, and survive. And, for better or worse, moods probably play a significant role in sexual attraction (or lack thereof). Yes, we certainly notice other attributes as well, such as looks, IQ, and values, but we also tend to be influenced by the mood of the persons we are. Is it conceivable that nature would want to pair up "mood partners" in some way? There are specific ideas about how mania or depression or both might help humans adapt in some fashion. For example, depression might warn us that there is trouble ahead when no one else sees it. There are about fifty theoretical reasons to claim why mania has survival value, at least for the species, if not for the individual . . . more energy, more fierceness, more confidence, more sex . . . oh, yes, did I mention more sex? Some or all of these might have merit, but it is also possible that the genes involved in mood disorders are also involved in other processes like the immune system or that it is their effect on normal moods, not in depression or mania, that has survival value. And of course, I haven't seen any good evidence yet that they have any survival value but I do wonder about it a lot.

Earlier in this book I wrote about how depressive illnesses disrupts and often destroys relationships. Yet, ironically, it turns out that moods (and genes) involved in these illnesses appear capable of actually enhancing relationships, too! How these genes bring couples together is a phenomenon that clinicians and researchers call assortative mating. For years psychiatrists and researchers observed that patients with depression and manic depression are two or three times more likely to marry someone else with the disorder than would be expected by chance. But how to account for this phenomenon? Consider my patients Valerie and John.

## Beyond the Practical: The Lessons of Assortative Mating

When she first came to me, Valerie was fifty years old and had suffered from bouts of intermittent and prolonged depression. As a teenager she'd experienced an episode of psychological or hysterical paralysis, which is thought to be rare in depression today. In her twenties and thirties she began to drink heavily, which is common in those with her illness. Valerie's condition was also fairly typical in that other members of her family had affective disorders as well. In fact, her family was riddled with them. All three of her sisters, her three brothers, her daughter, and her father have the same condition. In spite of her problems, however, Valerie was a bright, extroverted, and sensible woman of considerable achievement.

I later met John, who was about five years her senior, when he came at Valerie's urging for an evaluation. His history revealed that he had suffered exclusively from depressions: a unipolar disorder as opposed to his wife's Bipolar II illness. When he first became ill, the episodes of depression would last up to one to two years each time. It was all that he could do to get up in the morning and go to work. When he came home he would often crawl into bed. There was depression in his family, too: one of his sisters had manic depression and both his grandfather and an uncle had committed suicide. When I did a mental status examination I saw that John appeared to be depressed and withdrawn. He had no energy, he couldn't concentrate, and even a good night's sleep failed to refresh him. He also had an unrealistically low opinion of himself and viewed his future bleakly. So as it turned out, while Valerie and John had very different forms of mood disorders (or as I prefer to call them, affective disorders), they shared lots of depression.

John and Valerie were good observers of their own conditions once they understood their symptoms for what they represented. John, they both agreed, tended to have a more chronic low-grade depressive disorder. Valerie, on the other hand, had distinct periods during which she felt extremely well, even better than normal, for three to six months, followed by periods of equal time when she felt down. For John, Valerie embodied optimism. Her cheerful demeanor balanced out his tendency to look darkly at the world. For Valerie, John represented stability, an anchor that she could hold fast to against the emotional waves that buffeted her.

John didn't feel like a bastion of stability at all, far from it. Without Valerie's understanding and affection he felt he would be completely lost. But the need and commitment didn't work in only one direction. Valerie realized that John was committed to her as well, whatever the state of his mood, and in that way he was an anchor for her. I marveled at how their unusual but effective mutual support system worked. This isn't always the case in marriages between two affected persons.

According to several studies, when both husband and wife are depressed at the same time, the rate of divorce is very high.

Psychiatrists have been puzzling over why this apparent assortative mating occurs. A psychiatrist I know who comes from Hungary reported that he'd seen such couples in Budapest in the 1930s. His professor had asked him, "Do they meet in da vaiting room?" This would give us a simple and logical explanation, but, no, it turns out, it's not the case for the patients in the studies and it was certainly not true for Valerie and John. Neither of them, for instance, knew when they got married that the other was ill. For that matter, they didn't even realize that they were ill themselves!

Well, let's take a few steps back. What brings couples together to begin with? Perhaps it's stating the obvious to say that people are drawn to potential mates who come from similar backgrounds. And we know that people are more likely to marry someone who is of nearly equal intelligence. People seldom marry individuals more than fifteen points from their own IQ. Physical appearance, too, especially height, affects marriage choices. We also know similar values and religious views tend to be powerful influences in picking mates.

On the other hand, we also know that people are sometimes attracted to their opposites as well. Some women who are not themselves rebellious but are at heart sensation seekers tend to marry exciting, risk-taking men who get into a lot of trouble. These marriages tend not to last very long, as the women discover to their dismay that these men are just too exciting.

Valerie had no problem coming up with an answer about why she chose John from the several suitors she'd dated. "John saw me through a couple of bad periods," she said. "He didn't run away." Her response echoes that of many other patients I've known. One of the reasons that John didn't run away is because he'd seen members of his own family through similar emotional crises. Having supported parents or siblings when they were coping with depression, he might have been more motivated to stick by Valerie. It's also a tribute to John that he saw Valerie even then as his soul mate whom he would stand by through a dark night. (That's a point to bear in mind: as important as what a doctor can do for you with diagnosis and treatments for depression, nothing can substitute for a family member or a friend when you hang in there with a depressed person at their lowest point.)

Another observation that persuades me that the pattern of assortative mating is based on some attractive force is that so many patients who have married several times have married an ill person on each occasion. It's only after they've been married for a while that they express surprise that the same thing has "happened again." I can't tell you how many times my patients found someone new who seems perfect to them and, whether they were right or wrong about the perfection, they were certainly surprised to find depression or bipolar disorder just as they had in their previous spouse. And when things go wrong they go through the same arguments with them and endure the same crises. "Why do I always find the same man (or woman)?" One of my younger patients is on his third marriage at age thirty-seven. His first two wives had a so-called milder form of manic depression (Bipolar II) and the third had depression, which occasionally required treatment prior to their divorce. Thankfully, the relationships can be very positive even with two ill persons, as Valerie and John's has done for over thirty years now.

One of my psychiatrist friends argues that assortative mating behavior has nothing to do with my romantic view of a sympathy and support. He reminded me of what the satiric journalist H. L. Mencken once said: "When they say it's not about sex, it's always about sex."

All right, for argument's sake, let's say it's just about sex. What could make you sexually attracted to a person with a depressive illness rather than to a person who didn't have a serious mood problem? The answer is that we don't really know. We haven't studied the differences, if any, in the sexual lives of couples when both are depressed compared to ones where only one is depressed. I do know that while most people lose interest in sex when they are depressed, this is not a universal rule. Some patients want more reassurance of their partner's love, passion, or commitment when they are depressed compared to when they're feeling healthy and relatively secure. Still other patients say sex is what they need to take the "edge off" of their tension so they can fall asleep at night when they are depressed. But in the pit of depression most patients have no interest in "carnal fun" to quote William Styron.

Now you might ask, as many of my patients do, whether this a bad thing to have two depressed people becoming parents, both on genetic grounds and based on the problems they will have if there are any children because of their clinical symptoms. For now my answer (though it might change as I learn more) is that decisions about children should hinge less on the statistical chance of developing the illness at some point in life and much more on the level of commitment by the parents to each other and their commitment to have, raise, and care for children. A medical student conducted a survey of couples in which one spouse had the illness. She asked them whether, if one member of the couple had a gene (or genes) that carried depression or bipolar disorder, would they still have children? Their answer was a unanimous yes. Then she asked them whether, if a test performed during pregnancy, showed that their child had the genes for depression, they would have an abortion. Again the answer was unanimous—no.

## Temperament, Depression, and Genes

Now we come to a question that has perplexed scholars, scientists and doctors alike. Given the fact that the abnormal genes that cause depression and manic depression do so much harm—especially in relationships, work, and daily function—why on earth would they have survived for the thousands of years that it seems that they have been around? Do they somehow confer some advantage for survival to offset their clear disadvantage for survival? This question doesn't apply only to depressive disorders. Actually several other genetic conditions have a similarly double-edged effect on mankind. The best-known example involves individuals with one gene for the blood disease known as sickle-cell anemia, which is especially prevalent among northern African populations living along the Mediterranean. (A similar pattern is seen with two other blood disorders, Thallasemia and G6PD deficiency, in populations living around the Mediterranean.) A child has to be born with two copies of the sickle-cell gene to develop sickle-cell anemia, and when that happens he or she is destined to suffer from a terrible illness. However, in families with the mutation, a child is far more likely to inherit only one copy of the sickle-cell gene and one normal hemoglobin gene. When that happens the single sickle-cell gene has a decided advantage to the individual: it offers a natural immunity to malaria. So it's not surprising that people living in an environment where malaria is endemic—especially in coastal regions of Africa and Mediterranean countries— have maintained a higher rate of sickle cell genes than populations that have developed elsewhere.

Without knowing what the genes for mood disorders are and what they do, we can't answer the question of what survival value they might have. But many people have at least speculated about what the answers might look like. Since the genes for depression presumably will influence mood and emotional mechanisms in the brain, perhaps they will contribute to normal personality traits or temperament. In other words, if it takes variations in one or any of the three to five genes to cause a mood disorder, the variations in the genes themselves might contribute something positive to normal temperament in humans. How might that happen?

Well, some people never fantasize; they always see things as they really are. We call them realists, pessimists or skeptical types. They are all like Sergeant Friday from the old TV serial, *Dragnet,* asking for "Just the facts, ma'am. Nothing but the facts." We certainly need realists and pessimists, among whose number we find a lot of police officers, businesspeople, and scientists. But we don't want everyone on the team to be the same type. Imagine what sort of world it would be like if everyone were a confirmed realist. If each time we faced a particularly knotty problem and there was someone leaning over your shoulder saying, "You can't do this, better forget it," then where would we be? People sometimes overcome seemingly impossible odds, after all, defying the advice of realists. Possibly one or two genes for today's bipolar disorder might have helped produce extroverted, optimistic leaders who are as needed now as they were in the past. (We would have to hope, however, that any of these optimists today who get elected to higher office are wise enough to appoint a couple of realistic skeptics as their advisers.) In other words, if I were to select people on the basis of temperament—whether it was for a position in government, business, or even on my amateur basketball team—I would want to have a variety of types. So, from an evolutionary standpoint, to insure that there is sufficient variety, it might be critical to have ten to twenty genes affecting mood and optimism levels. However, the urgent task for us is to help the 5 to 10 percent of the population who have too many of these genes which cause clinical depression or bipolar disorder. After all, if this part of the theory is right, we could say that they have paid the evolutionary toll so we could have sufficient diversity in moods.

## Does Depression or Manic-Depression Provide Any Survival Benefit?

Beyond the genes, could there be some value for elements of the disease itself? So far we have lots of speculation and very little knowledge. However, with the strides we've made in our research, we're almost at the point where we'll be able to test some of our ideas. In time, we'll be better able to unravel some of these intriguing mysteries. One of the best-articulated theories, advanced by Dr. Kay Jamison and others, takes note of the fact that a significant number of highly creative artists, poets, and novelists have bouts of depression and manic-depressive illness. Jamison freely acknowledges that most poets and artists are not manic-depressive and that many manic-depressives have no demonstrable talent. All the same, she has found in her studies that four to five times as many poets and novelists have manic-depressive illness than is seen in the general population. This suggests that there's at least some truth to the observations linking genius with madness.

There are other theories, too, some of which suggest that depression evolved because it might have helped our ancestors survive in a world with predators and calamities. In this view, the genes are there to communicate an urgent warning. Depression genes might say: Don't put up a fight! Stop! Preserve your resources! Hunker down and wait for the storm (or the wooly mammoth) to pass. Maybe clinical depression is a result of that mechanism going awry like a red light that never changes to green, causing a rush-hour mess. This might be the stress-response system failing. It might even be possible to link this frozen stoplight theory with the theory linking depression to creativity. Perhaps people in the artistic professions, driven to inspired heights in their manic states, may not know when to stop trying to tap their creative juices even if they're running dry. That's where depression enters the picture. Depression may be the great editor that tempers the flight of artistic exhuberance by revealing the mistakes and misjudgments previously hidden by his or her intoxicated state. But great editors can get carried away, too, and start wielding their pencils too freely, leaving little or nothing behind. Maybe such editors' pencils should be colored depression blue instead of mania red.

The answers to these and other equally tantalizing questions are more likely to be found once we understand the basic genetic mechanisms, brain pathways and hormonal systems that cause periods of severe depression or manias when they are not working well. We hope that these discoveries will lead to powerful diagnostic, therapeutic, and preventative advances. That doesn't suggest to me that we will eradicate clinical depression or manic depression any time soon. (We have not eradicated cancer either, though we certainly can understand it and treat it much better than we did in the past.) What these discoveries do mean in practical terms is that we will be in a position to reduce the delay in diagnosing depression and manic depression and we will be able to make treatments more effective and less toxic.

In addition we will begin to develop better ideas about how to answer the questions patients ask themselves after they have recovered from an episode of disease: *Where is it that my disease ends and I (my normal self) begins? What is it about my brain that means I could lose control again?*

Even when we can answer these questions, we will still need wisdom that derives from experiences and not just from experiments. People are always going to need their doctors to help them deal with the ambiguous nature of these illnesses. To do that, doctors have to educate themselves. One thing I can assure you is that doctors learn most of what they know not in kindergarten or even in the labs of medical school. They learn from their patients. It is through their patients that doctors (experienced or new) come to understand that courage, patience, and grace, far from being exceptional qualities, are the norm even among patients who are suffering the most. Depression is in many ways the worst of diseases because it hits patients where they are the most vulnerable, by robbing them of their sense of self-worth and calling into question their very reason for being; that's why it's the more remarkable that they manage to demonstrate such courage and act with such grace, and still maintain their patience even when they feel that their illness will last for all eternity. But depression does lift eventually even when treatments fail. Obstetricians have their moments, certainly surgeons do, too, but for me the best place in the world isn't in a maternity ward or an operating room. I can imagine no better place than to be close to my patients when their depression finally relinquishes its grip and gives them back their lives.

# Appendix A: Insurance

Weaving through the ins and outs of any health care plan can be confusing and frustrating, but this is particularly true for the mental health provisions.

The major health plan types include traditional (or indemnity) HMOs, PPOs, Medicare, and Medicaid. The health insurance industry has gone through a period of "consolidation" so that fewer companies with larger portfolios are now left to compete with one another. Most of the large insurance companies offer health plans of every type and shape. They offer plans with varying benefits, premiums, and copays. HMOs have not become the dominant type of plan as expected. HMOs are structured to emphasize preventative care, and they have fulfilled this mandate more than other types of plans. But they have come under increasing pressure because of the fiercely competitive marketplace to act like other plans by limiting enrollment and benefits for the severely chronically ill, a category that includes those with serious psychiatric illnesses.

Medicaid is the federal health insurance program for people who are not senior citizens. Although it can appear excessively bureaucratic, in many ways it is superior to other insurance plans for individuals with serious mental illnesses. Supplemental Security Income is a related benefit for disabled individuals. If you qualify for this small monthly stipend, you automatically qualify for healthcare coverage via Medicaid.

Essentially health plans have "carved out" mental health care to contracting companies. The managers of these contractors will often oversee a separate group of providers that manage all psychiatric care. Even governmental-sponsored programs are moving to carve out their psychiatric care benefits. As a result, the patients' major insurance company has only an indirect responsibility for the care of depressive, manic depressive and other psychiatric conditions. This system requires families and patients to negotiate their way through a multistep chain of phone calls and forms during very stressful times when someone needs urgent psychiatric care. Patients are bounced

back and forth from the major carrier to the mental health manager
and to the health care professionals who can only be paid if the care
is approved in advance.

This "carve-out" results in one of the strangest quirks of the current cost-focused era of managed care where psychiatric care costs
and outpatient visit costs are paid for from funds which are kept separate from the larger general medical budget. These psychiatric
"carve outs" cover therapy and hospital costs but not outpatient medications. They are aggressively managed (i.e., reviewers are "encouraged" to say no to clinicians who believe a patient needs more days
in the hospital or more therapy sessions). The assumption seems to
be that it's far less expensive to prescribe drugs than it is to pay for
therapy. Up to now there have been relatively few limits on prescribing psychiatric medications most of which are written by the primary
care providers (GP's, etc.) not by psychiatrists. Such a policy creates
a health care system that strips humanity and empathy from care and
discourages the management of all aspects of the illness and its
impact on the patient. Psychiatrists are reduced to making a check-
list diagnoses and writing prescriptions on fifteen-minute sessions.
This policy effectively isolates the patient's care from the family as
surely as our misguided rules governing psychiatric confidentiality
ever did.

A number of mental health parity acts have recently been passed
by Congress and the state legislatures. In general, parity means that
basic healthcare plans have to offer benefits for mental health care,
which are considered comparable to those offered for physical disabilities. But because mental health care benefits are managed
through a separate carve-out mechanism, just because your policy
entitles you to a benefit doesn't necessarily mean that you can access
it because the rules for "medical necessity" are written in such a way
as to make denial of care quite easy. These rules, of course, work well
when it comes to preventing payments for unnecessary expensive
care; it's just that they also are likely to prevent payment for needed
care. These policies often restrict the number of visits you can make
to a mental health professional and/or raise your copayment for
such visits.

There are some important strategies to keep in mind when you
review and use your insurance coverage. First be informed. Document everything that happens when a decision goes against your clinician: in this regard your doctor or therapist can be very helpful. If
the situation warrants, appeal the insurer's decision. Above all,
remain calm but persistent.

It is especially critical to be informed of all of the items covered and not covered by your plan. Read it carefully before you join and before you are in a crisis. Be sure that you have a copy of the firm's master policy, not just the usual brief list of what is covered. Look at your plan's "out of network" clause, which would allow you to choose a professional other than those listed on their "network provider" or HMO list. Many individuals find it useful to maintain separate manila folders for their insurance and medical information and bills. You will probably need a separate folder for documents relating just to psychiatric care. Among the information, you should have telephone numbers of individuals to contact in case of a crisis situation, such as a hospitalization.

You should keep copies of all bills, reports, evaluations, tests, and other medical records. Also, you should document all phone conversations with insurance representatives. Be sure to ask for the full name (and spelling) of the individual you are speaking to and obtain the direct phone number. If you personalize the relationship, the representative will feel more accountable for resolving your problem. If something is promised during the phone conversation, it is a good idea to send a letter to the insurer documenting the conversation. It can work somewhat similarly to how you approach the gate attendants at the airport; you are rewarded for being nice but persistent

Needless to say, all this is very time-consuming work. In the long run an experienced psychiatrist will have had quite a lot of experience dealing with various insurance plans. But while health professionals are usually quite willing to help you with insurers, they are limited in the time they can give you if you want them to do more than fill out the necessary forms and give you advice on how to proceed. If you find that your provider is too busy to assist you with these issues, you might be able to seek advice and guidance from the support staff.

Many individuals simply accept insurance claim denials. In fact, nearly 70 percent of all claim denials are never appealed. All denied claims should be appealed if they are reasonable and should be covered under the original policy. I've found that most appeals are successful but usually require two or three levels of appeals after initial denial of benefits from a lower-level reviewer. You shouldn't hesitate to write a letter stating the grievance or claim that you wish to file with the company. Be emphatic and clear about your demand. Letters simply registering a complaint or expressing your unhappiness will most likely go unnoticed. In this context, the Internet can become an extremely valuable tool in helping you dispute claims. You can often find pertinent state laws, public policy statements, and possibly insurance commission rulings online (see www.naic.org or www.bazelon.org). If you still have difficulty, you can contact your state's department of health or insurance commission. Also, your state's NAMI chapter can be extremely helpful. They most likely have much of the information you need and are pros at dealing with insurance companies. As a last resort, you can resort to legal action. Consulting a lawyer can be useful. However, this process may be protracted and expensive.

In disputes, you should remain calm yet assertive when dealing with representatives at both the insurer's and the provider's level. Be sure to have all information (policy numbers, insurance and provider's phone numbers) accessible while speaking to any official about your case. You'll do far better if you are able to explain your situation in an organized manner. And remember that although at times the experience is frustrating, patience almost invariably helps your cause. Be restrained. Becoming angry over the phone or in a face-to-face meeting might make you feel momentarily better but it usually makes the situation worse. Remember that the representative you are speaking to is rarely involved in making the decisions about your case. If possible, you want the representative to be your ally, not your enemy.

# Appendix B:
# Helpful Organizations

1. American Academy of Child and Adolescent Psychiatry (AACP)
   (202) 966-7300
   www.aacap.org

   The AACAP is a professional medical organization comprised of the child and adolescent psychiatrists in the United States. Their stated missions are to treat and improve the quality of life for children, adolescents, and families affected by mental, behavioral, or developmental disorders. The organization offers information on child and adolescent psychiatry, current research, prevention programs, and managed care, as well as fact sheets for parents. You'll find the "Facts for Families" section on the web site particularly helpful.

2. American Association for Geriatric Psychiatry (AAGP)
   (301) 654-7850
   www.aagpgpa.org

   The AAGP is a national association mainly composed of psychiatrists with special training in geriatrics. The organization is dedicated to promoting the mental health of the elderly. Through education and research the AAGP hopes to enhance standards of practice in geriatric psychiatry. The organization also serves as an advocate for the mental health needs of older Americans. The web site is useful for the elderly and their families for its practical advice, including how to go about locating a psychiatrist who specializes in geriatric psychiatry. Clicking on "Consumer Information" will link you to sites for the public.

3. American Foundation for Suicide Prevention (AFSP)
   (888) 333-2377; National Suicide Hotline, (800) 999-9999
   www.afsp.org

   The AFSP is made up of a variety of professional and lay members who are dedicated to understanding and preventing suicide. The organization supports research projects that further the dissemination of information about depression and suicide and works to develop more treatment options. The group also educates the public through conferences and literature. Support groups are available nationwide, including those for suicide survivors. The web site offers moving stories written by individuals whose lives have been affected by suicide. Users can also find information here on National Suicide Survivor Day.

4. American Psychiatric Association (APA)
   (202) 682-6000
   www.psych.org

   The APA is a medical organization made up of psychiatrists primarily in the United States. Although the group's focus is directed toward the needs of professionals, it does offer a wide range of resources for the general public, including fact sheets, videos, publications, a suggested reading list on depression, bipolar disorder, and other conditions. They also have hotline numbers and phone numbers of other organizations that may be of help. Many of these materials are also available in Spanish. A section titled "Public Information" is available on the drop-down site guide menu.

5. American Psychological Association
   (800) 374-3120
   www.apa.org

   The APA is an organization whose objective is to advance psychology as a science, profession, and means of promoting human welfare. Although primarily a professional association, this APA provides some information for the general public. You'll find the help center on their Web site to be a very valuable tool. Of particular interest are articles on depression that are both interesting and timely.

6. Anxiety Disorders Association of America
   (301) 231-9350
   www.adaa.org

   The ADAA is a nonprofit organization of professionals and members of the general public whose mission statement says that they will promote efforts to cure and prevent anxiety disorders and improve the lives of people who suffer from anxiety disorders. In addition to its role in promoting patient advocacy, educating the public, and encouraging research, the ADAA also tries to eliminate discrimination associated with anxiety disorders. Users who are interested in the latest developments in research into anxiety disorders will find information on several interesting clinical trials on the web site.

7. Bazelon Center
   (202) 467-5730
   www.bazelon.org

   The Bazelon Center is a nonprofit legal advocacy organization that seeks to uphold national policies recognizing the legal rights of people with mental disabilities. The web site is especially useful for people who want to learn more about the legal ramifications of mental health issues. Lucid explanations can be found, for instance, for terms such as *medical necessity* and outpatient commitment. In addition, the web site offers insurance-related topics, including information on the National Disabilities Act.

8. Bipolar Genetics Collaboration Research
   www.bipolargenes.org

   This web site is a resource operated by researchers across the country who are collaborating in the search for the genes responsible for bipolar disorder. The site explains the nature of the study and offers information about how families can participate.

9. Bipolar Kids Homepage
   www.geocities.com/EnchantedForest/1068

   Bipolar Kids Homepage is a web site specially designed for children and their parents, teachers, doctors, and friends. There are several good links for children and their caretakers.

10. Bipolar Significant Others
    www.bpso.org/

    This web site contains an extensive list of resources, especially books and web sites, related to bipolar disorders. The information is useful for everyone, but has particularly excellent material for parents of bipolar children.

11. Boston University Center for Psychiatric Rehabilitation
    (617) 353-3549
    www.bu.edu/sarpsych/

    The Boston University Center for Psychiatric Rehabilitation provides information for patients and families about rehabilitation for psychiatrically disabled persons. At the user's request, announcements and news about special events can be e-mailed directly by filling out the form on the site.

12. Center for Disease Control and Prevention
    (404) 639-3534
    www.cdc.gov

    The Centers for Disease Control and Prevention, based in Atlanta, is a government agency responsible for monitoring and improving the health of Americans. Its major objectives include the investigation and prevention of illness. The CDC also performs a valuable advocacy role in health-related issues. The agency offers reports from the surgeon general on its web site, including two major reports on mental illness, one a comprehensive analysis of the problem of suicide in the United States and another on mental illness in youth and children. (Search: depression.)

13. Child and Adolescent Bipolar Foundation
    www.cabf.org

    The Child and Adolescent Bipolar Foundation strives to educate the public about the early onset of bipolar disorders, advocate for increased resources for affected families, and promote research on the nature, causes, and treatment of bipolar disorder in children and adolescents. This web site explains the importance of education and includes helpful hints for bipolar children and their families.

14. Dana Alliance for Brain Initiatives
    www.dana.org/

    The Dana Alliance for Brain Initiatives is a nonprofit organization composed of neuroscientists interested in educating the public and advancing research on the brain. The web site contains many articles for professionals, and the "Brainy Kids On-line" link is full of fun activities for children to learn more about the brain.

15. Depression After Delivery
    (800) 944-4773
    www.infotrail.com/dad/dad.html

    Depression After Delivery is a national organization providing support, education, information, and referrals for women coping with depression associated with the birth of a baby. The list of resources on the web site is full of links related to issues about postpartum depression as well as general parenting information.

16. Depression and Related Affective Disorders Association (DRADA)
    (410) 955-4647
    www.med.jhu.edu/drada

    DRADA is a fifteen-year-old nonprofit organization focusing on manic-depressive illness and depression that brings together individuals with affective disorders, family members, and mental health professions. The organization's mission is to alleviate the suffering caused by depression and manic depression by facilitating the formation of self-help groups, providing education and information, and lending support to research programs. DRADA works in cooperation with the Johns Hopkins University School of Medicine, which ensures the medical accuracy of the materials. An annual mood disorders research and education symposium is sponsored by both DRADA and Johns Hopkins University School of Medicine. The web site contains a list of excellent books and videos available about mood disorders.

17. Moodswing.org
    www.moodswing.org/

    This on-line resource is an extremely helpful guide for people suffering from bipolar disorder, their families, and friends. As a basic guide, the "frequently asked questions" link is particularly useful.

18. National Alliance for the Mentally Ill (NAMI)
    (800) 950-NAMI
    www.nami.org

    NAMI is America's largest self-help support and advocacy organization for people with serious mental illness and their families. It seeks to provide current information about all mental illnesses. It emphasizes the importance of research for mental illnesses to improve the lives of those affected. The web site offers information about how to contribute to its advocacy efforts. You'll also find an informative page on how to participate in a research study.

19. National Alliance for Research on Schizophrenia and Depression
    (NARSAD)
    (516) 829-0091
    www.mhsource.com/narsad

    NARSAD was founded by the National Alliance for the Mentally Ill, the National Mental Health Association, the National Depressive and Manic Depressive Association, and the Schizophrenia Foundation (now disbanded). This is the largest donor-supported organization in the world devoted exclusively to supporting scientific research on brain disorders. It is committed to ending mental illness through research on the causes, treatments, cures, and prevention. The NARSAD web site includes clear and basic explanations of the signs and symptoms of both depression and bipolar disorder.

20. National Association of Insurance Commissioners (NAIC)
    (202) 624-7790
    www.naic.org/

    The NAIC is an organization of insurance regulators representing all regions of the United States. The web site can help you contact information for your state insurance commissioner. From the home page click on the "Insurance Regulators" link, which will enable you to choose a "map" option. Once you select the state the web page of the state insurance commission will automatically appear.

21. National Association of State Mental Health Program Directors
    (NASMHPD)
    (703) 739-9333
    www.nasmhpd.org/

    The National Association of State Mental Health Program Directors represents state mental health authorities at the national level. Its mandate is to identify mental health policy issues, analyze trends, encourage research, and educate. A directory of state psychiatric hospitals can be found on the web site.

22. National Depressive and Manic-Depressive Association (NDMDA)
    (800)826-3632
    www.ndmda.org

    NDMDA is a patient- and family-based organization that views affective disorders as biochemical in nature, best treated with medication and adjunctive psychotherapy. This group educates the public, advocates for research, and fosters self-help for patients and families. In addition, NDMDA works to eliminate discrimination and stigma associated with these two illnesses. It also seeks to improve access to care. On the web site you can find a link to "patient assistance programs" that provides information about how pharmaceutical companies who offer prescription medication for free to impoverished patients.

23. National Institute of Mental Health
    (301) 443-4513
    www.nimh.nih.gov/

    The National Institute of Mental Health (NIMH) acts to diminish the burden of mental illness through research. By using powerful scientific tools, researchers at NIMH hope to better understand, treat, and eventually prevent mental illness. NIMH recently initiated a national public education campaign on depressive illness called Depression/Awareness, Recognition, and Treatment (D/ART). Information in Spanish can be found on the NIMH web site. If you need an explanation of the different medication options for depression and bipolar disorder, you can turn to the "For the Public Section" on the site.

24. National Mental Health Association (NMHA)
    (703) 684-7722
    www.nmha.org

    The National Mental Health Association is America's oldest and largest nonprofit organization concerned with all mental illnesses. This volunteer group works to improve mental health through advocacy, education, research, and service. The "depression screening" link on the web site not only contains a screening test, but also has information about which professionals in your area you should speak to in case you feel that you might be depressed.

25. Pendulum Resources
    www.pendulum.org/

    This web site provides information on books, organizations, and other web sites that are helpful for people with bipolar disorder. In addition, it offers up-to-date information about ongoing research studies and articles dealing with bipolar disorder.

26. Screening for Mental Health
    (781) 239-0071
    www.nmisp.org

    Screening for Mental Health is a nonprofit organization that coordi-
    nates mental health screening programs. The National Depression
    Screening Day (NDSD) was begun in 1991 with support from the Amer-
    ican Psychiatric Association. Their web site enables the user to find the
    date and location of the nearest screening center.

27. Stanley Center for the Innovative Treatment of Bipolar Disorder
    www.wpic.pitt.edu/stanley

    The Stanley Center is a research center dedicated to learning more
    about bipolar disorder and possible treatment options. Information on
    the many studies that the Stanley Center is conducting can be found on
    the web site.

28. Substance Abuse and Mental Health Services Administration
    (301) 443-8956
    www.samhsa.gov

    The Substance Abuse and Mental Health Services Administration was
    created by the U.S. Department of Health and Human Services to
    improve services for mental health and substance abuse. The agency is
    dedicated to the prevention, treatment, and rehabilitation of people
    with substance abuse and/or mental health needs. Their focus is to
    work to educate, eliminate stigma, improve services, and promote poli-
    cies emphasizing treatment. Statistics on drug, alcohol, and tobacco
    abuse, broken down by state, can be found on the web site, which also
    provides educational materials, fact sheets, and survivor information.

29. Walkers in Darkness
    www.walkers.org/

    Walkers in Darkness is a support organization for people affected by
    depression and bipolar disorder. The organization's Internet mailing
    list is particularly popular with individuals who wish to freely discuss
    issues of concern with those who have similar problems. The web site
    offers an excellent list of resources, including organizations, books, and
    web sites.

# Appendix C: Helpful Books

1. Barondes, S. *Mood Genes: Hunting for Origins of Mania and Depression.* New York: W. H. Freeman Company, 1998.

   Psychiatrist and neurologist Dr. Samuel Barondes has put together an interesting account of old and new research on the genetics of mood disorder. Because this disease tends to run in families, it has been long suspected that specific genes may be responsible. Barondes explains that finding these genes will provide an entirely new way of understanding manic depression. While the book is scientific in its approach, it is highly readable and accessible to nonscientific readers.

2. Beers, C. W. *A Mind That Found Itself.* Garden City: Double Day, 1908.

   This is a brilliant autobiographical account of one man's struggle with depression and bipolar disorder. Although Beers was writing in the early twentieth century, readers will find his story compelling and relevant. His book is remarkable considering the courage necessary to be forthcoming given the era and his privileged background. He details his delusions and depressions, his hospitalization, and eventual recovery with unusual clarity. He spent the rest of his life advocating for patients. He was the founder of the National Mental Health Association. This book is not very easy to find but Amazon.com does have it listed.

3. DePaulo, J. R. and K. Ablow, *How to Cope with Depression: A Complete Guide for You and Your Family.* New York: McGraw-Hill, 1988. Fawcett Crest Paperbacks, 1989.

   Dr. DePaulo's last book discusses depression from the perspectives of disease, personality, behavior, and life history in a readable and easy to-understand manner. He discusses the cause and treatments of mood disorders.

4. Fitzgerald, F. S. *The Crack-Up.* New York: J. Laughlin, 1945.

   F. Scott Fitzgerald suffered from a debilitating mental illness that led to his decline and possibly contributed to his untimely death. Shortly following his death, Fitzgerald's stories and essays about his own bout with mental illness were collected and published. The pieces in this collection paint a vivid portrait of his declining years.

5. Jamison, K. R. *An Unquiet Mind.* New York: Random House, 1997.

The author brings her own experience with manic depression in this illuminating and incisive study of the disease. She gives a clear, eye-opening account of her struggle with the disease.

6. Jamison, K. R. *Touched with Fire: Manic-Depressive Illness and the Artistic Temperament.* New York: Free Press, 1996.

This book explores the relationship between manic depression and artistic temperament. An overwhelmingly high percentage of poets, authors, musicians, and artists have been found to suffer from the illness. By drawing on the artists' personal accounts, Dr. Jamison clearly demonstrates the way in which they managed to produce great works in spite of their disabilities. She also makes clear the genetic nature of the disease by documenting the prevalence of manic depression in the family tree of each artist discussed.

7. Jamison, K. R. *Night Falls Fast.* New York: Vintage Press, 1999.

Dr. Jamison's moving book discusses suicide from a variety of perspectives, both as a historical and a biological phenomenon. She also examines suicide prevention—where it has worked and where it hasn't. The book explores what goes through people's minds and hearts as they contemplate suicide, making for an account that is both intensely personal and humane.

8. Manning, M. *Undercurrents: A Life Beneath the Surface.* San Francisco: HarperCollins, 1995.

A prominent clinical psychologist from Washington, D.C., describes her difficult but successful treatment for a severe clinical depression. This book offers an encouraging insight into the experience of depression and its treatment. Her account of how she benefited from treatment with electroconvulsive shock therapy (ECT) is particularly well written.

9. Mondimore, F. *Bipolar Disorder: A Guide For Patients and Families.* Baltimore, Johns Hopkins University Press, 1999.

Dr. Mondimore's readable and comprehensive book on bipolar disorder will help patients and families understand the latest scientific and medical information about the disease. Dr. Mondimore considers each of the various treatment options, discusses their advantages and disadvantages, and provides other pertinent information that will help patients make informed decisions about their care. He describes what it's like to live with bipolar disorder, examining such subjects as the importance of building a support system, how to plan for emergencies, and why people with the illness should give themselves permission to seek help.

10. Mondimore, F. *Depression: The Mood Disease.* Baltimore: Johns Hopkins University Press, 1990.

This book serves as an excellent introduction to depression and other mood disorders. Dr. Mondimore, a psychiatrist, writes a consumer guide to the diagnosis and treatment of depression and other mood disorders.

11. Morrison, A. *The Antidepressant Sourcebook: A User's Guide for Patients and Families.* New York: Doubleday, 1999.

Morrison, a practicing psychiatrist, explains the medical properties of antidepressant medications. He addresses topics that may not be covered in a patient's therapy session, such as drug interactions, stopping medications, the effects of alcohol and caffeine when taken with medication, and issues involving pregnancy. Patients can use the information offered by this book to become better informed and better able to work with their doctors toward successful treatment.

12. Papolos, D., and J. Papolos, *Overcoming Depression.* New York: Harper and Row, 1987. Revised version, 1997.

This book can be extremely educational for patients and their families. It explains the causes of depression, as well as the results of experimental work on the disease, through the eyes of a scientist. In addition, the book contains practical treatment information.

13. Pinsky, D. *Restoring Intimacy: The Patient's Guide to Maintaining Relationships During Depression.* Chicago: National Depressive and Manic-Depressive Association, 1999.

The National Depressive and Manic-Depressive Association developed this unique book to address difficult issues involving depression and relationships. This book provides insight for partners and advice for depressed individuals in such areas as getting help and validating the severity of the disease. It also offers information on the side effects of medications, particularly in terms of their impact on sexual and emotional intimacy. Separate sections are written by several experts including Dr. Martha Manning and her husband.

14. Sheffield, A. *How You Can Survive When They're Depressed.* New York: Harmony, 1998.

Anne Sheffield addresses the critical but often overlooked subject of how a depressed individual can affect family and friends. She discusses the emotional strains that are placed on those closest to a depressed or manic-depressed individual. Some of the coping strategies she suggests for people whose lives are affected by mental illness are truly eye-opening.

15. Stearns, A. *Living Through Personal Crisis.* Chicago: Thomas More Press, 1984.

This book has little to do with depression but is the best and most practical guide available on how to deal with disasters in your life. Stearns is also the author of *Coming Back*, a wonderful collection of exemplary stories of how different people come back from a personal crisis.

16. Styron, W. *Darkness Visible: A Memoir of Madness*. New York: Vintage Press, 1990.

This memoir is derived in large part from Styron's presentation at the Johns Hopkins/DRADA Second Annual Mood Disorders Symposium in 1989. Styron writes this harrowing account of his own experience with a debilitating episode of depression with the same drama and craft that has made him one of the best living American novelists. He offers a skeptical insight into the benefits and hazards of medication treatment and presents a very positive view of how hospitalization and superb nursing care aided his recovery.

# Glossary

**acetylcholine:** The main neurotransmitter involved in muscle activity and one of the principal neurotransmitters involved in bodily functions that are automatic (such as sweating). Tricyclic (and to a lesser extent other) antidepressants interfere with acetylcholine and cause symptoms such as dry mouth, blurred vision, constipation, and increased heart rate.

**affective:** Refers to mental experiences that include moods, emotions, appetites, and motivations. Affective experiences are often distinguished from cognitive abilities such as intelligence, memory, and reasoning.

**affective disorders:** Narrowly, the syndromes of depression, mania, or mixed states; more broadly, also includes anxiety states such as panic disorder.

**allele:** One of the variant forms of a gene at a particular locus, or location, on a chromosome. Different alleles produce variation in inherited characteristics such as hair color or blood type. For some genes, one form of the allele (the dominant one) may be expressed more than another form (the recessive one).

**amino acids:** The building blocks of proteins. There are twenty different kinds of naturally occurring amino acids. Some amino acids are synthesized within the body, while others (called essential amino acids) must be obtained in the diet.

**amygdala:** Part of the brain's limbic system, this primitive brain structure lies deep in the center of the brain, and is involved in emotional reactions, such as anger, as well as emotionally charged memories. It also influences behavior such as feeding, sexual interest, and the immediate "fight or flight" reaction to stress to help ensure that the body's needs are met.

**antipsychotic:** An unfortunate name given to neuroleptics medications. They are, in fact, helpful in relieving symptoms such as delusions and hallucinations, sometimes referred to as psychotic symptoms.

**atypical depression:** A moderately severe form of affective illness that combines long periods of depression with short intervals of relief. Sleep and appetite are often increased. The onset of atypical depression may seem closely tied to distressing life events. Its victims frequently come to suffer from prominent anxiety symptoms and abnormal behaviors (e.g., eating disorders).

**axon:** A long, single nerve fiber that transmits messages, via chemical and electrical impulses, from the body of the neuron to dendrites of other neurons, or directly to body tissues such as muscles.

**basal ganglia:** Structures deep in the brain that are involved in muscle tone, and movement, cognition, and affective responses. These structures are injured in Parkinsonian patients and probably also patients with a variety of depressive and bipolar disorders.

**base pair:** Two bases which form a "rung of the DNA ladder." A DNA nucleotide is made of a molecule of sugar, a molecule of phosphoric acid, and a molecule called a base. The bases are the "letters" that spell out the genetic code. They are paired selectively, adenine (A) with thymidine (T) and guanine (G) with cytosine (C).

**behavioral therapy:** Psychotherapy that attempts to extinguish or diminish abnormal behaviors by changing the consequences of those behaviors.

**bipolar disorder:** Affective illness with episodes of mania as a defining feature. In more than 90 percent of patients there are also episodes of depression. People with only manic episodes are also referred to as bipolar.

**bipolar II disorder:** An affective disorder in which recurrent or persistent depressions predominate, but the defining features are brief periods of hypomanic mood.

**brain stem:** A part of the brain that connects the brain to the spinal cord. The brain stem controls functions basic to the survival of all animals, such as heart rate, breathing, digestive processes, and sleeping.

**bright-light therapy:** Also called phototherapy, a treatment for depression in which the patient is exposed to bright lights for several hours each day. Seasonally depressed individuals, who experience depression during winter months when sunlight is less plentiful, inspired this therapy.

**candidate gene:** A gene whose function or location in a chromosome region makes it a likely suspect for involvement in the causal pathway of a disease.

**carrier:** An individual who possesses one copy of a mutant allele that causes a trait or disease only when two copies are present (a recessive disorder or trait). Although carriers are not affected by the disease, two carriers can produce a child who has the disease.

**cerebrum** (also called **cerebral cortex**): The largest brain structure in humans, accounting for about two-thirds of the brain's mass and positioned over and around most other brain structures. The cerebrum is divided into left and right hemispheres, as well as specific areas, called lobes, that are associated with specialized functions.

**chromosome:** A structure found in the cell nucleus that contains most of the genes; chromosomes are composed of DNA and proteins. Each parent contributes one chromosome pair, so children get half of their chromosomes from their mother and half from their father.

**cognitive therapy:** Psychotherapy for depression designed to confront and correct what is seen as an inappropriately dismal self-image and view of the world. Through techniques including discussion, role playing, and the demonstration of success in assigned simple tasks at home, the therapist attempts to expose the distortions in the patient's negative mindset.

**computed tomography (CAT or CT):** An X-ray technique introduced in the early 1970s that enables scientists to take cross-sectional images of the body and brain. CT uses an Z-ray beam passed through the body to collect information about tissue density, then applies sophisticated computer data and mathematical formulas to create an anatomical image from that data.

**congenital:** Any trait or condition that exists from birth.

**cortex:** The outer part of the brain's cerebrum, which is organized in layers and regions. For example, the motor cortex lies just to the front of central sulcus in the frontal lobe, that is involved in movement and muscle coordination. Scientists have identified specific regions in the cortex that manage information of specific types or representing specific parts of the body (for sensation or motor actions).

**cortisol:** A steroid hormone produced by the adrenal glands, that controls how the body uses fat, protein, carbohydrates, and minerals and helps reduce inflammation. Cortisol is released in the body's stress response; brain scientists have found that prolonged exposure to cortisol has damaging effects on the brain.

**Cushing's disease:** A disease in which the adrenal glands are overstimulated and, therefore, produce an overabundance of the hormone cortisol. Symptoms of mania or depression often accompany the round, moonlike facial appearance, unusual distribution of fat, diabetes, and high blood pressure usually seen in this condition.

**delusion:** A false, unshakable belief held by a person despite overwhelming evidence to the contrary. The false belief is not a widely shared one among those in the individual's religious or cultural group. A person may become convinced, for example, that he or she is dying of cancer despite a battery of tests showing that the person is completely well.

**dendrite:** Short nerve fibers that project from a nerve cell, generally receiving messages from the axons of other neurons and relaying them to the cell's nucleus.

**depression:** A mood or affective disorder characterized by disruptions in one or more of the brain's neurotransmitter systems, including those related to serotonin and dopamine. Clinical depression is a serious condition that can be effectively treated with medications and/or behavioral therapy.

**DNA (deoxyribonculeic acid):** The material from which the forty-six chromosomes in each cell's nucleus is formed. DNA contains the codes for the body's approximately 100,000 genes, governing all aspects of cell growth and inheritance. DNA has a double-helix structure-two intertwined strands resembling a spiraling ladder.

**dominant:** A gene that almost always results in a specific physical characteristic even though the patient's genome possesses only one copy. With a dominant gene, the chance of passing on the gene, which may cause a condition or disease, to children is 50–50 in each pregnancy.

**dopamine:** A neurotransmitter involved in the brain's reward, or pleasure, system and in the control of body movement. Some addictive drugs increase brain levels of dopamine, causing the "high" associated with illicit drug use.

**ECT (electroconvulsive therapy):** The application of electric current to one or both sides of the scalp as a treatment for severe depression (or mania).

**endocrine:** Pertaining to the body's network of glands or the hormones they produce.

**endocrine system:** A body system composed of several different glands and organs that secrete hormones.

**epinephrine:** Also called adrenaline, this hormone is secreted by the adrenal glands in response to stress and other challenges to the body. The release of epinephrine causes a number of changes throughout the body, including the metabolism of carbohydrates, to supply the body's energy demands. See also *cortisol,* the other stress hormone released by the adrenal lands.

**frontal lobe:** The front part of the brain's cerebrum, beneath the forehead. This area of the brain is associated with higher cognitive processes, such as decision-making, reasoning, and planning.

**functional MRI, or Magnetic Resonance Imaging:** A brain imaging technique based on conventional MRI, but which uses sophisticated computer programs to create images that show which areas of the brain are functioning during certain tasks, behaviors, or thoughts.

**gene:** The basic unit of inheritance. A distinct section of DNA in a cell's chromosome that contains the codes for producing specific proteins involved in brain and body function. Gene defects (genetic mutations) are thought to cause many brain disorders.

**genetic code (ATGC):** The language in which DNA's instructions are written. It consists of triplets of nucleotides, with each triplet corresponding to one amino acid in a protein's structure or to a signal to start or stop protein production.

**genome:** The complete genetic map for an organism. In humans, this includes about one hundred thousand genes whose codes are written in our DNA, the spiraling chain of proteins that makes up the forty-six chromosomes in each cell. More than fifty thousand genes relate to functions of the brain.

**genotype:** The genetic identity of an individual that does not show as outward characteristics.

**hallucination:** A perception without a stimulus. Hallucinations may be visual, auditory, olfactory (smell), gustatory (taste), or tactile (touch).

**hemisphere:** Literally, half of a sphere. In brain science, it refers to the left or right half of the brain.

**heterozygous:** Possessing two different forms of a particular gene, one inherited from each parent.

**homozygous:** Possessing two identical forms of a particular gene, one inherited from each parent.

**hormone:** A chemical released into the blood stream by the body's endocrine glands (including the adrenal glands). Hormones act on receptors in many parts of the body to influence bodily functions or behavior.

**Human Genome Project:** The government-funded scientific initiative that has now completed the draft sequence of all the DNA in the complete human genome, including the 34,000 or so genes that are the basic units of inheritance. Completion of the finished sequence and identification of all human genes are the next goals of the project.

**hypothalamus:** A small structure located in the midbrain, which plays an important role in the interaction of the brain and the hormonal systems. It plays important roles in many behaviors that depend on brain and hormonal signals.

**inherited:** Transmitted through genes from parents to offspring.

**limbic system:** A brain system located in the inner aspects of the frontal and temporal lobes, encircling the top of the brain stem. The limbic system plays an important role in emotions, memory, and physiologically reinforced behaviors.

**Magnetic Resonance Imaging (MRI):** A brain imaging technique that uses powerful magnets to create sharp anatomical images of the brain or body. During an MRI scan, the person is placed inside a scanner, where the strong magnetic field causes the atoms in the body to line up in a particular fashion (just as the needle of a compass lines up in the Earth's magnetic field). The machine then sends out pulses of radio waves, which cause the atoms to release radio signals. The pattern of signals provides information about the number of particular types of matter present and the chemical environment. Sophisticated computer programs are then used to reconstruct the data into images of anatomical structure. MRI is also used to measure brain activity, (see *functional MRI*).

**major depression:** The official *DSM* term for a serious clinical depression. When major depression occurs in the setting of past manic episodes, the patient is said to have bipolar disorder. Otherwise the patient is classified as having a unipolar illness.

**mania:** The syndrome or cluster of symptoms that are the defining features of bipolar disorder. Sometimes referred to as a high phase or mood swing.

**Manic-Depressive Illness:** The traditional term derived from Kraepelin's term "Manic Depressive Insanity" for the illness in which episodes of both mania and depression have occurred (i.e., bipolar disorder). In this volume the terms manic depression, manic-depressive illness, and bipolar disorder are used synonymously.

**metabolize:** To break down or build up biochemical elements in the body, effecting a change in body tissue. Brain cells metabolize glucose, a blood sugar, to derive energy for transmitting nerve impulses.

**Mixed Affective Disorder:** An affective disorder in which symptoms of depression and mania exist simultaneously.

**mutation:** A change in the usual sequence of base pairs in the DNA. In most cases, mutations to DNA sequences within or near genes either have no effects or cause harm, but occasionally a mutation can improve an organism's chance of surviving. When mutations occur in the germ lines (either sperm or egg cells) but don't prevent reproduction, they may be passed on to offspring and their descendants.

**neuron:** A nerve cell. The basic unit of the central nervous system, neurons are responsible for the transmission of nerve impulses. Unlike any other cell in the body, a neuron consist of a central cell body, a single axon (which can have many branches), and dendrites. The axon transmits nerve impulses from the neuronal cell body to the synapse attaching to receiving neuron or neurons. Dendrites receive messages from sensory end organs or from other neurons and transmit them to the cell body of the neuron. Scientists estimate there are more than 100 billion neurons in the brain.

**neurotransmitter:** A chemical that acts as a messenger between neurons, and is release into the synaptic space or cleft, where a nerve impulse reaches the end of an axon and sends a message across the synapse to one of the dendrites of the adjacent neuron. Several dozen neurotransmitters have been identified in the brain so far, each with specific but numerous receptors for receiving a complex array of signals.

**phenotype:** The observable traits or characteristics of an organism, for example, hair color, weight, or the presence or absence of a disease.

**postsynaptic neuron:** The neuron on the receiving end of a nerve impulse transmitted from another neuron.

**prefrontal cortex:** The area of the cerebrum located in the forward part of the frontal lobe, which is thought to control higher cognitive processes such as planning, reasoning, and "social cognition"—a complex skill involving the ability to assess social situations in light of previous experience and personal knowledge, and interact appropriately with others. The prefrontal cortex is thought to be the most recently evolved area of the brain.

**presynaptic neuron:** In synaptic transmission, the neuron that sends a nerve impulse across the synaptic cleft to another neuron.

**protein:** A molecule made up of a number of amino acids arranged in a specific order determined by the genetic code. Proteins are essential for all life processes.

**psychiatry:** A medical specialty dealing with the diagnosis and treatment of mental disorders.

**psychoanalysis:** A theory of psychological development, as well as a form of psychotherapy based on Sigmund Freud's ideas.

**psychology:** A field of study concerned with the normal and abnormal mental functions and behavior of humans and other animals.

**psychosis:** Implies loss of contact with reality. The term is usually used to describe conditions that include symptoms such as delusions or hallucinations.

**psychotherapy:** A general term used to describe treatments which use psychological or symbolic means for helping patients. The basic elements include clarification, reassurance, interpretation, and education of the patient.

**rapid cycling:** An affective illness in which episodes of mania or depression occur at least four times within a year.

**receptors:** Molecules on the surfaces of neurons whose structures precisely match those of chemical messengers (such as neurotransmitters or hormones) released during synaptic transmission. The chemicals attach themselves to the receptors, in lock-and-key fashion, to activate the receiving cell structure (usually a dendrite or cell body).

**recessive:** A genetic condition that appears only in individuals who have received two copies of a mutant gene, one from each parent.

**Seasonal Affective Disorder (SAD):** An affective illness that seems to recur at a particular time during the year. The term is usually applied to conditions in which depression occurs during fall and winter, when daylight hours are shortest.

**serotonin:** A monoamine indolamine neurotransmitter made from the amino acid tryptophan.

**Steroids:** A family of naturally occuring adrenal or gonadal or man-made molecules with a range of hormonal activities. These include the stress hormone action of decreasing inflammation as well as the toxic effect of inducing symptoms of mania or depression when either produced in excess amounts or taken as medication.

**synapse:** The junction at which an axon approaches another neuron or its extension (a dendrite or axon); the point at which nerve-to-nerve communication occurs. Nerve impulses traveling down the axon reach the synapse and release neurotransmitters into the synaptic cleft, the tiny gap between neurons.

**synaptic transmission:** The process of cell-to-cell communication in the central nervous system, whereby one neuron sends a chemical signal across the synaptic cleft to another neuron.

**syndrome:** A group of symptoms that occur together and often herald the presence of an underlying disease.

**temporal lobes:** The parts of the cerebrum that are located on either side of the head, roughly beneath the temples in humans. These areas are involved in hearing, language, memory storage, and emotion.

**thalamus:** A brain structure located at the top of the brain stem, the thalamus acts as a two-way relay station, sorting, processing, and directing signals from the spinal cord and midbrain structures to the cerebrum, and from the cerebrum down.

**unipolar:** An affective illness in which only major depressive episodes occur. It is synonymous with the term major depressive disorder, recurrent type.

# Bibliography

American Psychiatric Association. *Diagnostic and Statistical Manual of Mental Disorders* (4th ed.). Washington, D.C.: American Psychiatric Press, 1994.

Anon. A practising psychiatrist: The experience of electro-convulsive therapy, *Brit. J. Psychiatry* 111:365–367, 1965.

Barondes, S. *Mood Genes: Hunting for Origins of Mania and Depression.* New York: Oxford University Press, 1998.

Bloom, F. E., Kupfer, D. J. (eds.). *Psychopharmacology: The Fourth Generation of Progress.* New York: Raven Press, 1995.

Bowden, C., et al. Efficacy of divalproex vs. lithium and placebo in the treatment of mania. The Depakote Mania Study Group, *JAMA* 1994, 271: 1830.

Brodaty, H, et al. Age and Depression, *J Affective Disord* 23:137–149,1991.

Calabrese, J. R., et al. A double-blind placebo-controlled study of lamotrigine monotherapy in outpatients with Bipolar I depression, *Journal of Clinical Psychiatry,* 60, 79–88, 1999.

Casey, N. (ed.). *Unholy Ghost: Writers on Depression.* New York: William Morrow, 2001.

Cheng, A,Chen, T., Chen, C., Jenkins, R. Psychosocial and psychiatric risk factors for suicide: Case-control psychological autopsy study, *The British Journal of Psychiatry* 177:360–365, 2000.

Cooper, B. Nature, nurture and mental disorder: old concepts in the new millennium, *The British Journal of Psychiatry* 178:s91–s101, 2001.

Cooper-Patrick, L., et al. Identification of patient attitudes and preferences regarding treatment of depression, *Journal of General Internal Medicine, 12,* 431–438, 1997.

Corrigan, P. W., Penn, D. L. Lessons from social psychology on discrediting psychiatric stigma, *American Psychologist, 54,* 765–776,1999.

Daly, I. Mania. *Lancet* 349:1157–1160, 1997.

Delgado P, et al. Serotonin and the neurobiology of depression. Effects of tryptophan depletion in drug-free depressed patients. *Arch Gen Psychiatry.* 51:865–74,1994.

DePaulo, J., and Ablow, K. *How to Cope with Depression.* New York: Fawcett Crest Books,1989.

Dowling, C. *You Mean I Don't Have to Feel This Way?* New York: Bantam Books, 1993.

Federoff, J. P., et al. Phenomenological comparisons of major depression following stroke, myocardial infarction or spinal cord lesions, *J Affective Disorders* 22:83–89,1991.

Fink, M. *Electroshock: Restoring the Mind*. New York: Oxford University Press,1999.

Fischbach, G. D. Mind and brain. *Scientific American,* 267:48–57,1992.

Folstein, M. F., McHugh, P. R. Dementia Syndrome of Depression. In *Alzeimer's Disease: Senile Dementia and Related Disorders.* Edited by Katzman, R., Terry, R. D., Bick, K. L., New York: Raven Press, 7:87–96, 1987.

Food and Drug Administration. *Center for Drug Evaluation and Research Handbook* [on-line], 1998. www.fda.gov/cder/handbook/index.htm

Frank, J. D., Frank, J. B. *Persuasion and Healing: A comparative study of psychotherapy.* Baltimore, Md.: The Johns Hopkins University Press, 1991.

Frasure-Smith, N., Lesperance, F., Talajic, M. Depression following myocardial infarction: Impact on six-month survival, *Journal of the American Medical Association, 270,* 1819–1825,1993.

Frasure-Smith, N., Lesperance, F., Talajic, M. Depression and eighteen-month prognosis after myocardial infarction, *Circulation,* 91:999–1005, 1995.

Freud S. *Mourning and Melancholia.* Standard Edition, London: Hogarth Press,14: 243–258, 1957.

Gazzaniga, M. S., Ivry, R. B., Mangun, G. R. *Cognitive neuroscience: The biology of the mind.* New York: W. W. Norton, 1998.

Goldberg, D. and Huxley, P. *Common Mental Disorders: A Biosocial Model.* London: Tavistock/Routledge, 1992.

Goodwin, F. K., Jamison, K., *Manic Depressive Illness.* New York: Oxford Press, 1990.

Grob, G. N. *From Asylum to Community: Mental Health Policy in Modern America.* Princeton, N.J.: Princeton University Press, 1991.

Grob, G. N. *The Mad Among Us: A History of the Care of America's Mentally Ill.* New York: Free Press, 1994.

Hanson, K. W. Public opinion and the mental health parity debate: Lessons from the survey literature, *Psychiatric Services,* 49, 1059–1066, 1998.

Harlow, S. D., Goldberg, E. L., Comstock, G. W. A longitudinal study of the prevalence of depressive symptomatology in elderly widowed and married women, *Arch Gen Psychiatry,* 48:1065–1068, 1991.

Heginbotham, C. UK mental health policy can alter the stigma of mental illness, *Lancet,* 352:1052–1053, 1998.

Hirsch, S. R., Shepherd, M. (eds.). *Themes and Variations in European Psychiatry: An Anthology.* Bristol: John Wright, 1974.

Hudson J. I., et al. Fibromyalgia and major affective disorder: a controlled phenomenology and family history study, *Am J Psychiatry* 142:441–446, 1985.

Jamison, K. *Touched with Fire: Manic-Depressive Illness and the Artistic Temperament.* New York: The Free Press,1993.

Jamison, K. *An Unquiet Mind.* New York: Vintage Books, 1995.

Jamison, K. *Night Falls Fast: Understanding Suicide.* New York: Knopf, 1999.

Jaspers, K, *General Psychopathology, Volumes 1&2* (transl. J. Hoenig, M. W. Hamilton, 1962), Baltimore: Johns Hopkins University Press, 1997.

Johns, A. Psychiatric effects of cannabis, *The British Journal of Psychiatry* 178: 116–122, 2001.

Kraepelin, E. *Manic Depressive Insanity, and Paranoia.* Translation of selections from the Eighth German Edition of the *Textbook of Psychiatry, volumes iii and iv,* (transl. by R. Mary Barclay and edited by George M. Robertson, MD, FRCP), Edinburgh, E & S Livingstone, 1921.

Kupfer, D. J., Frank, E., Perel, J. M. The advantage of early treatment intervention in recurrent depression, *Arch Gen Psychiatry* 46:771–775, 1998.

Lewis, A. J. States of depression: Their clinical and aetiological differentiation, *Brit Med Journal* 2:875–878, 1938. (Reprinted in Lewis, A. J., *Inquiries in Psychiatry,* New York: Science House, 133–140,1967).

Lewis, A. *Inquiries in Psychiatry: Clinical and Social Investigations.* New York: Science House, 1967.

Lidberg, L., et al. Suicide attempts and impulse control disorder are related to low cerebrospinal fluid 5-HIAA in mentally disordered violent offenders, *Acta Psychiatr Scand* 101: 395–402, May 2000.

Lish, J. D., et al. The National Depressive and Manic-Depressive Association (DMDA) survey of bipolar members, *Journal of Affective Disorders* 31: 281–294, 1994.

Llewellyn, A., Stowe, Z, Strader, J. The use of lithium and management of women and bipolar disorder during pregnancy and lactation, *J Clin Psychiatry* 59 Suppl: 57–64,1998.

Lopez, A. D., Murrey, C. J. L. The global burden of disease, 1900–2020, *Nature Medicine* 4:1241–1243, 1998.

McMahon, F. J., DePaulo, J. R. Clinical features of affective disorders and bereavement, *Current Opinion in Psychiatry* 5:580–584,1992.

Manning, M. *Undercurrents: A Life Beneath the Surface.* San Francisco, CA: HarperSanFrancisco,1995.

McElroy, S., Keck, P. Pharmacologic agents for the treatment of acute bipolar mania, *Biol Psychiatry* 48: 539–546, 2000.

McGovern, G. *Terry: My Daughter's Life-and-Death Struggle with Alcoholism.* New York: Random House, 1996.

McHugh, P. R., Slavney, P. *The Perspective of Psychiatry, 2nd edition.* Baltimore, Md.: The Johns Hopkins University Press, 1998.

McHugh, P. R. Physician-assisted suicide—the ultimate right? *N Engl J Med.* 336:1525–1526, 1997.

McHugh, P. R. A structure for psychiatry at the century's turn—the view from Johns Hopkins. *Journal of the Royal Society of Medicine* 85:483-487,1992.

McHugh, P. R. William Osler and the new psychiatry. *Ann Intern Med.* 107:914–8, 1987.

McHugh, P. R., The *DSM*: gaps and essences. Psychiatric research report, 17(2):1–3, 14–15, 2001.

McHugh, P. R., The death of Freud and the rebirth of psychiatry: an anthropologist misdiagnoses the profession's current ills. *The Weekly Standard,* 5:41–42 (July 17), 2000.

Mondimore, F. *Depression: The Mood Disease.* Baltimore, Md.: The Johns Hopkins University Press, 1990.

Mondimore, F. *Bipolar Disorder: A Guide for Patients and Families.* Baltimore, Md.: The Johns Hopkins University Press, 1999.

Mukherjee, S., Sackeim, H., Schnur, D. Electroconsulvie therapy of acute manic episodes: a review of 50 years' experience. *Am J Psychiatry* 151:169–176, 1994.

Murray, C. J. L., Lopez, A.D. (eds.). *The Global Burden of Disease: A Comprehensive Assessment of Mortality and Disability from Diseases, Injuries, and Risk Factors in 1990 and projected to 2020*, Cambridge, Mass.: Harvard School of Public Health, 1996.

NIMH Consensus Development Conference Statement. Mood disorders: pharmacologic prevention of recurrences, *Am J Psychiatry* 142:469–76, 1985.

Papolos, D., Papolos, J. *Overcoming Depression*. New York: HarperCollins, 1997.

Parker, G. New and old antidepressants: all equal in the eyes of the lore?, *The British Journal of Psychiatry* 179:95–96, 2001.

Penn, D. L., Martin, J. The stigma of severe mental illness: Some potential solutions for a recalcitrant problem, *Psychiatric Quarterly*, 69:235–247, 1998.

Piccinelli, M. Gender differences in depression: a critical review, *The British Journal of Psychiatry* 177:486–492, 2000.

Pope, H. G., Katz, D. L. Affective and psychotic symptoms associated with anabolic steroid use, *Am J Psychiatry* 145:487–490, 1988.

Price, L., Heninger, G. Drug therapy: lithium in the treatment of mood disorders. *N Engl J Med* 331: 591–598, 1994.

Regier, D. A., et al. Comorbidity of mental disorders with alcohol and other drug abuse. Results from the epidemiological catchment area study, *Journal of the American Medical Association*, 264: 2511–2518, 1990.

Regier, D.A., et al. The de facto U.S. mental and addictive disorders service system. Epidemiologic catchment area prospective one-year prevalence rates of disorders and services, *Archives of General Psychiatry*, 50: 85–94, 1993.

Resnick, W. *The Manual for Affective Disorder Support Groups*. Baltimore, Md.: DRADA, 1988.

Ring, H. A., Trimble, M. R. Affective disturbance in Parkinson's disease, *Int J Geriatric Psychiatry* 6: 385–393, 1991.

Robins, L. N., et al. Lifetime prevalence of specific psychiatric disorders in three sites, *Arch Gen Psychiatry* 41: 949–958, 1984.

Robinson, R. G., et al. Mood disorders in stroke patients: importance of location of lesion, *Brain* 107: 81–93, 1984.

Robinson, R. G., Coyle, J. T. The differential effect of right versus left hemispheric cerebral infarction on catecholamines and behavior in the rat, *Brain Res* 188:3–78, 1980.

Rosenthal, N. *Winter Blues: Seasonal Affective Disorder: What It Is and How to Overcome It.* New York: Guilford Publications, 1998.

Ross, E. D., Rush, A. J. Diagnosis and neuroanatomical correlates of depression in brain-damaged patients: implications for a neurology of depression, *Arch Gen Psychiatry* 38: 1344–54, 1981.

Rovner, B. W., et al. Depression and mortality in nursing homes, *JAMA* 265:993–996, 1991.

Schaffer, C. B., Donlon, P. T., Bittle, R. M. Chronic pain and depression: a clinical and family history survey, *Am J Psychiatry* 137:118–20, 1980.

Sheffield, A. *How You Can Survive When They're Depressed: Living and Coping with Depression Fallout.* New York: Random House, 1998.

Skevington, S., Wright, A. Changes in the quality of life of patients receiving antidepressant medication in primary care: validation of the WHOQOL-100, *The British Journal of Psychiatry* 178:261–267, 2001.

Stoff, D., Mann, J. (eds.). *The Neurobiology of Suicide.* New York: The New York Academy of Sciences, 1997.

Stoll, A., et al. Omega-3 fatty acids in bipolar disorder: A preliminary double-blind placebo-controlled trial, *Arch Gen Psychiatry* 56: 407–412, 1999.

Storosum, J. G., et al. Short term efficacy of trycyclic antidepressants revisited: a metaanalytic study, *Eur Neuropsychopharmacol:* 11: 173–80, 2001.

Wells, K. B., et al. The functioning and well-being of depressed patients; results from the Medical Outcomes Study, *JAMA* 262: 914–9, 1989.

Zisook, S., Shuchter, S. R. Depression through the first year after the death of a spouse, *American Journal of Psychiatry,* 148:1346–1352, 1991.

West, E. D., Dally, P. J. Effects of iproniazid in depressive syndromes, *Brit Med J* i:1491–1494, 1959.

Videos

Art Buchwald. DRADA, 1998. (40 minutes) *Uncut videotape. Describes this columnist's touching, sincere, and humorous account given at the 1997 symposium.*

Day for Night: Recognizing Teenage Depression. Vanderpool Films, 1999. (26 minutes) *Sponsored by DRADA and the Johns Hopkins University School of Medicine. Offers an in-depth look at the symptoms and treatment of teenage depression with teenagers who have dealt with depression and bipolar disorder as well as their families and friends, and interviews with professionals. Includes a fifteen-page instructional pamphlet. An award winner—Time Inc. 2000 FREDDIE AWARD in the area of coping.*

Dick Cavett. DRADA, 1993. (43 minutes) *The talk-show host describes his experiences with depression for the 1992 symposium.*

Downtime: A Work Site Guide to Understanding Clinical Depression. DRADA in cooperation with the Wellness Councils of America (WELCOA), 1993. (16 minutes, VHS [comes with a 34-page meeting guide]) *Portrays the on-the-job story of employees with depression, and gives additional information. Outlines, in printed guide for presenters, a work site training session. An award winner with commentary by Dick Cavett.*

Mike Wallace. DRADA, 1992. (40 minutes) *Shows the CBS correspondent describing his experiences with depression for the 1991 DRADA Mood Disorders Symposium.*

# Index